Greenhill Books

LUFTWAFFE BOMBER ACES

LUFTWAFFE BOMBER ACES

Men, Machines, Methods

MIKE SPICK

GREENHILL BOOKS, LONDON
STACKPOLE BOOKS, PENNSYLVANIA

Greenhill Books

Luftwaffe Bomber Aces
First published 2001 by Greenhill Books
Lionel Leventhal Limited, Park House, 1 Russell Gardens,
London NW11 9NN
and
Stackpole Books, 5067 Ritter Road, Mechanicsburg,
PA 17055, USA

British Library Cataloguing in Publication Data
Spick, Mike
Luftwaffe bomber aces : men, machines, methods
1. Germany. Luftwaffe 2. Bomber pilots – Germany
3. World War, 1939–1945 – Aerial operations, German
I. Title
940.5´44943

ISBN 1-85367-444-3

Library of Congress Cataloging-in-Publication Data available

Edited, designed and typeset by Roger Chesneau
Printed and bound in Great Britain by
Creative Print and Design (Wales), Ebbw Vale

CONTENTS

ILLUSTRATIONS AND TABLES

7

Diagrams (drawn by John Richards)

Tables

PROLOGUE

There were hundreds of guns firing at us, as if they'd been brought here from the entire Empire to guard the artery of world power. Flashes appeared from all over the island. It was a veritable wasp's nest. Through the glass of the cockpit I could see the airfield at Luqa steep below me. We were not going to make it! Then Helbig's aircraft tilted down, and the entire Staff Flight went with him. The light blue underbellies of all the aircraft showed simultaneously. No waverers! A second later I lowered my dive brakes, put the nose down, and throttled right back. Out of the corner of my eye I watched my wing men. I looked ahead. I was right behind Helbig in the vic of the Staff Flight. The Staff Flight aircraft were racing down ahead of me but seemed to be poised, motionless, over the target area, their wings like narrow lines, as if on an aerial photograph. Press on! . . .

At last! Ahead and below me there was movement in the formation. Almost as if they were rocket-propelled, the staff aircraft, pulling out of their dive, swept out from the target, so that in a flash I could see the imperial crosses on the upper surfaces of their wings. Our turn now! I held my aim down to the smallest ring of light in my sight. The alarm klaxon blared out: that meant that I was 800 metres above the ground. I could see my target clearly . . . I pressed the bomb release.

This was the first sortie by Hans-Joachim (Hajo) Herrmann against Malta in February 1941. A Junkers Ju 88 pilot, he had flown the He 111 against Poland and Norway with *KG 4*, then the Ju 88 against France and England. A holder of the *Ritterkreuz,* he was now *Kommandeur III/KG 30,* and was destined to go on to still greater things. Malta was at this time defended by anti-aircraft guns and a handful of RAF Hurricanes, and was not yet the hornet's nest it later became. Leading the raid was Joachim Helbig, at this time *Kommandeur I/LG 1* (Ju 88), who already held the *Ritterkreuz* with *Eichenlaub,* and who, a little more than one month earlier, had led attacks on the British aircraft carrier HMS *Illustrious* in the Mediterranean which had all but sunk her, putting her out of the war for eighteen months.

Malta was just beginning to win her reputation as 'the unsinkable aircraft carrier'—a reputation which would be justified by future events. The raid described was recorded as having destroyed eight Wellington bombers and severely damaged another seven, thus helping to secure the supply lines to North Africa, where the *Deutsches Afrika Korps* under Erwin Rommel, combined with the Italian Army, battled with the British Empire for control of Egypt and the Suez Canal. Had Rommel been successful in this undertaking, the *Wehrmacht* would have been free to advance to the oilfields of the Middle East. The loss of oil—the life blood of war—would have been critical to the Empire. Nor would German difficulties have been extreme: Iraq, in particular, was to a degree anti-British.

The primary air weapon was the bomb. When one considers it, this was an extremely primitive weapon. If released in straight and level flight, it accelerates downwards at the rate of 32ft/sec^2 while retaining to a degree the forward speed of the releasing aircraft. Given that it is correctly sighted, and in still air conditions, a lapse of one-tenth of a second from an altitude which gives a falling time of 30 seconds and a forward speed of 180mph (290kph) will give an error of 792ft (241m). Given a crosswind of 30mph (48kph), the bomb will drift a considerable distance to the downwind side of the target. The counter to this is to establish the wind direction on the ground, then to bomb directly into it, or directly against it. This should in theory counterbalance crosswind error. It does not always do so because wind direction tends to vary at different altitudes. But even if the wind direction does not vary, and the attack is made directly into, or with, the prevailing wind, its strength is still an unknown quantity. Assuming a wind strength of 30mph (48kph) in either direction, even with precise aiming a significant longitudinal error is incurred. Level bombing was therefore an inexact science. It must also be appreciated that what could be achieved on the range from a moderate altitude bore little relationship to actual combat conditions. When the bomb aimer was being shot at, and in imminent danger of extinction, the margin of level bombing error increased by a factor of three.

In the Second World War there was just one possible alternative. Dive bombing radically decreased the relative speed over the ground; in fact, if a 90-degree dive angle could be achieved, it became zero. At the same time, the release height of the bomb was greatly reduced and, with it, the time of flight. This made for tremendously increased accuracy, allowing pinpoint attacks.

Ironically, the *Luftwaffe* adopted this—ironically for two reasons. First, while it paid lip service to the idea of a strategic bomber force, dive bombers could be little other than tactical aircraft supporting the surface forces, whether army or navy. Secondly, stressing aircraft for dive attacks involved weight increases, which significantly reduced payload/range capacity. The *Luftwaffe* never succeeded in producing a true strategic bomber in the entire war—an omission that it came to regret.

The fact is that the dive bomber was extremely vulnerable to anti-aircraft fire. Tipping over into a dive against a defended target made it a fairly easy, slow, no-deflection shot for ground fire. The supreme irony of this was that Germany led the field in *Flakartillerie*. Had Poland, France or Britain had the numerical and technical equivalent of the '88, the dive bomber would have been shown for what it was—a slow and unhandy non-starter. But they did not! And so, in the early days of the Second World War, the Ju 87 Stuka and the Ju 88 built a legendary reputation, which was to a large degree founded on the weakness of their opponents.

On the Russian Front, matters were even worse. Many German Ju 87 pilots notched up more than 1,000 sorties. The historical record shows that they could not have done this in the West.

1. THE STORM CLOUDS GATHER

When Germany lost the First World War, various factors came into play that virtually ensured that the Second World War would take place. The Treaty of Versailles in 1919 imposed crippling sanctions on the German economy, while military power, not least that of aviation, was forbidden. However, it contained three inherent flaws. First, Germany was not occupied, which allowed all sorts of undercover activity to flourish, not least the emergence of the *Luftwaffe*. Secondly, there were no restrictions on civil aviation after 1926, which permitted warplanes to be developed in the guise of civilian aircraft. Thirdly, and most importantly, the disastrous state of the German economy created conditions which positively aided the rise of a totalitarian state. Underlying this was the fact that the German Army had not been chased all the way back to Potsdam. The myth quickly spread that the defeat of 1918 had not been due to the defeat of the German Army in the field; it had been due to betrayal at home. The sight of British and French troops marching down the Unter den Linden in a victory parade would quickly have killed this canard, but it simply did not happen. This allowed militant organisations such as *Stahlhelm* to flourish unchecked. With hindsight, the rise of the National Socialist (Nazi) Party, led by Adolf Hitler, seems to have been almost inevitable.

Germany quickly became the most air-minded nation in the world. As early as 1928, Lufthansa was an extremely efficient airline. Even before this, Germany had negotiated for military training facilities at Lipetsk in Russia—something that 'Uncle Joe' Stalin would deeply regret in the future. Then there was the *Deutscher Luftsportsverband*, which offered cheap gliding for the youth of the country; virtually everywhere else, aviation activities were the preserve of the idle rich. When the time came to reveal the *Luftwaffe* to the world, it had a tremendous pool of actual and potential flyers on which to

15

draw, and when it was finally revealed, the Allies, faced with a *fait accompli*, could do little about it. Propaganda—otherwise known to Anglo-Saxons as bull**** (the current term for which is now 'spin-doctoring')—played its part in presenting the new service as much more powerful, both numerically and technically, than it actually was, to discourage potential opponents. To a remarkable degree it worked.

Training for war is inherently unrealistic. In war, people get killed, although at the end of the millennium the attitude is that this must be minimised, if not altogether eliminated. It was not always so! In the first half of the twentieth century, the fact that there would be casualties was easily accepted: war was about inflicting casualties, and it was only to be expected that they would also be sustained. However realistic the training, the participants return to their wives or girlfriends each night, or the bar: rarely is anyone killed, and then only by accident. Given this relatively safe training environment, those involved tend to perform well. What this fails to indicate is how well they would perform if someone was shooting back at them! Faced with the prospect of imminent extinction, individual performance suffers. As a modern rule of thumb, bombing accuracy degrades by a factor of three, to give but one example. Even more important is leadership. How an individual performs in the stress of battle is a completely unknown quantity until it happens. The outbreak of the Spanish Civil War in 1936 provided the *Luftwaffe* with an ideal opportunity to test men, tactics and hardware, under truly operational conditions.

The Planes in Spain...

The Spanish Civil War was essentially a conflict of ideologies—the Nationalists (Fascists) versus the Republicans (Communists). While Hitler's sympathies were obviously with Franco, direct military intervention was not a viable political option for Germany for fear of a confrontation with France. If, in the light of later events, this seems overcautious, it must be remembered that in 1936 the fledgeling *Luftwaffe* was still small and relatively ill-equipped. By September 1939 the situation had changed out of all recognition.

Assistance to Franco was duly provided by forming the Condor Legion. To preserve the appearance of legality, this was theoretically a part of the Spanish Nationalist forces, with Spanish uniforms and insignia and its aircraft carrying Spanish markings. Personnel, both air and ground crews, were initially all German volunteers, flying German aircraft. In practice, the volunteer aspect was soon dropped, not because volunteers were in short supply but because the advantages of 'live training' were so great. Many promising young *Luftwaffe* aircrew were seconded to the Condor Legion, some of whom were later to become household names. A typical tour of duty was about six months—long enough for the flyers to become battle-hardened but short enough to allow a high turnover of personnel. By the time Republican resistance collapsed, at the end of March 1939, the Condor Legion had provided the *Luftwaffe* with a nucleus of experienced warriors and leaders for the major conflict to come.

This apart, the Spanish Civil War was an invaluable proving ground for tactics and equipment for the *Luftwaffe*. Of course, this should equally have applied to the *Regia Aeronautica*, which also fought for Franco, and the Soviet Air Force, fighting on the Republican side. But for various reasons the *Luftwaffe* was by far the major tactical beneficiary of the war.

Condor Legion fighter operations are covered in some detail in this book's companion volume *Luftwaffe Fighter Aces*. But the Legion was in fact a miniature air force, with bomber and reconnaissance units, attack units and its own flak. At the end of November 1936 the bomber element consisted of *Kampfgruppe 88* with three *Staffeln* of Ju 52/3m bombers.

These good-natured and reliable trimotors were excellent transports, but less than perfect as bombers. Large and slow, with a cruising speed of barely 100mph and a service ceiling of less than 10,000ft, they were easy targets for flak or fighters. Defence was minimal—a single machine gun in an open dorsal position and another in a retractable ventral dustbin. The engine in the nose obscured the pilot's view of the target, and on the bombing run the observer let down the ventral turret, from which he not only aimed the bombs but also steered the aircraft using a direct link to the rudder. This was often not to the pilot's liking.

Hajo Herrmann's first ever bombing sortie was an attack on shipping off the coast of Morocco. His observer on this occasion was a naval officer, Walter Storp, destined to become famous with the *Luftwaffe*. He made a frontal attack from 5,000ft, and the first three bombs were near misses. As Herrmann later recalled:

I didn't like this intervention from below at all, because my rudder bar seemed to develop a will of its own . . . After the third bomb there was such fierce flak around me—we were right in the middle of the flotilla—that I kicked the rudder bar to the left in order to take evasive action, but Storp steered me in the other direction with the strength of a bear.

The second attack was made from much higher, about 8,200ft. Again there were three misses. At the very end, a piece of shrapnel lodged in the cooling vanes of the engine directly in front of Herrmann, who was forced to contemplate it on the long haul back to base, low on fuel.

As was becoming evident, a level bombing attack on a ship in open water was a thankless task, even without the pilot and observer struggling for control. In harbour things were slightly easier. On 13 August 1936 a Ju 52/3m hit the battleship *Jaime I*, which was anchored off Malaga, with two 250kg bombs, badly damaging it.

By the beginning of 1937 Russian-built and -flown fighters outclassed the He 51, which was able to offer little protection to the lumbering Junkers, and the addition of extra machine guns did little to help. Daylight bombing was temporarily abandoned. The answer was, of course, more modern aircraft, and at the end of that month they started to arrive—He 111Bs, Do 17Es and Ju 86Ds. The last, which were diesel-engined, were unreliable, but the two other types, much faster and with higher ceilings than the Ju 52, proved far more difficult for the Republican fighters to intercept. At the same time, new fighters arrived to give better protection. The He 51s were relegated to ground attack, where they achieved a certain amount of success. One of their tactics was the *Cadena*, or chain, where they played 'follow my leader', diving on targets to strafe before climbing away to repeat the process. Each aircraft carried nine 10kg bombs which, when they were expended, were followed up by strafing with guns. A handful of Hs 123 biplanes also appeared. While these were designed as dive bombers, in Spain they were used for strafing.

On 26 April 1937 occurred the most emotive air attack of the entire war. Guernica was a rail terminus and communications centre on the Oca river. It also contained a small-arms factory, although it appears that this was unknown to the attackers. The main target was the Rentaria Bridge, while blocking the roads to the south and east were secondary tasks. Faulty reconnaissance suggested that enemy troops were massing in the town, but it appears that the bulk of these were refugees.

Late in the afternoon 26 bombers showered 40 tonnes of bombs on to the helpless town. There was no anti-aircraft defence, so target marking was carried out from 4,000ft, a comparatively low altitude. Despite this, many of the bombs fell wide, causing massive devastation and up to 1,500 casualties, most of them civilians. World opinion condemned this as a terror attack. But was it? Guernica contained at least three legitimate military targets—the station, the bridge (which was not hit) and the arms factory. It would appear that the true culprit was inaccurate bombing, for whatever reason. This was far from the first instance. To quote but one, Durango had, just weeks before, suffered heavy loss of life as a result of inaccurate attacks on an arms factory. The main difference was one of scale, and the fierce international reaction to the raid.

Meanwhile, from January 1937, the He 59s of *AS/88* started to carry torpedoes, and stepped up their attacks on shipping and coastal targets. This campaign was intensified from early 1938 when Martin ('Iron Gustav') Harlinghausen took command. A tactic developed at this time was to approach coastal targets from seaward with engines throttled right back, descend gently and almost silently to about 1,000ft, then release the bombs and pour on the coals for a rapid if noisy escape.

Meanwhile yet another new aircraft type had joined the fray—the Ju 87 Stuka—although this was only ever present in penny packets. As the war continued, the Condor Legion was increasingly used to soften up the defences prior to an attack by surface forces. When the war ended in March 1939, Condor Legion bomber losses were stated to be 15 to enemy action and 39 in accidents.

For the *Luftwaffe* bombers, what were the lessons of Spain? In fact, many were the wrong ones. What coloured the entire conflict in the air was that, for the most part, the opposition was of low quality, while enemy anti-aircraft defences were minimal. This gave the Condor Legion bombers and attack aircraft a much easier ride than they would have had against top-class opponents, with the effect that while their new bombers, the He 111 and Do 17, had certainly performed adequately, they perhaps looked better than they actually were.

A major factor was the relative ease with which the new generation of fast bombers could evade interception. This applied not only to the Heinkels and Dorniers: Russian-built SB-2 bombers used by the Republicans were equally hard to intercept, which emphasised the advantages of speed. Only standing patrols of fighters stood much chance of catching them, and there were never enough fighters available for these to be really effective. At the same time, defence against fighter attack was not completely neglected: extra machine guns were added to the standard bomber types to increase the crossfire from a formation, although events in 1940 were to prove that this upgrading was still woefully inadequate. Be that as it may, the front end of the Do 17 was completely redesigned in the light of Spanish experience. A deeper front fuselage section was adopted, which allowed a greater field of fire for the ventral gun position. The pilot's position was raised and fully glazed, making room for a fourth crew member. In front, the distinctive 'beetle eye' glazed nose, made up of optically flat panes, provided an undistorted view forward and downward. This did nothing for the aerodynamics; it was entirely an operational change.

One thing was certain: the accuracy of level bombing was often abysmal, and only so much could be done by improving sighting systems. This reinforced the need for the dive bomber, which gave much greater accuracy, particularly against moving targets such as ships. The ability to make diving attacks began to feature more and more in German bomber specifications.

The new wonder bomber, the Ju 88, which entered service in mid-1939, had been conceived as a fast bomber, able to hold off, if not outrun, fighters altogether by sheer speed. It soon had the ability to make steep diving attacks added to its requirements. The same need bedevilled the development of the Heinkel He 177, of which more later.

The accent on speed was in some ways counter-productive. Whilst it could allow lone raiders to penetrate the defences, bombers were only really effective *en masse*. This demanded a cruising speed at which formation could be comfortably kept. But this was well within the capabilities of the new generation of fighters. On the other hand, fighter escort would provide what protection was needed. The *Luftwaffe* High Command can hardly be blamed for failing to foresee the effect of radar detection and ground controlled interception, which would allow enemy fighters to concentrate on incoming raids. The *Luftwaffe* striking force had many other failings, but these were due to causes other than the Spanish experience.

Equipment

Bomber ace Werner Baumbach, in his book *Broken Swastika*, stated that the *Luftwaffe* strike force at the outbreak of the Second World War was part tactical and part strategic. This is frankly untrue. The essential difference between strategy and tactics is that the former is intended to win the campaign or the war, whereas the latter are purely aimed at winning the engagement or the battle. Therefore the role of the strategic bomber is to carry heavy munitions loads over long distances, to strike at enemy warmaking capacity—i.e. aircraft and munitions factories, oil facilities, sources of raw materials and fuel etc. The fact is that the *Luftwaffe* never really produced a strategic bomber during the entire war. A few raids were carried out which could be described as strategic, but using what were essentially tactical bombers, relatively short-ranged, and with small bomb loads. The current expression is 'a box of matches the length of a cricket pitch!'

Given this, they had little chance of success. Strategic bombing was considered in the mid-1930s, its chief proponent being *Generalmajor* Walther Wever. His requirement was for a bomber, operating from bases in Germany, to be able to reach the north of Scotland in the West and the Ural mountains in the East, while carrying a worthwhile bomb load. Two prototypes were developed,the Dornier Do 19 and the Junkers Ju 89, both four-engined.

The Do 19 was, unsurprisingly for the era, seriously underpowered. Maximum speed was just 199mph while range was 994 miles, giving an operational radius of about 400 miles at most. Maximum bomb load was 3,000kg. Unless more powerful engines could be fitted, and the fuel capacity increased, this was a loser. The Ju 89 was rather better, with a maximum speed of 242mph and a bomb load of 4,000kg, although range was similar to that of the Dornier. Not that maximum speed was particularly important: the real crunch was payload/range, for which the delineator was economical cruising speed, probably about 155mph for the Dornier and 180mph for the Junkers. Neither was developed into an operational aircraft. The primary reasons were twofold. First,

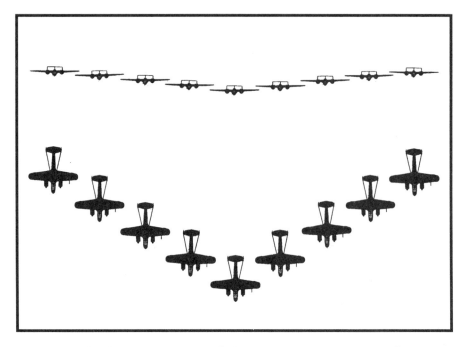

Standard Luftwaffe *flight formations at the beginning of World War II (1):* Staffelwinkel

Germany was lacking in raw materials. This meant that at least four twin-engined bombers could be produced for the same expenditure of effort and *matériel* required by three strategic bombers. Secondly, Wever died in an air accident on 3 June 1936. A novice pilot, he tried to take off from Dresden with his aileron locks still in place. His successors chose numbers rather than quality.

It has been suggested that, had the *Luftwaffe* possessed a strategic bomber fleet in 1940, Britain might have lost the war. This is patent nonsense. In daylight, strategic bombers would have been far too vulnerable to fighter attack, as USAAF raids on Germany later demonstrated. In the night Blitz of 1940–41, whilst they could have carried heavier bomb loads, the reduced numerical strength would have largely offset this advantage. When in late spring of 1941 radar-equipped RAF Beaufighters backed by GCI started to make serious inroads into the *Luftwaffe* bomber force, their task would have been simplified by having fewer targets to handle! The only area in which they might have made a real difference was in the Atlantic, ranging far out to interdict convoys to the beleaguered British Isles.

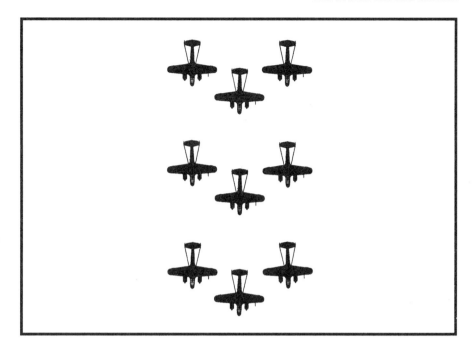

Standard Luftwaffe *flight formations at the beginning of World War II (2):* Staffelkolonne

The idea was not, however, completely dead. In 1938 a specification was issued for a heavy bomber able to carry two tonnes of bombs to an operational radius of 1,000 miles at a speed of 310mph. Initially it had to be stressed for medium angle dive bombing; this was later increased to a 60 degree dive angle. The aircraft eventually emerged as the fairly disastrous He 177, which although it had very advanced design features, not only failed to meet the specification but was too late to play anything more than a peripheral role in the war to come.

Crises

Other crises occurred, apart from the Spanish Civil War. On 7 March 1936 Hitler decided to occupy the Rhineland. Militarily this was a gigantic bluff: Hajo Herrmann, at the time with *KG 4* (Ju 52/3m) was briefed to fly against Paris if necessary, while three *Staffeln* of *StG 165* (Ar 65) stood ready to intervene, even though their aircraft were not combat-ready. France and Britain backed off, although opposition would have almost certainly toppled Hitler and prevented the holocaust to come. The other crisis in 1938 was the *Anschluss* with Austria. Both were backed with demonstrations of armed might by the *Luftwaffe*, in the latter case including leaflet drops by *Stab, II* and *7/KG 155* (Do 17). *KG 255* (Do 17) and *I/StG 168* (Ju 87) were also prepared, while Hajo Herrmann's *KG 4*, now equipped with the Ju 86, was with one of the units which was ready to strike in the West if Britain and France intervened. In the event, both operations were bloodless, and many Austrians joined the *Luftwaffe*. Bluff had prevailed, and the major war in Europe was still to come.

Then, in 1939, came the two-stage occupation of Czechoslovakia, backed by *StG 165* and *KG 155, KG 255* and *KG 355*. Again, the occupation was bloodless. The obvious next step, laid out in *Mein Kampf*, was the invasion of Poland.

Level Bombers

The two major types of level bombers with which the *Luftwaffe* started the Second World War were the Do 17Z and the He 111H. The chronic unreliability of the Ju 86 saw it phased out at an early stage, even though when Hajo Herrmann complained of two engine failures in the space of thirty flying hours he was reprimanded and accused of inexperience. His war record was later to show that this was hardly true in terms of ability.

The Dornier Do 17Z was widely known as the 'Flying Pencil', owing to its slim fuselage. Unusually, it was powered by two Bramo 323P air-cooled radial engines which, with their lack of radiators and plumbing, were far more resistant to battle damage than the more common inlines. With a wing loading at maximum weight of less than 32lb/sq ft, the aircraft was remarkably agile for a bomber, and accounts exist of Dornier pilots attacking fighters in Poland and in France. Normal cruising speed was about 180mph at operational altitude, but its great weakness was payload/range—one tonne of bombs for a normal radius of little more than 200 miles. By the summer of 1940 it was already being phased out in favour of the Ju 88, and by 1943 it had virtually vanished from the scene.

The Heinkel He 111H was powered by two Jumo 211 liquid-cooled inline engines, which, although rather more powerful than those of the Dornier, gave a power/weight ratio about one-third worse. Wing loading, at 33lb/sq ft, was slightly higher than that of the Dornier, but it was an easy and safe aircraft to handle, even with one engine out. Formation cruising speed was 180mph. The crew was five in daylight, when an extra gunner was carried, but four at night. Normal defensive armament consisted of six machine guns, while the maximum bomb load was two tonnes. Operational radius was in excess of 300 miles. One unique feature was the all-glazed cabin, which restricted the view of the pilot considerably, making close formation flying rather difficult. For take-off and landing, his seat and the flying controls could be raised to the point where his head protruded through a hatch to give him a good all-round view. Another strange feature was the bomb bay, from which the bombs were released tail-first, toppling until they reached a nose-down attitude. This can have done nothing for bombing accuracy. The He 111 was the workhorse of the *Luftwaffe* until 1944.

Level Bombers/Dive Bombers

The Ju 88 was without doubt the most versatile German aircraft of the war, used for level bombing, dive bombing, torpedo bombing, reconnaissance and night fighting. Powered by two Jumo 211 inline engines, with annular radiators which gave the appearance of radials, it was designed as the ultimate fast bomber. Even then, its typical formation cruising speed was only 190mph, although when flying solo this increased to 230mph. Wing loading, in excess of 45lb/sq ft at normal combat weight, was high for the time, and handling was considered tricky to the point of being dangerous, especially with one engine out. As a dive bomber, the normal attack angle was about 60 degrees, with dive brakes controlling acceleration. Maximum bomb load was initially 2.5 tonnes, but this was later increased by external carriage. Operational radius was in excess of 500 miles.

Dive Bombers

The Junkers Ju 87 Stuka (a contraction of *Sturzkampfflugzeug*) was slow, single-engined and short-ranged. Its adoption was at first opposed by many in the *Luftwaffe*, as it was thought that its almost vertical diving attack would make it easy meat for quick-firing anti-aircraft guns, which would be presented with an almost zero-deflection shot. This was the factor which led to its eventual demise, but not until the Allies and Russians had got up to speed with their

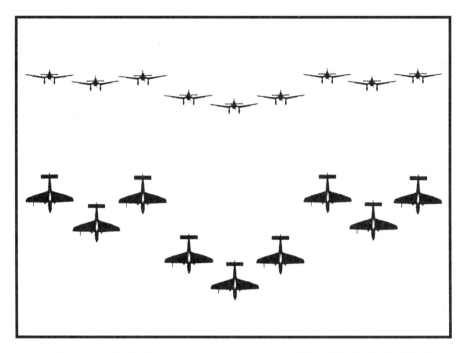

Standard Luftwaffe *flight formations at the beginning of World War II (3):* Staffelkeil

guns and gunnery. It must be remembered that, prewar, Germany led the world in anti-aircraft guns, and this coloured the view of the opponents of the Stuka. In practice it proved to be an outstanding success in Poland and France, in the Balkans and Crete, and, until the final year of the war, against the Soviet Union. Its one failure was in the Battle of Britain, where it was conclusively proved that it could not live without air superiority having first been gained. Formation cruising speed was just 160mph; maximum bomb load was one tonne. It was used as a tactical close air support machine, based close to the front lines, and its short operational radius was hardly relevant.

Organisation of Flying Units

The organisation of *Luftwaffe* flying units differed greatly from those in the West, and although many commentators have used Western terms to describe them, true equivalents did not exist.

In the West, the captain of a bomber crew is the pilot. This is the case even if the pilot is a sergeant and he has a squadron leader as a tail gunner. In

German bomber units, it was not unknown for an observer to be the commander, although this naturally did not apply to the Stuka units, where the two-man crew consisted of a pilot and a radio operator (the latter also doubled as a gunner, as did all other members of a bomber crew apart from the pilot). It was therefore not unusual for a pilot to become an observer as his career advanced. Only as the war progressed did it become the norm for the pilot to be the aircraft commander.

The smallest unit was the *Staffel*, with a nominal strength of nine aircraft, although this was later increased. The commander, who could be anything from a *Leutnant* to a *Hauptmann*, was known as the *Staffelkapitän*. This was an appointment, not a rank. The nearest RAF equivalent was the acting rank bestowed on a commander who had insufficient seniority to merit promotion.

The *Staffelkapitän* was responsible for administration and discipline, and the myriad other tasks of any commander. There were of course times when an appointee lacked experience in the air, and in this case a *Staffelführer* led the unit in combat. The title *Staffelführer* could be used to denote a probationary leader, or even a non-commissioned officer as a temporary measure.

The *Gruppe* was the basic flying and adminstration unit, and normally consisted of three *Staffeln* and a *Stab*, or headquarters unit, generally of three or four aircraft. The *Stab* was often equipped with a different type of aircraft from that of the *Gruppe*, and carried out different functions—perhaps reconnaissance or target location for the main force. A *Gruppe*, led by a *Kommandeur* whose rank could be anything from *Hauptmann* to *Oberstleutnant*, although nominally part of a larger formation, often operated autonomously.

The largest unit was the *Geschwader*, which normally comprised three *Gruppen* and a *Stab* and was led by a *Kommodore*, whose rank was anything from a *Major* to a full *Oberst*. With his command sometimes spread over three fronts and perhaps two continents, his administrative task must have been very difficult, and sometimes impossible. He was, however, still expected to lead his men in the air. In the event of the *Gruppen* being dispersed, the *Geschwaderstab* was attached to one of them. Nothing was totally consistent. Late in the war some *Gruppen* operated a fourth *Staffel*, while some *Geschwader* had a fourth, or even a fifth, *Gruppe*. Then there were various

27

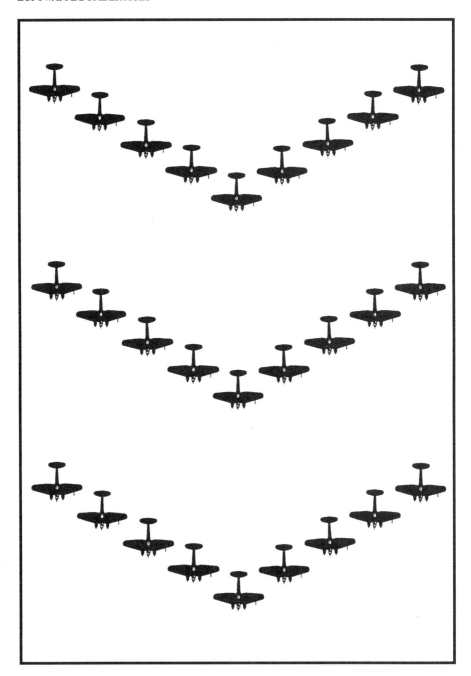

Standard Luftwaffe *flight formations at the beginning of World War II (4):*
Gruppenkolonne aus Staffelwinkeln

specialist *Staffeln*, notably the railway attack units which included *Eis* (for *Eisenbahn*) after the *Staffel* numeral.

Nomenklatur

Unit designation was generally by function. A *Zerstörer Geschwader (ZG)* was a twin-engined fighter unit, usually equipped with the Bf 110 but often engaged in ground attack. For the record, the author has chosen to use the term 'heavy fighter' for these: there are many references to navy destroyers being attacked or sunk, and this avoids confusion. Bomber units were *Kampfgeschwader (KG)*. Where an autonomous *Gruppe* exists, this is a *Kampfgruppe (KGr)*. Then there are the dive bomber units, the *Stukageschwader (StG)*, the *Schnellkampfgeschwader (SKG)* fast bomber units, usually equipped with FW 190s, and the attack units or *Schlachtgeschwader (SG)*. *Nachtschlachtgeschwader (NSG)* were night attack units.

Most units were numbered. *Staffeln* were identified by arabic numerals, for example *7/KG 54*, while *Gruppen* within *Geschwader* used roman numerals, for example *III/KG 54*. However, independent *Gruppen* were also allotted arabic numerals, e.g. *KGr 100*. As a general rule, *Staffeln* 1–3 were part of the first *Gruppe*, *Staffeln* 4–6 the second and *Staffeln* 7–9 the third. The *Stab* was always identified with its parent *Gruppe* or *Geschwader*, the latter using arabic numerals.

A few units fell outside this system. There were the two operational evaluation units, the *Lehrgeschwader*, each *Gruppe* of which flew a different type. *Erprobungsgruppe 210 (EprGr210)* was formed to evaluate the Bf 210, although it never did so. The suffix *(J)* to a *Kampfgeschwader* denoted that it flew the Me 262 as a fighter-bomber. Then there was the *Kommando (Kdo)*, which was a small detachment formed for a specific purpose.

Finally we must deal with what constitutes a bomber ace. In the companion volume *Luftwaffe Fighter Aces,* this was fairly simple: the number of confirmed victories was the decider. But for bombers, matters were not so clearcut. The German system of awards started off with the *Eiseners Kreuz* Class II and Class I, but these were so common as to be regarded as coming round with the corn flakes.

The next step up was the *Ritterkreuz*, or Knight's Cross of the Iron Cross. This has been the basic yardstick adopted. Even then, the selection of entries

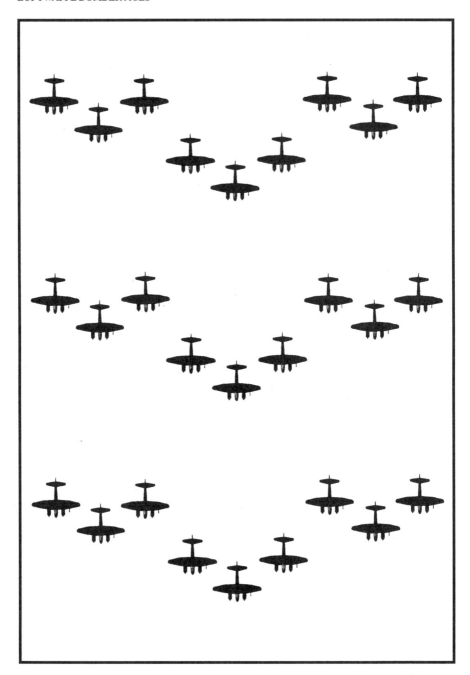

Standard Luftwaffe *flight formations at the beginning of World War II (5):*
Gruppenkolonne aus geschlossenen Staffelkeilen

has been far from easy. Unlike the RAF system, where bars are awarded to medals and orders, the *Luftwaffe* progressed in stages. After the first year or so of war, it was decided that the *Ritterkreuz* was in danger of being devalued, and the *Deutsches Kreuz in Gold* was instituted as a sort of halfway house. The *Ritterkreuz* became the next stage, followed by the *Eichenlaub* (Oak Leaves), *Schwerten* (Swords)—the last two irreverently known as the 'cabbages and knives and forks'—and the *Brillianten* (Diamonds). Only one higher award was issued, the Golden Oak Leaves, won by just one man.

The *Ritterkreuz* was awarded to more than 660 *Luftwaffe* bomber, dive bomber and attack pilots. Consequently the author has had to be selective with individual entries but he has tried to strike a balance, depending on what is known. In accordance with the author's usual practice he has ignored ranks, with the exception of NCO crewmen, who are noted as such.

2. BLITZKRIEG

By August 1939 the *Luftwaffe* was largely committed to dive bombing as a form of close air support to the ground forces, mainly due to the inherent accuracy of this form of attack. Whereas a level bomber might under ideal conditions place 50 per cent of its bombs within 250m of the target, a dive bomber might achieve an order of magnitude less than this, for example 25 yards. Whilst this was a great improvement, how effective was it?

Bomb damage was achieved in three ways: a direct hit that involved penetration of the target, which was rare: shrapnel damage, which, whilst it covered a larger area, depended on a piece of the bomb casing hitting the target with sufficient velocity to penetrate whatever the target was—which, except in the case of 'soft' targets such as trucks or troops, was not always sufficient to cause lethal damage; and blast. Blast spread out as the formula $1.33 \times 3.1416 \times r^3$ (where r = radius), which meant that it dissipated very rapidly with distance; it was not very effective in the case of near misses against hardened targets such as tanks, but was rather more so with soft targets. The area where a near miss might do considerable damage was at sea. In a dense medium such as water, blast effect was greatly multiplied, often causing lethal damage to freighters or lightly armoured warships such as frigates or destroyers by springing their plates. Not for nothing were the latter referred to as 'tin cans'!

Let us examine the method used in dive bombing with the Ju 87. The approach was typically made from about 12,000ft and a speed of 160mph. Operational ceiling was of little significance, as from much higher than this the target could not be identified with any degree of accuracy; in cloudy or hazy conditions, when the target could not clearly be seen, the attack had to be commenced from much lower.

Just in front of his seat, the Ju 87 pilot had a clear-view panel in the floor of his aircraft. When he was over the target he pulled a lever which deployed the underwing dive brakes to the maximum drag position, at the same time trimming the aircraft to compensate for a steep nose-down position. At this point the Ju 87 was launched into a steep dive, typically at a 70- to 80-degree angle. Like most *Luftwaffe* aircraft of the era, it was fuel-injected, and not subject to negative-g fuel carburation problems, so could bunt over without the need to peel off first. It built up speed to a maximum of about 350mph after about an 8,000ft loss of altitude, which was its terminal velocity with dive brakes deployed. As the Ju 87 passed a preset altitude, typically about 4,300ft, a warning klaxon sounded in the cockpit. When this ceased—which signalled the bomb release altitude, typically at about 2,300ft—it was time to drop the bombs. At the moment of release, the main bomb, which was always carried centrally, was swung clear of the propeller arc on a trapeze. Once the bomb was released, pull-out was automatic, subjecting the crew to grey-out as the blood drained from their heads.

There were, naturally, variations in the method of attack. Ideally, the dive was made into wind. There were two reasons for this: first, it prevented the aircraft from 'crabbing' in a crosswind, which in turn aided aiming accuracy; and secondly, the bombs did not drift sideways after release under the influence of a crosswind. While the falling time of the bombs was only about five seconds, sideways drift could make the difference between a direct hit and a near miss. Wind direction on the ground was sometimes indicated by smoke, but more often the forecast of the wind direction was the only means available.

Against a heavily defended target, the safest course was to attack from the direction of the sun, trusting it to blind the ground gunners and accepting the inherent inaccuracies of a crosswind. Against pinpoint targets such as bridges, the attack was made in line astern. Against area targets such as factories or airfields, *Ketten* of three Stukas attacked simultaneously. These had one basic weakness: with all aircraft coming down the same 'chute', as it were, ground fire could be concentrated on the line of the attack, with a correspondingly greater chance of scoring hits—and a single hit from a 40mm Bofors gun was usually lethal. Prewar, this had been the greatest argument against the adoption of the Stuka, and later in the war it was primarily responsible for its demise. The inevitable was held off for a while by units attacking in quick succession from different angles. On the other hand, the dive bomber was the best anti-shipping weapon of the entire war because of its inherent accuracy against small moving targets, as not only the *Luftwaffe* discovered, but also the US Navy and Imperial Japanese Navy in the Pacific.

Against shipping taking evasive action in open water, the aiming problems were magnified. Often a stepped dive was used, the aircraft pulling out at about 6,000ft before circling and picking a new target. Then, when the final attack dive was commenced, less speed built up, giving the pilot more time to refine the aim. At the same time, the sight could often be kept on target by aileron-turning the Stuka in its dive. Against enemy fighters, the Ju 87 was extremely vulnerable. With only a single, and later a twin, rifle-calibre machine gun for defence astern, the crossfire of a formation was negligible. This made fighter escort essential. The two fixed forward-firing machine guns in the wings were essentially for strafing; in air combat their lethality was questionable.

The area in which the Ju 87 was least vulnerable was in the attack dive. With speed brakes extended, velocity built up slowly, whereas a following fighter quickly built up speed and more often than not overshot its intended victim before it could bring its sights to bear. The really vulnerable time came at the pull-out after the dive. Formation cohesion had been lost, speed had been bled off by the pull-out and at low level there was little room for manoeuvre. The result was a gaggle of Stukas homeward-bound perhaps only a few feet above the unforgiving land or sea. There were two chances of survival. The first lay in pouring on the coals and trying to get to the front of the gaggle, where the aircraft would be protected by those astern. The second lay in a hard break into the direction of the attack to give the most difficult high-deflection-angle shot possible to the fighter. This did not always work. Radio operators/gunners sometimes felt that they were little more than body armour for the pilot: they would stop bullets aimed for him!

This apart, the task of the radio operator/gunner in a Ju 87 was unenviable. During the attack he faced backwards and upwards, unable to see what his crazy driver was doing, except that he was hurling their little pink bodies towards the unyielding ground at a rate of knots. Half the time he did not know whether the pilot had been hit, in which case he was on a one-way trip. Then, after the pull-out, struggling against the effects of grey-out, he was expected to note the effect of the bombs, while keeping a sharp eye open for enemy fighters, ready to repel a heavily armed assailant with what was little more than a peashooter! Ju 87 gunners not only earned their flying pay, but also the few Knight's Crosses that came their way.

Shortly before the outbreak of war, Stukas were involved in a training disaster. On 15 August 1939 *I/StG 76* was scheduled to make a practice bombing mission on the range at Neuhammer. A weather reconnaissance aircraft had reported 7/10ths cloud over the area between 2,500 and 6,000ft but clear sky below it. Walter Sigel led the *Stab* of three aircraft, followed by the three *Staffeln*. Starting from 12,000ft, they launched down towards, then into, the cloud, intending to acquire, then bomb, the target, when they emerged from underneath. Alas, the weather had changed. What had appeared to be cloud was actually ground fog. The rapidly unwinding altimeter was of little or no help as Sigel strained his eyes, expecting to burst out of cloud at any second. But what he saw was the ground, far too close. Shouting a warning over the radio, he heaved back on the stick, pulling out into a forest ride with barely feet to spare. To left and right, his wingmen crashed into the trees. Following closely behind, the nine aircraft of *2 Staffel* hit the ground; *3 Staffel* had just that extra bit of clearance, and all except two managed to pull out safely; *1 Staffel*, even higher, were spared the carnage. Thirty aircraft took off, only seventeen returned, and 26 young crewmen were dead. There was, however, no time to brood: the Second World War was about to commence.

Low-Level Attacks

Level bombing inaccuracy stemmed from two factors—speed and altitude. The faster the bomber, the more room there was for inexactitude, and the higher it was, the same applied. Less of either one or the other, and accuracy improved. At the outbreak of war, the *Luftwaffe* had one specialised ground attack aircraft type, the Henschel Hs 123 biplane. It was slow but agile, and its bomb load was a mere 200kg.

The level bombers also attacked selected targets at low altitude on occasion, while there were two *Staffeln* of slightly modified Dornier Do 17Zs, whose crews were specially trained in low-level attack, although they also flew standard medium-altitude attacks with their parent *Gruppen*. Fighters could also be modified to carry bombs, aiming with the Revi gun sight and releasing at low level in a shallow dive. This gave only moderate results.

Assault on Poland

At dawn on 1 September 1939 the German invasion force stood ready to cross the border into Poland. It was backed by Air Fleets 1 and 4, which contained a strike element of roughly 850 bombers, dive bombers and attack aircraft, of which about 88 per cent were serviceable. The *Blitzkreig* concept of war, in which speed of movement on the ground by armoured columns, bypassing strongpoints and penetrating deep into the enemy rear areas, spearheaded by air power, was paramount. Cut off, the strongpoints were left to be mopped up by the second (mainly infantry) echelon.

In fact, it was not quite like this. The first task of the *Luftwaffe* was to gain air superiority by destroying the Polish Air Force on the ground, and, to this end, large raids were aimed at known Polish airfields. The problem lay in the fact that the essential element of surprise had been lost. The Germans had telegraphed their punch, with the result that, when the blow fell, the target was no longer there. The Polish Air Force, technically and numerically inferior, had dispersed to secondary airfields. It could now only be ground down by attrition, mainly in the air.

The first *Luftwaffe* sortie of the war was flown by a *Kette* of *3/StG 1* led by Bruno Dilley. In all, five armoured thrusts were planned, but one of them was from East Prussia, which was cut off from Germany proper by the Danzig Corridor, ceded to Poland after the Great War. This made the restoration of supply and communications links of vital importance. The key position was the twin bridge over the Vistula at Dirschau. The Poles, well aware of this, had set demolition charges. Dilley's mission was to prevent the bridge's destruction long enough for an armoured train to cross and secure the bridge. The key was a Polish blockhouse on the far bank which housed the detonation equipment. If this could be destroyed, there was a chance that the bridge might be saved. Dive bombing was not an option—fortunately as it turned out—because ground fog shrouded the front on the first day of the war.

The *Kette*, each aircraft armed with a 250kg bomb beneath the fuselage and four 50kg bombs beneath the wings, raced over the countryside and through the drifting tendrils of fog at barely 10m. Fortunately, flying time to the target was only eight minutes, and the Vistula was an unmistakable landmark. The bridge stood out clearly, the blockhouse could be seen, and the attack was pressed home successfully. The time was 04.30.

Dilley's attack was followed up by the Dorniers of *III/KG 3*, but these were hampered by the fog. The interval gave the Poles time to reconnect the wiring and blow the bridge before the armoured train arrived. Such are the fortunes of war!

The fog also delayed the massive air strikes that had been planned, not only against the Polish Air Force but also against the capital, Warsaw, in an attempt to destroy the will of the Polish nation to continue the struggle. In fact, the attack on Warsaw was called off.

Further south, in the Air Fleet 4 area, conditions were rather better and the Heinkels of *KG 4* bombed Krakow airfield and rail links. This was not in the original plan, but, to the north, bad weather prevented some units from finding their briefed targets and they were redirected south. This was not done without opposition: on 2 September Hajo Herrmann's Heinkel had one of its engines knocked out by a frontal attack from a Polish fighter. He limped back to base on his remaining engine.

The level bombing attack on Krakow airfield was followed by the dive bombers of *I/StG 2* led by Oskar Dinort. But when the Dorniers of *I* and *III/ KG 77* arrived, dust and smoke obscured the target and aircraft of the latter unit were forced by the poor visibility to drop their load of 50kg bombs from very low level—barely 50m. Fitted with impact fuzes, the bombs exploded when the aircraft were still overhead. Although none was lost, many of the Dorniers were damaged by shrapnel from their own bombs.

Many other airfield targets were attacked in the first days, but, as related earlier, the bird had flown. However, while dispersal had saved the Polish Air Force from almost instant annihilation, it was not a panacea. As supply routes and communications centres were either attacked from the air or overrun by the advancing Panzers, so confusion reigned and the organisation collapsed, rendering the Polish Air Force virtually impotent. Of course, the *Luftwaffe* High Command was naturally slow to realise this.

With control of the air, the Stukas really came into their own, attacking and sometimes routing the Polish ground forces. Part of the effect was psychological. One of the ugliest aircraft ever built, the Ju 87 exuded an air of menace. When it commenced its attack dive, the engine and propeller noise increased as speed built up, even though it was throttled back. The noise grew even more as the range reduced. Against unseasoned troops, this sound of vicious intent was unnerving. This effect had been noticed in Spain, with the result that small wind-driven sirens were attached to the undercarriage legs, adding a piercing shriek to the overall effect. These became known as the 'Trumpets of Jericho', although the only walls they demolished were mental ones. Finally, a soldier on the receiving end of a diving Stuka always felt that he personally was the target, even though the bombs might eventually land hundreds of metres away. It was in Poland that the Stuka started to build up its formidable, almost legendary (and to a degree undeserved) reputation.

Günter Schwartzkopff, often called the 'Father of the Stukas' for his work in developing and forming the dive bomber units, and *Kommodore* of *StG 77*, was so unhappy about the decision to delay take-off on the first morning that he carried out a solo attack on Polish positions. A matter of honour, or foolhardy? Schwartzkopff had been born in the previous century and seriously wounded at Verdun in the Great War, and his attitudes were not those of today. At the same time, in leading from the front in such a manner, he set an inspiring example. On the other hand, the average Stuka pilot was not well versed in instrument flying: had the pilots been sent out in such conditions a disaster may well have ensued.

As a dive bomber, the Stuka was not used in the close air support role. For this, its crews had to be able to distinguish between friendly and enemy troops—in the confusion of battle an almost impossible task from a high perch two miles up. The aircraft's greatest use in supporting the Army was to attack targets behind the lines—supplies, troop concentrations etc—in what is now known as battlefield air interdiction. It could of course be used for close air support, but this entailed flying at relatively low altitudes where positive identification could be made.

As there was little future in swanning about over hostile territory at low altitude, attacks were almost invariably commenced from the German side of the lines in a shallow dive. There were two basic ways of establishing German positions. One was to lay out coloured panels in the front lines, although this was only of use when the lines had been stabilised. The other was for the tanks to carry large white crosses on their backs. These showed up fairly well in most circumstances, and helped to minimise the risk of 'own goals', although inevitably the latter occurred from time to time. The usual close air support load consisted of 50kg fragmentation bombs, which gave maximum effect against troops, soft vehicles and, where the Polish Army was concerned, cavalry. Discharge of the bombs was followed by strafing with the two fixed machine guns.

During the first week of the war, only sporadic attacks had been launched against Warsaw, without great success. Whilst these were intensified on 8 September, a critical situation arose. The German Eighth Army in the north had failed to keep up with the Tenth Army. Its right flank exposed, it was attacked by the Polish Army of Poznan on 9–10 September.

The Hs 123 biplanes of *II(Schlacht)/LG 2*, led by Werner Spielvogel, had been in action from the first day, giving close air support to the troops with fire bombs. Spielvogel himself was shot down on 9 September while on a reconnaissance flight in a Fieseler Storch. Although he force-landed safely, he was shot on the ground while attempting to rescue his pilot. Otto Weiss, *Staffelkapitän* of *4(Schlacht)/LG 2*, replaced him as *Kommandeur*. The *Staffelkapitän* of *5(Schlacht)/LG 2*, Spanish veteran Adolf Galland, would shortly become famous as a fighter ace.

Now *II(Schlacht)/LG 2* was thrown in against the Army of Poznan. The two rifle-calibre machine guns and the pair of 50kg bombs were not very effective, but one of the main weapons of the Hs 123 was pyschological: at above 1,800rpm its engine sounded like heavy machine gun fire, although at these revs it could not fire a shot without risking tearing off its propeller. Attacking from just 10m, it spread alarm and despondency among their enemies. Joined by the Stukas, then by the Heinkels of *KG 1*, *KG 4* (under Martin Fiebig) and *KG 26*, it halted the Polish counter-attack.

The first so-called terror raid of the Second World War took place on 13 September. Organisationally it was a shambles. General von Richthofen, commanding the Stukas, later recorded:

> Chaos over the target was indescribable. Not a single unit attacked at its appointed time, and aircraft nearly collided in the act of bombing. Below there was just a sea of flame and smoke, so that accurate assessment of results was impossible.

Was this in fact a terror raid? The French air attaché in Warsaw later stated that the *Luftwaffe* operations had conformed with the rules of warfare, and that civilian casualties had been caused only because the victims were close to military targets.

While most *Luftwaffe* bomber commanders followed the directives they were given, *Oberst* Seywald, *Kommodore* of *KG 77,* was a 'wild man', not amenable to discipline, who wanted to fight the war his way—and on moralistic lines. If he disagreed with the targets he was given, he substituted others. Tasked to raid the city of Warsaw on 13 September, he chose instead to attack strictly military targets. He was relieved of his command that same evening. Not all German bomber pilots conformed to the popular image of ruthless automata raining death and destruction on women and children, and Seywald was probably the first exception. So much for the postwar excuse of *'Befehl ist befehl'*—orders are orders—used by the Nazis to explain many atrocities.

Few night raids took place in the Polish campaign, and these were mainly carried out by *LnAbt 100* (He 111), the *Luftwaffe* Pathfinders, using the *X-Gerät* blind bombing system described later. Redesignated *KGr 100,* this unit later became notorious in the Blitz on Great Britain. Only four raids were mounted, the first on the night of 3/4 September and the last, which destroyed a munitions dump, on 10/11 September.

Leaflet raids on Warsaw followed, warning the Poles that further resistance was useless, but these were ignored. Warsaw was fortified. By now, knowing that the Polish campaign was as good as won, the *Luftwaffe* began to pull back first-line units, and also to restrict the use of heavier bombs, saving them for the inevitable war against France and Britain. When, on 25 September, the annihilation of Warsaw began, in addition to the Stukas 30 Ju 52 transports circled over the city. In the back of each, two soldiers literally shovelled out incendiaries with no attempt at obtaining accuracy. Some of them landed

40

on German infantry, but the deed was done. Two days later Poland capitulated.

Hermann Goering's boast of 'lightning speed and undreamed-of might' appeared to have been fulfilled in the Polish campaign. The admittedly not very strong nor modern Polish Air Force had apparently been crushed within days. While this was more in the appearance than the reality, it remained a fact. Then, with air superiority established, the German bomber force ranged the length and breadth of the country virtually unchallenged, cutting supply routes and communications. German air power, notably the Stukas, reduced strongpoints and spearheaded the advancing Panzers, while guarding the flanks of the ground forces. Finally, overwhelming air power resulted in the surrender of the Polish capital, and shortly afterwards that of the entire nation. If Stukas gained an undeserved reputation during this conflict, it was largely due to the Propaganda Ministry of Josef Goebbels, and the world press who believed his lies. Less than a year later, the Stuka myth would finally be laid to rest.

 **3. ANTI-SHIPPING OPERATIONS, 1939–40**

The British Empire, global in its extent as it then was, was founded on sea power. The Royal Navy had not only reigned supreme around the world for more than a century and a half, it had also been the model for all other navies whose political masters had harboured ambitions of empire. This included both Germany and Japan. Many of the latter's capital ships, notably a unit of the *Kongo* class, were actually built in British yards!

When Britain and France declared war on Germany shortly after the invasion of Poland, it posed problems for the Third Reich, although these were not at first fully appreciated. France, like Germany, was a land power, and could therefore be theoretically overcome by the same *Blitzkrieg* tactics as had been used against Poland. The island nation was, however, quite a different matter, separated from mainland Europe by the tricky waters of the English Channel and defended by a powerful navy which not only outnumbered but also outgunned the *Kriegsmarine*. However, this was not seen as a problem by *Herr* Hitler, who at the time assumed that he could reach an accommodation with the British while he turned his attention eastwards. Later scurrilously dubbed the '*Gröfaz*' by the *Luftwaffe*—a contraction of *Grösster Feldherr aller Zeiten*, the greatest military commander of all time—he here made his first, and arguably his greatest, mistake.

It was of course widely accepted at this time that warships were potentially vulnerable to air attack, although to what degree was a matter for debate. During trials in the United States in July 1921, the ex-German battleship *Ostfriesland* had been sunk by air attack, but only under the most favourable (and unrealistic) conditions: first, it was a static target, with its watertight doors left open, and secondly, it had no defences, which allowed a low-level attack, with no excitement to distract the bomber crews. On the first day fifty-two 600lb bombs were dropped from 1,500ft, with little or no effect; on the second day the vessel survived sixteen direct hits by 1,100lb bombs before finally succumbing to a final attack of eight 2,000lb bombs All this really proved was that bombing and sinking a defended moving battleship in open water, probably ringed by a screen of other warships, would be both difficult and expensive. Smaller ships, such as destroyers, could sustain far less damage, but, being smaller and faster, were more difficult to hit.

For Germany, this was academic unless enemy warships were within range of land-based aircraft, although dive bombing promised to supply the necessary accuracy.

German Carrier Aviation

The answer to the range problem, as convincingly demonstrated later in the war by the British, Americans and Japanese, was the aircraft carrier. Germany ordered her own, the *Graf Zeppelin*, although in the event this was never commissioned. How effective could it have been? The short answer must be: not very. Even if it had managed to put to sea, as a singleton it would have been overmatched by the numerous Royal Navy carriers which would inevitably have been sent against it. Its projected complement of aircraft consisted of Bf 109T (*Träger*, or carrier) single-seat fighters and Ju 87C dive bombers. While both were decidedly superior in these roles to their contemporary Royal Navy equivalents, how might they have fared in action? One suspects not very well. The basic Bf 109 did not handle well at low speeds, and the modifications for carrier usage—an arrester hook, greater wing area, wing folding and spoilers—would have added extra weight and drag, reducing performance and penalising low-speed handling, so important for deck landings.

Once in the air, it would have been a match for virtually every contemporary land-based fighter, but for how long? If later British experience with the Seafire, a navalised Spitfire, is anything to go by, not long at all. The Seafire proved to be too delicate for carrier operations: losses as a result of accidents were far greater than those brought about by enemy action. Even though its low-speed handling was far better than that of the Messerschmitt, its undercarriage was simply not up to the job. Another factor was very limited endurance. For operational reasons, carrier aircraft need far greater safety margins of fuel than their land-based equivalents, if only because they first have to find 'mother' in the trackless wastes of the ocean; then they have to wait their turn to land in an orderly queue. There can be no doubt that the Bf 109T would have suffered heavily from operational attrition.

The Ju 87C was a much more sturdy machine, but the same strictures on performance and endurance apply. Furthermore, the ship having an onboard complement of only twelve Stukas, how could it have have flown off the necessary searches and still have maintained a valid striking force? It was probably a wise decision not to have introduced the German carrier into service, as, having sailed, it would have immediately become a prime target—as in fact was the *Bismarck* a year later—for everything that could have been flung against it. The only conclusion is that it would have been of little more than nuisance value.

Küstenflieger

The *Luftwaffe* was therefore reduced to flying from land bases, which in the first eleven months of the war meant bases in Germany itself. The means to hand were also limited: the Heinkel He 111s of *KG 26*, many of the pilots of which were previously naval men; the slow but benign He 115 floatplane, the main function of which was minelaying but which was later used as a torpedo bomber; and the Ju 88, which, initially plagued by technical problems, was only just coming into service. The last at least had a dive bombing capability, which greatly increased its usefulness against shipping targets. All were lacking in operational radius.

The only type with a really useful range, the FW 200 Condor, was a converted airliner. It was conceived as a long-range maritime reconnaissance machine, but it was many months before it became a serious anti-shipping aircraft. Its airliner ancestry also meant that it was structurally inadequate as a warplane—a factor which led to many landing accidents and an inability to sustain much battle damage.

In the West, the war on the ground had stultified as both Germany and France watched each other carefully from either side of the fortified Siegfried and Maginot lines respectively. It was the period known respectively as the *Sitzkrieg* and the *drôle de guerre*, and, in Britain, as the Phoney War. Apart from reconnaissance, little offensive action could be taken, as both adversaries were anxious not to escalate the situation by causing civilian casualties.

Trial and Error

The one exception was ships at sea, or in the roadsteads, which meant in effect that the only possible targets were British or German warships. The Heinkels of *KG 26*, just two *Gruppen* strong, were pulled out of Poland in mid-September and deployed to the West for anti-shipping operations. *EprKdo 88*, the development unit for the Ju 88, was redesignated *I/KG 25* in August 1939, but then barely a month later became *I/KG 30*.

Its first operation was against the British Home Fleet on 26 September, when reconnaissance Dornier Do 18 flying boats sighted the latter at sea off the Firth of Forth. On this day, three Do 18s of *2/KüflGr 106* were shadowing the British Fleet, which consisted of the carrier *Ark Royal*, the battleships *Nelson* and *Rodney* and several cruisers and destroyers. One of the Dorniers was intercepted and shot down by Skuas from *Ark Royal*, but the other two escaped, radioing back the sighting and position.

A *Staffel* of He 111s of *1/KG 26* took off, led by Martin Vetter, followed by four Ju 88s from *I/KG 30*, commanded by Spanish Civil War veteran Martin Storp. Among the latter's crews was the former test pilot Carl Francke, serving as a humble NCO in the *Luftwaffe* reserve. It seems incredible that such a famous and gifted test pilot should fly in such a lowly capacity, but his was far from being the only case. In fact, it was very difficult for a reserve pilot to be commissioned into the regular *Luftwaffe*.

There was 8/10ths cloud over the target area. Francke sighted the carrier, which was of course the primary target, and tried a diving attack, but on the way down this was baulked by cloud. After an interval of several minutes he tried again, diving into a storm of flak to release two SC 500 bombs. As he pulled out and up, one of his crew observed a bomb near-miss *Ark Royal*'s bows. What about the second bomb? As he curved away there was a flash on the bows of the carrier. Could this have been a hit, or was it gunfire?

Francke's radio report was carefully worded, but when the next reconnaissance aircraft in the area failed to sight the carrier, and patches of oil were seen, the propaganda ministry, eager for success, reported her sunk. It had not

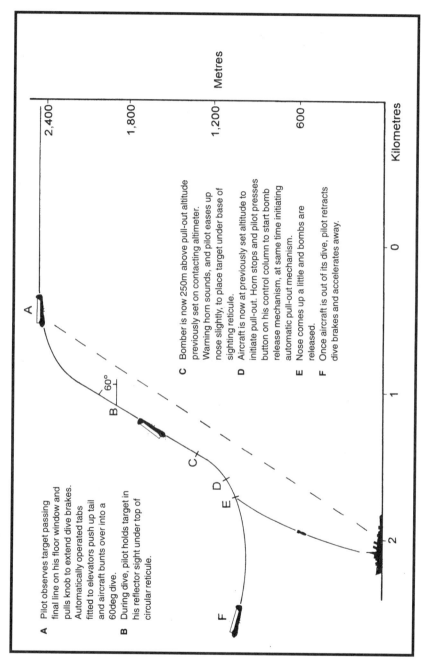

Metres

Kilometres

A Pilot observes target passing final line on his floor window and pulls knob to extend dive brakes. Automatically operated tabs fitted to elevators push up tail and aircraft bunts over into a 60deg dive.

B During dive, pilot holds target in his reflector sight under top of circular reticule.

C Bomber is now 250m above pull-out altitude previously set on contacting altimeter. Warning horn sounds, and pilot eases up nose slightly, to place target under base of sighting reticule.

D Aircraft is now at previously set altitude to initiate pull-out. Horn stops and pilot presses button on his control column to start bomb release mechanism, at same time initiating automatic pull-out mechanism.

E Nose comes up a little and bombs are released.

F Once aircraft is out of its dive, pilot retracts dive brakes and accelerates away.

Typical dive bombing attack by a Junkers Ju 88.

in fact been touched. For many weeks afterwards, German broadcasts asked, 'Where is the *Ark Royal*?', to which its crew, now heading for the South Atlantic and the pocket-battleship *Graf Spee*, delightedly chortled 'We're here! We're here!' But even at full volume, the message failed to reach Dr Goebbels! Only when the *Ark Royal* was finally sunk in the Mediterranean by a U-boat on 14 November 1941 were the German records altered.

Barely three weeks later, on 16 October, the battlecruiser *Hood* was sighted near the Firth of Forth and a *Staffel* of *I/KG 30* was launched to attack before the ship could reach sanctuary. This was nothing unusual; often they failed to find the enemy. On this occasion they arrived only to find that *Hood* had already berthed and was therefore untouchable.There were, however, other warships in the roadsteads, which the rules of engagement allowed to be attacked.

Staffelkapitän Helmut Pohle selected the cruiser *Southampton* as his target. He attacked in a steep dive and scored a hit, but the bomb did not go off; instead it penetrated three decks before emerging through the side of the cruiser. Pohle had been informed that there were no Spitfires based in the area, but at this point the RAF proved him wrong. From being the hunter, he became the hunted, and, in spite of desperate evasive action, his aircraft was badly shot up. His radio operator, flight mechanic and gunner were all killed or seriously wounded, and one engine was knocked out. Pohle, himself badly wounded and about to lose consciousness, ditched in the sea near a British trawler and was rescued, the only survivor. It was five days before he regained consciousness, to sit out nearly six years as a prisoner of war.

Another Ju 88 went down, reportedly to anti-aircraft fire, and a third had a lucky escape. Horst von Riesen only managed to near-miss his target, the destroyer *Mohawk*. As he pulled out, the Spitfires attacked. At full throttle, he sped away, just a few metres above the sea, jinking frantically to make himself a difficult target:

> . . . I thought I was finished. Guns were firing at me from all sides, and the Spitfires behind seemed to be taking turns at attacking. But my speed gave them all a bit of a surprise—I was doing more than 400kph [about 250mph].

Here it should be noted that while the maximum quoted speed of the Spitfire was far higher, this was at optimum altitude. In the denser air at sea level, it was much slower. In a different context, RAF fighter ace Bob Stanford Tuck was later to comment: 'Once it had unloaded its dirt, and was homeward bound with a Spitfire up its a***, the Ju 88 was a wonderfully fast kite!'

Desperately, von Riesen headed out to sea. Looking down, he could see what looked like raindrops hitting the water ahead. Then he realised—these were bullets aimed at him! At this early stage in the war, the eight machine guns of British fighters were harmonised to cover a large area at a relatively long range. This gave the average pilot a sporting chance of scoring just a few hits, but penalised the marksman. Given the later practice of all guns converging on a point at about 750ft range, von Riesen would probably not have survived. As it was, he was lucky. After a pursuit lasting more than twenty minutes, the Spitfires, far from home, turned back. But, in what was probably the final attack, bullets pierced the coolant system of his starboard engine. As he shut it down, his speed dropped to a mere 180kph—barely above stalling. The Ju 88, considered tricky to fly at the best of times, was even worse with the asymmetric thrust of just one engine. Nor was it supposed to be able to maintain altitude in this condition. But it did, even gaining a little as fuel was burned off. After four hours, it limped back into Westerland.

To emphasise von Riesen's feat in bringing back his stricken bomber, it is necessary to recall its handling flaws. Former civilian test pilot Peter Stahl, who first flew the type on 30 April 1940, likened it to a temperamental and capricious diva. At low speeds the rudder was not very effective. This made it touchy to land, with an approach speed of 250kph, flaring at 215kph—both very high for the period and well above the maximum that von Riesen could coax out of it on one engine. Asymmetric handling must have made this situation much worse. Turning into the live engine was extremely difficult, while even recovery from a turn in the other direction could not be achieved with any precision. As a former test pilot, Stahl was very experienced and well above average in ability. He commented: 'It is capable of suddenly doing quite surprising things without the slightest warning.'

Neither was take-off a bed of roses. Once the tail was lifted, a hard swing to port often resulted, which only an instantaneous bootful of rudder could correct. However, in the higher speed range it was very responsive—almost fighter-like, with light and well-harmonised controls. In a diving attack with air brakes extended it was very stable, unlike the Ju 87, which tended to oscillate and needed continuous corrections.

All in all, the *Luftwaffe* anti-shipping campaign in the first months of the war was not terribly successful. As has been seen, *I/KG 30* achieved little against British warships, dive bombing accuracy or no. The far more numerous Heinkels of the specialist anti-shipping unit *KG 26* also achieved little. Between them they lost thirteen aircraft in October 1939 for little result. Not until December did they open their account, losing three aircraft for the meagre return of two freighters (total tonnage 714) and eight minesweepers sunk.

KG 26 had also set an unenviable precedent when an aircraft of the *Stab* became the first *Luftwaffe* machine to be shot down on British soil, south of Edinburgh, on 28 October 1939. A potential intelligence windfall for the British (although it was eight months before they discovered all the details), this carried *Lorenz* blind landing receivers tuned to the *Knickebein* precision navigation and attack frequency. *Knickebein*, usually translated as 'Bent Leg', was actually a magic raven from folklore, although not to be confused with Hugin and Munin, the ravens which comprised the intelligence service of Wotan. It will be described in detail later.

Much of the work of *KG 26* consisted of armed reconnaissance—prowling the English coast, looking for shipping targets of opportunity. The weather was terrible, and while successes were few, so were losses to RAF fighters. If ships were difficult to find in these conditions, so were German bombers!

On 2 February 1940 *II/KG 26* was ordered off to intercept a convoy steering south near the north-eastern coast of England. The aircraft flew in pairs at three-minute intervals, and at least one pair was expected to make contact. This would then shadow the convoy, and vector the rest in. At any rate, that was the plan.

At 09.03 hours two aircraft were detected by radar, 60 miles offshore at 1,000ft. Shortly afterwards, a ship came under attack off Whitby. By this time, three Hurricanes of No 43 Squadron were already airborne and heading for the scene. Just offshore, the leader sighted a Heinkel and made a climbing attack from the front quarter and opened fire.

The first to spot the Hurricane was observer Peter Leushake, lying in the nose. His last words on this earth were *'Achtung, Jäger!'* The cockpit was a shambles, the flight mechanic was mortally wounded and the radio operator was hard hit. Trailing smoke, the Heinkel headed for land, with blood drops marking its passage over the snow as it crash-landed south of Whitby. It was the first German aircraft to fall on English soil.

The greatest fiasco of *KG 26* came on 22 February 1940 when *4* and *6 Staffeln* attacked a destroyer flotilla, sinking one ship with a single hit by an SC 50 bomb. Ironically it was the *Leberecht Maas*—a German destroyer. Given such a small weapon, of only 50kg, it had to be a fluke, but it underlined the vulnerability of destroyers to air attack. Less than half an hour later the German destroyer *Max Schultz* hit a mine in the general confusion and also sank. As the old saying goes, the average flyer couldn't tell his (HMS) *Argus* from his elbow! Ship recognition was a closed book to most of them. It should not have been so, because many of the *KG 26* aviators were ex-Navy men. This was, however, a common failing with all air forces.

With the invasion of Norway and Denmark scheduled for the following day, Heinkels of *II/KG 26* were sent to attack the British Fleet at Scapa Flow at dusk on 8 April. They were supported by communications jamming on the British fighter wavelength, but all this did was to alert the RAF that a raid was imminent. As a result, the Hurricanes of No 43 Squadron, now based at Wick, were at cockpit readiness. Four Heinkels of the 26 despatched were lost.

At this point a Heinkel 111 of *6/KG 26* took part in one of the most hilarious incidents of the entire war. The aircraft was damaged by Darky Hallowes of No 43 Squadron, and the pilot turned back to crash-land. Having in misty conditions mistaken the airfield flarepath for lights on the sea, he belly-landed in the middle of the runway. The fuselage door was opened, a dinghy was thrown out, and two of the crew, having removed their boots, dived out, only to find that they were on dry land!

Previous to this, another blunder had been committed. A Heinkel He 115 floatplane of *KüFlGr 106* dropped a magnetic mine in too-shallow water off the Thames Estuary. Recovered at low tide, it was defused by Lt-Cdr Ouvry of the shore-based unit HMS *Vernon* at Portsmouth. Its secrets revealed, British anti-mine countermeasures followed in due course. Ouvry was a remarkable man. Blinded while defusing a mine off Gibraltar—from memory, in 1941—

he remained in the service postwar, giving recruiting lectures to schools. A tall and immaculate figure armed with a long wooden pointer with which he indicated graphics with great precision to his audience, his blindness appeared no handicap. But we digress.

Meanwhile *I/KG 30* continued to attack British Fleet anchorages in the Orkneys and Shetlands, without much success. On 16 March they raided Scapa Flow at last light, but damaged only the cruiser *Norfolk* and the gunnery training ship *Iron Duke*.

Another unit destined to become famous had also joined the fray. *LnAbt 100*, which was equipped with the *X-Gerät* system and had carried out the handful of precision night bombing raids on Poland, was redesignated *KGr 100* on 18 November 1939. Commanded by Joachim Stollbrock, a former Lufthansa pilot, it carried out armed reconnaissance missions against shipping, and also unarmed *X-Gerät* trials in the West, gaining valuable experience with the system.

These were brought to a premature end on 13 February 1940 when Stollbrock himself was intercepted at dusk over the Thames Estuary by three Spitfires of No 54 Squadron. Fortunately for the *Luftwaffe*, his aircraft fell into the sea. Horrified by the thought that the latest blind bombing system could have been compromised, the authorities quickly ordered that *X-Gerät* equipment be removed from all aircraft. Stollbrock's replacement was Artur von Casimir, formerly *Staffelkapitän* of *1/KG 55*. His comment on navigation over the North Sea was 'It was by guess or by God!' Von Casimir himself was shot down and captured in the later stages of the Norwegian campaign, but British Intelligence failed to realise the importance of their prisoner and the opportunity was for interrogation was lost.

The pace was stepped up in March 1940 when both individual ships and convoys in the North Sea and the Channel Narrows came under attack, again with little success. Naval wisdom says that it is more effective to let water into the bottom of a ship with a torpedo than to let air into the top of it with a bomb. This is of course to ignore two essential facts. The first is that bombs let fire rather than air into the top of a ship. The second is that torpedoes tend to have a rather long running time. This puts a premium on the fine judgement of the torpedo-bomber pilot while giving the target plenty of time to take evasive action. Early German torpedoes were not very effective: they were relatively slow, giving a long running time from operational ranges, typically 1,500m, and they also had a tendency to run too deep, taking them under the target ship. They were used in this period by He 115 floatplanes and to a lesser degree by He 59 seaplanes, without success. Not until the following year did more effective torpedoes become available.

Operation 'Weserübung'

This was the simultaneous invasion of Denmark and Norway on 9 April 1940. Germany was deficient in natural resources, notably iron ore, and much of this came from Swedish mines at Gällivare. The obvious way to transport such heavy and bulky material was by sea, but for much of the winter the northern Baltic was frozen up and impassable. The easy way was to send it over a relatively short rail link to the port of Narvik in Norway, and then by ship. The British and French needed to halt it; to the Germans it was vital that the trade continued.

On 8 April the British had laid three minefields in Norwegian coastal waters. The purpose was to force the iron ore carriers out into international waters, where they could be attacked without causing an international incident. The analogy is that of giving a pig a pill. The method is to place the pill in a tube, insert the tube in the pig's mouth, and blow! But the pig blew first! The Germans, their plans more advanced, invaded on the following day with a bold combination of seaborne and airborne landings.

The bomber component of the *Luftwaffe* for '*Weserübung*' was not particularly large, as resources had to be kept back against a French offensive. It consisted of *I/StG 1* with the long-range anti-shipping Ju 87R; *II* and *III/KG 4* (He 111P), commanded by Martin Fiebig; *KG 26*, commanded by Robert Fuchs, a Spanish veteran and the first bomber pilot to be awarded the *Ritterkreuz*; *KGr 100* (He 111); and *KG 30* (Ju 88), commanded by Walter Loebel, the first well-known bomber pilot in the *Luftwaffe*. The accent was on anti-shipping specialists, as it was rightly expected that the Royal Navy would intervene in force.

When the invasion proper started, in the first wave were the Heinkels of *III/ KG 30*, not yet converted to the Ju 88. The target was the island fortress off

Kristiansand. At the controls of the leading aircraft was Hajo Herrmann; at his side was his *Staffelkapitän*, Erich Bloedorn, future *Kommodore* of the *Geschwader* and *Ritterkreuz* winner. On board were bombs for the fortress, set to drop at 10m intervals, and containers of pamphlets calling for surrender.

Now came one of those odd incidents on which the fortunes of war so often turn. An observer in one of the other aircraft had mistakenly set 100m intervals for the bombs instead of 10, with the result that the final two fell in the city. Whilst the fortress withstood the bombing, the Mayor of the city, expecting more bombing, ordered its commander to surrender.

As if this were not enough, while the afternoon raid, on a barracks near Oslo, went according to plan, Herrmann's aircraft was damaged by flak from the German cruiser *Blücher*. Then, on the following day, the *Gruppe*, tasked to attack British units farther north, was ordered to land and refuel at Fornebu. The longest runway was partially blocked by crashed aircraft from the airborne landing of the previous day. Herrmann attempted to put down on the shorter one, but his Heinkel, with a full load of bombs on board, could not be halted in the available distance and was wrecked. As a fitting finale to this comedy of errors, a G.38 airliner landed, bringing not reinforcements but a military band!

Meanwhile Denmark, taken by surprise, had fallen with barely a shot fired in its defence. For the Germans, little more than a show of strength was needed. A leaflet raid on Copenhagen by *I/KG 4*, in which one Heinkel was slightly damaged by machine-gun fire from the ground, was the sole contribution of the bomber force. Denmark's value lay in the fact that it commanded the narrows into the Baltic, which to Germany made it strategically important.

On 9 April intensive air reconnaissance over the North Sea soon located the British Home Fleet off Bergen, and elements of *KG 26* and *KG 30* were launched against it. A 500kg bomb hit the battleship *Rodney* without penetrating its armoured belt, three cruisers were damaged and the destroyer *Gurkha* was sunk. This was a fair return for the loss of four Ju 88s from *III/KG 30* and proved conclusively that, without fighter cover, ships were very vulnerable to air attack.

Meanwhile British and French troops had landed in Norway, and in many places the German Army was hard-pressed to hold its positions. Much of the available air power now had to be allocated to attacking port facilities and supply routes. As the campaign dragged on, reinforcements were sent—the Ju 88s of *II(K)* and *III(K)/LG 1*, the Heinkels of *I* and *II/KG 54* and the solitary FW 200 *Staffel, 1/KG 40*.

The most difficult task was supporting German forces at Narvik, in the far north of the country, until such time as an intermediate airfield could be captured. This was where the Condors scored. They alone had the range and endurance to reach the area from bases in Germany. On 11 April three of them made the round trip, bombing British shipping in a sortie that lasted seventeen hours. They also flew a few resupply missions.

Meanwhile Allied shipping casualties mounted, despite the presence of aircraft carriers on occasion. The cruiser *Suffolk* survived two hits on 17 April, the carrier *Furious* was damaged on the following day by a Condor and a French destroyer was hit on the day after that. May saw the sinking of a Polish destroyer, the anti-aircraft cruiser *Curlew* and the troopship *Chobry* and the damaging of the battleship *Resolution* and the cruiser *Aurora*. As the Norwegian campaign finally drew to its close, on 27 May there was one unusual gleam of humanity. *KGr 100* raided the town of Bodø. In 1920, many starving Viennese children had been evacuated to the town until normal conditions were restored in their homeland. He 111 pilot Horst Goetz had been one of these children. As a token of thanks, he dropped his bombs in the sea! We shall meet Goetz again: although he was never awarded the *Ritterkreuz*, he was one of the Pathfinders who led the infamous Coventry raid; he flew the stratospheric Ju 86R bomber over England in 1941; he flew on the Russian Front; and he ended the war flying the Ar 234 jet reconnaissance bomber in the West.

4. VICTORY IN THE WEST

Even while the campaign in Norway remained undecided, on 10 May 1940 Germany launched an all-out assault in the West. The heavily fortified Maginot Line, which ran the entire length of the Franco-German border and was regarded with some justification by the French as impregnable, would have been difficult and costly to take by storm. But it ended with one flank in the air at the Franco-Belgian border. Given a total disregard for international law, it could be turned by the simple expedient of violating the neutrality of Luxembourg, Belgium and Holland.

The expedient was simple; the execution was not. Luxembourg was virtually defenceless, but the Belgians and Dutch were ready and waiting. So was a French army group, with the British Expeditionary Force attached, which, immediately on the onset of hostilities, crossed into Belgium in support. But once again the *Blitzkrieg* concept, spearheaded by air power, would prove decisive.

Predictably, the German onslaught in the West followed the pattern set in Poland eight months earlier, but on a considerably larger scale. The first essential was to gain air superiority by knocking out the Allied air assets—bases and facilities as well as catching the aircraft on the ground—in conjunction with attacks on supply routes and communications, to hamper the movement of enemy ground forces, which, in this case, as British troops were involved, had to include ports. Attacks on Allied army camps and depots were assigned a high priority. Then, if the advancing Panzers hit stiff resistance, the way had to be cleared and their exposed flanks protected.

From dawn onwards, the armada of black-crossed bombers started to swarm across northern France and the Low Countries. In all, 47 airfields in France, fifteen in Belgium and ten in Holland were attacked, with mixed success.

Luftwaffe Strike Units in the West, 10 May 1940

Unit	Aircraft type	Commanders later awarded *Ritterkreuz*
Luftflotte 2, commanded by Albert Kesselring		
I, II, III/LG 1	He 111, some Ju 88	*Kdre* Alfred Bülowius
IV(StG)/LG 1	Ju 87	
II(Schlacht)/LG 2	Hs 123	*Kdr* Otto Weiss
I, II, III/KG 4	He 111	*Kdre* Martin Fiebig
I, II, III/KG 27	He 111	
I, II, III/KG 30	Ju 88	*Kdre* Walter Loebel
I, II, III KG 54	He 111	
I, II, III/KG 77	Do 17	
I, III/StG 2, I/StG 76 attached	Ju 87	*Kdre* Oskar Dinort
I, II/StG 77	Ju 87	*Kdre* Günter Schwartzkopff
Luftflotte 3 commanded by Hugo Sperrle		
I, II, III/KG 1, III/KG 28 attached	He 111	
I, II, III/KG 2	Do 17	*Kdre* Johannes Fink
I, II, III/KG 3	Do 17	*Kdre* Wolfgang von Chamier-Glisczinski
I, II, III/KG 51	He 111/Ju 88	
I, II, III/KG 53	He 111	
I, II, III/KG 55	He 111	*Kdre* Alois Stoeckl
I, II, III/KG 76, III/StG 51 attached	Do 17, Ju 87	*Kdre* Stefan Frölich
Stab StG 1, II/StG 2 and 1/TrGr 186 attached	Ju 87	

Martin Fiebig, who had been awarded the *Ritterkreuz* just two days earlier, led the He 111s of *KG 4* out to sea shortly after take-off. His targets were Amsterdam Schipol, Ypenburg near Den Haag and Rotterdam Waalhaven. Well away from land, he turned them south before approaching the coast of Holland from the west—as the least likely direction from which an attack would be expected. In practice this proved to be rather too clever, as his long detour, not unnaturally, caused a delay. By the time *KG 4* arrived, the Dutch defences were thoroughly alert, and the Heinkels were greeted with a storm of anti-aircraft fire and fighters.

Results were moderate to fair. About 75 Dutch aircraft were destroyed on the ground, including four of the eight modern T.5 bombers, but the cost was high. Eleven Heinkels were shot down, including that of the leader, Fiebig. He had celebrated his 49th birthday just three days before, escaped by parachute and was held prisoner, but only until the Dutch capitulation a few days later. It was a feature of the early *Luftwaffe* that many bomber commanders were quite elderly by combat standards.

In fact, *KG 4*, more by luck than judgement, had cut things remarkably fine. At Waalhaven, hardly had the bombing by *II/KG 4* ceased than paratroops were dropping to take the airfield. This was one of five airfield operations on the day in which bombing preceded an air landing. Only two of these were successful, and part of an effort to secure bridges over the Maas (Meuse) river in Rotterdam. At least as important was the seizure of the Albert Canal bridges to the south-east, in Belgium. The waterway was a considerable barrier to the German advance, and three bridges had been earmarked for capture. The Belgian Army had set demolition charges on all three, and, unlike the Vistula crossing in Poland, there was no chance of forestalling their destruction by air attack.

This area of Belgium was good tank country—flat and open, and ideal for the Panzers—but unless the bridges could be secured the advance would quickly grind to a halt. Another factor was the Belgian Army fortress of Eben Emael, which, with its heavy guns, dominated the approaches. This had to be neutralised. Paratroops were not a viable option. The troop transports droning overhead would alarm the Belgians, who would immediately blow the bridges. Added to that, the paras would take time to reach the ground, gather their equipment, and re-form to attack.

The answer was glider-borne troops. In one of the war's more spectacular operations, the gliders were released on the German side of the frontier, to approach silently and land precisely on top of the Belgian positions. It was a great success. Eben Emael was finally neutralised on the following day, and two of the three bridges were taken intact. But the German forces involved were small and vulnerable to counter-attack. They were supported by Stukas, notably by *StG 2* and *StG 77* led by Günter Schwartzkopff and the Henschels of *II(Schlacht)/LG 2* led by Otto Weiss, which hammered the advancing Belgian 7th Infantry Division with precision bombing and strafing until the Panzers arrived to consolidate the bridgehead.

Meanwhile *LG 1*, mainly with He 111s but having some Ju 88s, and with a *Gruppe* of Stukas, had been tasked with neutralising the Belgian Air Force. Led by Alfred Bülowius, they found four of the seven Belgian fighter squadrons on the ground at Schlaffen and took out three of them. Barely seconds beforehand, the Fiat CR.42 biplanes of *4/II/2* had escaped to Brusthem.

Not for long. In mid-afternoon, strafing Messerschmitts preceded yet more Stukas. Belgian fighter pilot Jean Offenberg recalled:

> Stukas dived on us, with their sirens wailing, hurting the ear drums as the bombs burst with a dull thud. I could hear crackling on the other side of the farm, which lay behind us . . . My heart seemed to have shrunk to the size of a cherrystone as I waited there powerless for the storm to abate. Then one by one the Stukas left for the east and a great calm descended upon the peaceful countryside.

Eight Fiats, all that remained of Offenberg's Group, redeployed to an emergency airfield at Grimbergen, near Brussels. But under the continued *Luftwaffe* onslaught, the Belgian Air Force was out of the fight after four days. Offenberg arrived in England via France, Corsica, Algeria and Gibraltar, to continue the battle. With five confirmed victories and two shared, he was killed in a mid-air collision with a Spitfire on 29 January 1942.

The Burning of Rotterdam

Meanwhile the battle for the Rotterdam river crossings was on. The paras from Waalhaven, supported by troops landed direct from He 59 flying boats on the river, were in the centre of the city, but their hold was tenuous. On 14 May a signal was sent to the Dutch commander to surrender, but to him this seemed a bluff.

At that very moment, the Heinkels of *KG 54* were on their way to Rotterdam, tasked to deliver a knock-out blow to the defenders on the north bank. The recall signal, to be given if the Dutch had capitulated, would be by radio. Failing this, it would be indicated by red Very lights fired from the ground.

As *KG 54* approached the city, it divided into two columns. The first, led by *Kommodore* Lackner, came straight in. The second, led by Otto Höhne, *Kommandeur II/KG 54*, turned away to approach from the south-east. Meanwhile the Dutch had agreed to surrender the city.

Visibility was poor, and Lackner took his unit down to 700m. The bombers wound in their trailing aerials, thereby reducing their radio reception range. Despite repeated attempts, no recall signal was received by the bombers, nor were any red Very lights from the ground visible. Given the combination of haze and Dutch anti-aircraft fire, this was hardly surprising. Lackner's column bombed accurately, starting intense fires.

The other column did not bomb. As Otto Höhne, awarded the *Ritterkreuz* on 5 September, later recalled:

> Never again did I fly an operation accompanied by such dramatic circumstances. Both my observer, prone in front of me manning the bomb sight, and my radio operator, seated behind, knew the signal I would give in the event of the bombing being cancelled at the last moment!

Even as his first *Kette* bombed, Höhne saw a couple of faint red lights and gave the cancellation signal. He then led his column south to the alternative target—British troops near Antwerp.

Rotterdam was designated a 'terror raid' by the Allies, but, as we have seen, efforts were made to prevent it. The heart of the city was burnt out, but the two contributory factors in this appear to have been the fact that the majority of the buildings were timber-framed, while the antediluvian Rotterdam fire brigade was totally inadequate to deal with a major conflagration.

France

The attack on French air bases was far less effective, owing to faulty *Luftwaffe* intelligence. Of the 91 airfields in northern France which housed front-line units, only 31 were attacked on the first day. Even then, fourteen of these were occupied by corps (liaison and spotting units), although one did have an RAF squadron in residence. The other attacks were squandered against airfields that were of secondary importance. Nearly three-quarters of the eighteen French bomber airfields were not attacked, and, of those that were, only two sustained significant damage.

That afternoon, cloudy skies coupled with an appalling navigational error caused a spectacular 'own goal'. *III/KG 51* was tasked to raid the French airfields of Dijon-Longvic and Dole-Tavaux. A *Kette* of Heinkels from *8/KG 51* became separated from the main formation in cloud and failed to re-join.

Many miles off course, they misidentified Freiburg in Germany as their target and bombed it. Among the dead were 57 civilians.

The *Luftwaffe* was not about to admit so monstrous an error, even though the Heinkels had been seen and identified from the ground. As a number of bombs had failed to explode, their German origin could not be denied. The Propaganda Minister blamed the RAF, and this incident was subsequently used as an excuse for German raids on civilian targets. This being the case, it was obviously impossible to court-martial the leader of the *Kette*, Paul Seidel, without giving the game away. He was not even grounded. Having converted to the Ju 88, he was shot down and killed off Portsmouth on 12 August.

The furious pace of the air assault on Allied airfields and communications targets on 10 May could not be maintained. On 11 May only 23 airfields were attacked, but one of these was Vaux, north of Reims. The raid was assigned to the Do 17s of *4/KG 2*, one of the few low-flying specialist *Staffeln*. Contour-chasing, the nine Dorniers crossed the Maginot Line before the French anti-aircraft gunners could react, and, after a superb piece of navigation—no easy task in the rolling country east of Rethel—they erupted across the airfield.

As luck would have it, they caught the Blenheims of No 114 Squadron RAF on the ground, bombed up, with engines running, lined up and ready to take off. It was a recipe for disaster. Pulling up to a safe release height (about 50m) for their 50kg bombs, *4/KG 2* swept in. Six Blenheims were destroyed and all the rest rendered unserviceable, while losses among the British aircrew were also high. So rapid was the attack that the ground defences remained silent. Even afterwards, things remained so quiet that Dornier pilot Walter Bornschein, a future *Ritterkreuz* winner, was able to circle the airfield while his radio operator took a cine-film of the devastation.

Breakthrough at Sedan

The decisive breakthrough on the Western Front came at Sedan, north-east of Reims, once again on the River Meuse (Maas). Although it was close to the Belgian frontier, the river line had been fortified with pillboxes and protected gun emplacements. The French High Command had anticipated an attack here, but thought that the Germans would not attempt the river crossing until they had brought up enough artillery support to breach the fortified line. This was estimated to take eight days, which would allow ample time to reinforce the reservists who manned the defences.

They had reckoned without two factors: the rapidity with which a massive German armoured force could cross Luxembourg and the Belgian Ardennes—hilly, heavily wooded country, considered impassable by armour; and the flying artillery in the form of the Stuka. In fact, the Panzers were in position after barely three days. It was not done without loss: a *Gruppe* of *StG 1* mistakenly attacked a Panzer division on 11 May, but the Allied bombers failed to intervene at all, mainly because the few reconnaissance reports were largely disbelieved.

The bombardment commenced in the late afternoon of 13 May, with continuous attacks by waves of Stukas on pre-briefed bunkers and other 'hard' targets. This kept the heads of the French gunners down, almost completely neutralising them. The French defenders, deafened by constant explosions, buffeted by shock waves and intimidated by the howling of the dive bombers' engines and the shrieking of the 'Trumpets of Jericho', were quickly reduced to impotence. Much of the effect was, of course, psychological, but it took a heavy toll of fighting efficiency, especially against the French second-line troops.

It was not only the Stukas: level bombers also flew many sorties in support of the Sedan operation, adding their sound and fury to the overall effect under which the initial river crossing began. By the next day, temporary bridges had been erected, and the Panzers poured across the river in force. Soon they had broken through the slender defences. But it was the Stukas that had unlocked the gate for them.

At a cost. As the Polish campaign had clearly demonstrated, liaison between air and ground was still sadly lacking. *I* and *II/StG 77* had been transferred to the Sedan sector in time for the offensive. On 14 May they attacked a Panzer division in error. Several senior officers were among the casualties. But the *Kommodore*, Günter Schwartzkopff, was given little time to atone. His Ju 87 received a direct hit from French anti-aircraft fire near Sedan on the following day. Thus perished the 'Father of the Stukas'.

The Race for the Sea

Following the breakthrough at Sedan, the Panzers were out and running, with little in their way to hinder them. Operations in the Low Countries had pulled the Allied armies too far north; they were in no position to intervene. The short-ranged Stukas now moved forward to advanced bases in occupied territory. For a while, their well-organised logistics units managed to keep up with them, but, with moves sometimes on a daily basis, they became ever more hard-pressed. With individual crews flying six or more sorties a day, the requirement for bombs was enormous, and for fuel only slightly less so, while the sheer wear and tear involved, to say nothing of battle damage, made huge demands on spares and also on the overworked ground crewmen.

The level bombers—and the Ju 88 is included in this category, despite its diving abilities—were in slightly better condition in that their sorties, of which rarely more than two a day were flown from well-stocked peacetime bases, just took a little longer to carry out, owing to the extra distance.

The French had no effective early warning and fighter control system, which meant that contact usually occurred only when German bombers happened to encounter enemy fighter patrols, or when it became obvious that a certain area was to be the target, which was not often. In the first three weeks of the German offensive, French fighters claimed 350 victories, although not all of the victims were bombers. There were, however, isolated German disasters. On 12 May five Curtiss Hawk 75s intercepted Stukas bombing French troops near Sedan and claimed sixteen victories. The perennial bugbear of overclaiming is evident here—only fourteen Stukas were shot down in the first four days of the conflict—but there can be little doubt that the Hawks scored heavily. Then, on 19 May, *KG 54* lost fifteen Heinkels to fighters, including that of its *Kommodore*, between Lille and Arras.

With Germany on the attack, the *Luftwaffe* had the initiative and the Allies could do little more than respond to threats as best they could. Then, as the Panzers sped across France, threatening to cut the Allied armies in two, the situation worsened. British and French fighter units in their path were forced to fall back, often to emergency landing grounds with few facilities and poor or non-existent communications.

At this time, the level bombers and the Ju 88s were primarily concerned with attacking communications targets such as railways and ports, army camps and stores depôts. Meanwhile the Stukas not only spearheaded the armoured thrusts, but ranged their open flanks. On the rare occasions when the British or French launched a counterattack, they stopped it.

A typical example took place at Montcornet, north-east of Laon, on 18 May. A French tank division, led by Charles de Gaulle, had taken up ambush positions but was spotted by German reconnaissance aircraft. Waldemar Plewig of *II/StG 77* later commented:

> . . . [I] was to attack some French tanks which were well hidden in farmyards. With the newly developed fragmentation bomb we achieved great success. The French tanks were all ready to attack, but we managed to disable them all by damaging their tracks.

Tanks needed nothing less than a direct hit to destroy them completely, and they were of course very small targets. But, in a battlefield situation, a 'mobility kill'—tearing off tracks or bogeys—was almost as effective.

Plewig was shot down and seriously wounded by Hurricanes over the English Channel on 8 August. Taken prisoner, he was awarded the *Ritterkreuz* while in captivity.

By now both Holland and Belgium had surrendered, and on 21 May the Panzers had reached the sea at Abbeville, cutting the Anglo-French forces in half. The British Expeditionary Force, with considerable French units, was trapped, encircled in an area based on the Channel ports of Boulogne, Calais and Dunkirk. The campaign in the West continued for another month, but at this stage it was won and lost irretrievably.

Assault on the Ports

Shipping, particularly that which brought supplies and reinforcements to France from Britain, had long been a legitimate target for the *Kampfflieger*. With the German invasion of 10 May, ports and dock facilities became of equal, if not greater, value, with Rotterdam in Holland, Ostend and Antwerp in Belgium and Le Havre and Cherbourg in France added to the three already named.

That the defences were fierce was attested to by Peter Stahl, who joined *5/ KG 30* at Oldenburg, arriving at noon on 10 May. He recorded that he had never seen such intense activity, with Ju 88s taking off and landing almost continuously. One aircraft had just returned after sustaining 70 hits. Another made an even deeper impression on the unblooded young pilot:

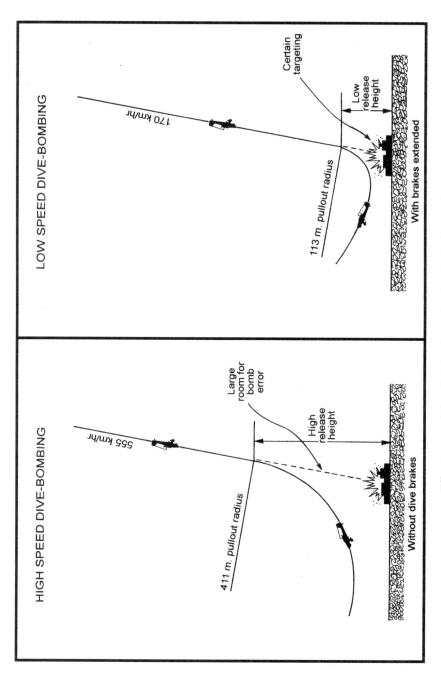

HIGH SPEED DIVE-BOMBING

555 km/hr

411 m. pullout radius

Large room for bomb error

High release height

Without dive brakes

LOW SPEED DIVE-BOMBING

170 km/hr

113 m. pullout radius

Certain targeting

Low release height

With brakes extended

Effectiveness of slatted air brakes as fitted to the Junkers Ju 87.

One Ju 88 taxies directly towards the command post where I am standing . . . The entry hatch opens and I see a bloodied hand groping around underneath. Ground crewmen run up to the machine and carefully pull out the badly wounded gunner from the ventral gondola. He is hit in the neck, and collapses on the field. An ambulance is on hand right away, and the casualty is whisked away to the hospital. More movement around the machine, and they carry out the observer—dead. It seems almost like a war film, but this is stark reality . . .

Mere numbers and percentage figures of losses are only half the story— that of the aircraft which failed to return to base. But of those that did return, many crewmen would never fly again. The two *Gruppen* of *KG 30* lost six aircraft on this day alone. Six days later they were pulled out of the battle to refit.

On the ground, part of the army turned north towards Boulogne and Calais. The former in particular was a tough nut to crack, and Oskar Dinort's *StG 2* was called in. Heavy raids were mounted on the morning of 25 May, and the garrison capitulated, but only after a number of British troops had been evacuated.

Calais, some twenty miles further up the coast, was the next objective. Here resistance was stiff, and British destroyers added their weight of fire to that of the defenders. The initial raids, on 24 May, were made by *StG 1*, which attacked the citadel. Then, in the late afternoon, the assault was switched to the bombarding destroyers, three of which were close inshore. The Polish destroyer *Burza* was hit and forced to retire to Dover, and *Vimiera* was damaged by near misses but survived. Not so lucky was the elderly *Wessex*, which, while it avoided the first two attacks by zig-zagging at full speed, took three direct hits from the third. Both boiler rooms were wrecked, and hull damage caused flooding. Shortly afterwards, she sank—the first of many destroyers to be lost in the coming days.

Attacks on Calais, by Stukas and level bombers, continued on the following day, but they were now within range of RAF fighters based in England. Oskar Dinort's *StG 2* was tasked with dealing with the destroyers. Behind him were future *Ritterkreuz* winners Hubertus Hitschhold, *Kommandeur I/StG 2*, and Heinrich Brücker, *Kommandeur III/StG 2*. For them, attacking fast-moving and agile destroyers was a new venture.

More than two miles below, the ships appeared, tiny spots difficult to see against the sun-drenched ocean. Dinort commenced his dive, aiming for one of the larger spots, but as his target took evasive action it vanished beneath his engine cowling. There was little else to do but pull out and re-acquire the target before diving again. Once more he dived, only to see the destroyer turn to port through 180 degrees. Unable to follow it, he pulled out to start again. Like those of most of his *Geschwader*, Dinort's bombs fell in the sea, raising impressive columns of water which sparkled in the sun, but not much else. More than 40 Stukas could claim only a single guard boat sunk, and two hits on a freighter.

Whilst the pull-out was automatic, immediately afterwards the pilot was kept busy, retracting the dive brakes, opening the radiator shutter, cancelling the bomb release switches and changing the propeller pitch and elevator trim. Just when the Stukas were at low speed and low altitude, the Spitfires struck.

Hearing a warning from his radio operator/gunner, Oskar Dinort throttled back, and at little above stalling speed he turned hard to starboard. The pursuing Spitfire overshot and missed him. His two wingmen were not so lucky: both were shot down.

StG 77, now commanded by Clemens *Graf* von Schönborn-Wiesentheid, another future *Ritterkreuz* winner, who had replaced Schwartzkopff as *Kommodore*, had previously been engaged against French armour which had counterattacked the German flank near Amiens. Now it was switched to reinforce *StG 2* in the assault. Owing to losses brought about by British-based fighters on the previous two days, the Stukas were escorted by the Bf 109s from *JG 27*. First in was *StG 77*, attacking the citadel and harbour. Its bombs left so much smoke and dust that the following *StG 2* could hardly see its targets. Then the 10th Panzer Division attacked. Calais surrendered late that afternoon. Only Dunkirk was left. If, like Boulogne and Calais, this could be overrun in double-quick time, the rout, not only of the French in the north but also of the BEF, would be complete.

Two Miracles

The British often refer to the successful evacuation of Dunkirk as a miracle. When one considers that more than 338,000 Allied troops were evacuated from the beaches in the teeth of the *Luftwaffe*, this was certainly one of them. But the first and most important miracle had occurred earlier: the *Führer* had halted his advancing Panzers on 24 May.

The titular head of the *Luftwaffe*, Hermann Goering, had offered to reduce the Dunkirk pocket by air attack alone. With hindsight, this was an appalling error—but only with hindsight! From the point of view of the *Gröfaz*, the French Army, now in the south of the country and operating on interior lines, was offering increasingly stiff resistance. The campaign appeared to be far from over, and anything which would save his Panzers unnecessary casualties was to be welcomed. Another factor here was the weather. It is hardly possible that Hitler could have taken this into his calculations, but in 1940 it was unusually benign in terms of sea state rather than cloud. Given normal conditions, barely one-seventh of the actual numbers evacuated could have been taken off the beaches.

The evacuation began on 27 May. At first light, Heinkels of *KG 1* and *KG 4* attacked. They were followed by the Heinkels of *KG 54* and the Dorniers of *KG 2* and *KG 3*, after which the docks became virtually unusable. Only the beaches remained. But, on that first day, German level bomber losses exceeded 10 per cent, the majority falling to fighters. To give just one example, a *Staffel* of Dorniers from *III/KG 3*, bombing the oil storage tanks west of the harbour, lost half of their number to Spitfires. A similar fate befell *III/KG 2*. At this point the Ju 88s of *II/KG 30* had been withdrawn to refit, while the anti-shipping Heinkels of *KGr 100* and *KG 26* were still in action off Norway.

Between 27 May and 2 June *Luftwaffe* bombers flew just over 1,000 sorties, losing 45 aircraft. One of these was a Ju 88 of *III/KG 30* flown by Hajo Herrmann, flying his 40th sortie. On 31 May his *Gruppe* set out to attack shipping at Dunkirk. Selecting a target, he began his dive, but the air brakes failed to deploy. His speed built up and, having overshot his comrades, he gently pulled his overladen aircraft out to try again.

Suddenly Hurricanes were on the scene. A burst of fire whipped through the fuselage and hit the instrument panel. A second burst knocked out his port engine, which trailed brown smoke. He aimed at a medium transport, but his bombs narrowly missed. More Hurricanes! His starboard engine was hit!

I cringed down behind my armour plate. The *coup de grâce* must come now. There was a sound of cracking, but I didn't know where it was coming from. Water burst in through the brittle cockpit, causing my breath to stick in my throat.

His aircraft had crashed in shallow water just off the beach. As the land battle was in full swing, he and his crew crawled through the water away from the fighting. On the way, they encountered a shot-down Hurricane pilot. Outnumbered four to one, he surrendered to them. Still crawling, they finally reached the German lines and safety.

Just two days earlier another Ju 88 ace, Joachim Helbig of *II/LG 1*, had also narrowly escaped from Hurricanes over Dunkirk. Wounded in one arm, he just made it back to base. He later commented: 'We called it the Hell of Dunkirk. We met terrific resistance from the British fighters and anti-aircraft fire from warships. Now we knew what the enemy's mettle was like!'

The Stukas flew slightly more than 800 sorties, for a mere ten losses. However, they failed in their aim of forcing the Allies to surrender. While they sank or severely damaged no fewer than 89 ships, no attempt was made to interdict traffic in mid-Channel.

The Capitulation of France

With the Dunkirk pocket finally in German hands, the *Luftwaffe* turned its attention to the south, where the battered but as yet undefeated French armies had concentrated. Two major operations were mounted, the first on communications targets in the Rhône valley and around Marseilles and the second, Operation *'Paula'*, on the airfields and aircraft factories in the region of Paris.

The first resulted in the loss of six He 111s of *KG 53* to Swiss fighters when the German aircraft inadvertently crossed the frontier. The French fighter force was still far from finished. On the morning of 5 June, Heinkels of *KG 4* raided troop concentrations near Rouen. Assailed by five MS 406 fighters, the Heinkel of Hans-Georg Bätcher was hit in both engines. With no power he was forced to land behind the French lines and was taken prisoner. Released at the armistice, he went on to have a distinguished career on all fronts.

Operation *'Paula'* took place on 3 June and consisted of 640 bombers drawn from *LG 1* and *KG 1, 2, 3, 4, 30, 51* and *54*, with strong fighter cover. *KG 51*, now equipped with the Ju 88, raided Etampes, only to lose its *Kommodore*, Josef Kammhuber, who had trouble with his air brakes. Straggling behind his formation, he fell victim to fighters. He survived, to become Chief of Staff of the new *Luftwaffe* postwar.

'Paula' was at first hailed as a great victory, but this was not borne out by results. Sixteen airfields were attacked but only six sustained heavy damage, while a mere twenty French aircraft were destroyed on the ground. Fifteen factories were slightly damaged. The cost was four German bombers.

The German forces now turned their attention southwards, hammering troop concentrations and rail links as they went. The end was inevitable: France capitulated on 25 June, freeing more than 400 *Luftwaffe* prisoners.

 **5. ASSAULT ON ENGLAND, JULY 1940–MAY 1941**

With France out of the fight, what was to become known as the Battle of Britain was about to begin. In fact this was less a battle than a campaign—the first ever to be fought entirely in the air. In its later stages it passed from being mainly daylight operations to almost exclusively night actions, known as the Blitz. It ceased only when German units were withdrawn to take part in the attack on the Soviet Union in June 1941.

To the Third Reich, it seemed hardly possible that Britain would continue the war; if she did, it could not be for long. The BEF had been chased ignominiously home from Dunkirk, leaving all its tanks and most of its heavy equipment behind. The RAF in France had taken a heavy beating. Most bomber squadrons had been decimated, while fighter losses were tremendous, and many damaged and unflyable Hurricanes had been abandoned on their airfields in the face of the onrushing Panzers.

To the victorious *Luftwaffe*, the task now seemed simple—to gain air superiority by destroying the RAF on its airfields or in the air, as had been done in Poland, France and the Low Countries. This would create favourable conditions for a landing by surface forces, spearheaded by paratroops and glider-borne troops. The greatest obstacle was the Royal Navy, but without cover from protecting fighters this would be vulnerable to air attack. However, it was hoped that, faced with the full 'lightning speed and undreamed-of might' of Goering's airmen, the islanders would sue for peace before an invasion became necessary. But first, the *Luftwaffe* needed to put its own house in order.

The campaign in the West had been costly: 147 Stukas and 635 bombers had been lost, and hundreds more had suffered varying degrees of damage. Machines and men—and the latter included the hard-pressed ground crewmen as well as the flyers—had been pushed to the limit. Maintenance and rest were sorely needed, while many units needed to withdraw to re-equip and to train new air crewmen.

Provision had to be made for bases in France and Belgium, to allow the short-legged Bf 109 fighters and Ju 87 Stukas to reach across the English Channel. This in itself was a major undertaking: repair and servicing facilities, stocks of spares and fuel, and sufficient bombs to avoid shortages in highintensity operations; oxygen; ammunition; logistics support—the list of requirements was endless. It took planning, but most of all it took time. And time gave Britain a much-needed breathing space.

The *Luftwaffe* was now up against a unique problem, something totally outside its previous experience. A cardinal principle of war is security of base, and lack of this had been a major factor in the downfall of their previous opponents. Now, with the Panzers halted by the English Channel, the *Luftwaffe* faced an opponent whose airfields could not be overrun, or even threatened by ground forces. It was of course true that no airfield within bomber range could be completely immune to air attack, but even here the goalposts had been moved. RAF Fighter Command had a finely honed detection and control system. Radar looked out to sea to give early detection; inland, a network of observers tracked intruders. With only a short delay, inbound raids were plotted on situation maps and measures were taken to deal with them. Such a system existed nowhere else in the world. It was not perfect, but it ensured that only in exceptional circumstances would units be caught on the ground. The RAF fighter control system also had a further advantage. By enabling squadrons to be directed to where they were most needed, it ensured that a far higher proportion of interceptions could be achieved than by any previous means. It was, to use the modern term, a 'force multiplier'. This ensured that the *Luftwaffe* had largely lost the vital element of surprise, and only rarely would its mass daylight raids elude the defending fighters.

The greatest British defensive weaknesses were a chronic shortage of anti-aircraft guns and, initially, an almost total inability to counter night raids. An effective night fighter, backed by radar-directed ground control, was still many months in the future, while experienced German bomber crews treated the guns with contempt, even over London.

The official date for the start of the Battle of Britain is 10 July 1940, but small raids on mainland targets had started five weeks before this, mainly harassing attacks at night. Targets included airfields, aircraft factories and ports. Little damage was done, but German casualties were light. At the end of June a comprehensive air reconnaissance of British airfields was begun. This gave the RAF fighter control system valuable practice, and losses of *Luftwaffe* reconnaissance aircraft rose unacceptably. They were forced to ever higher altitudes to survive, but this degraded photographic definition. Consequently, while the *Luftwaffe* knew which airfields were in use, most of the time they did not know whether they housed fighters, trainers, coastal aircraft or what. When in mid-August the time came to launch an all-out assault on Fighter Command's airfields, all too many raids were wasted on non-fighter bases.

The Channel Battles

Merchant shipping had been a legitimate target for the *Luftwaffe* since the outbreak of war. Most of the early attacks had been mounted off the North Sea coast of England and Scotland by lone raiders, and small raids had been made on ports. In addition, mines had been laid in harbours and their approaches. The fact was that, in addition to deep-sea convoys carrying imports and exports, Britain was heavily dependent on coastal traffic for transporting bulky cargoes such as coal and raw materials. The alternative was rail transport, but this was comparatively inefficient and uneconomic.

Even as the *Luftwaffe* took up forward bases in France, shipping continued to use the Channel. Attacking it was an obvious move, not only to damage the British economy but also as a prerequisite to establishing air superiority. At the same time, ports and harbour installations were targeted.

On 2 July, Johannes Fink, *Kommodore KG 2* (Do 17), was appointed *Kanalkampfführer*, a title quickly amended to Chief Sewer Worker by his colleagues. The Channel campaign began in earnest on 4 July, when the Stukas of *III/StG 51* raided Portland naval base, sinking the anti-aircraft auxiliary *Foyle Bank* and three freighters and damaging nine other vessels, including a tanker set ablaze in Weymouth harbour. The cost was meagre—one Stuka shot down and another damaged, both by anti-aircraft fire.

Gradually the pace mounted. Vessels in convoy were unable to take hard evasive action owing to the proximity of other ships. In any case, lumbering freighters were not terribly agile. Bomber losses were slight, and well worth the effort involved. At the same time, German escort fighters were inflicting casualties on Fighter Command.

On 9 July *I/StG 76* was redesignated *III/StG 77*. Led by its *Kommandeur*, Friedrich-Karl *Freiherr* von Dalwigk zu Lichtenfels, it set out to attack Portland and a convoy offshore. At the latter they succeeded only in damaging a large freighter before being intercepted by Spitfires. Protected by Bf 109s, the Stukas lost one aircraft, that of their *Kommandeur*. He was awarded a posthumous *Ritterkreuz*.

The pot came to the boil on 10 July, marking the official opening of the Battle of Britain. A large convoy passing Dover in the early afternoon was attacked by Dorniers of *I/KG 2*. A huge dogfight between British and German fighters erupted, and while only two Dorniers were lost and a third badly damaged in this action, only one direct hit was scored from 150 bombs dropped.

As July passed, the tempo increased. In terms of attrition, Britain was not doing well. All too many fighters were being lost while shipping losses were gradually becoming unsustainable. The fact was that, in the Channel narrows, the warning time given by radar was too short for effective reaction, and the fighter control system could not be used to its best advantage. The *Luftwaffe* bomber force, increasing in strength all the time as re-equipped units joined the front, could afford casualties. Almost inevitably, the *Luftwaffe* closed the Channel to convoys. It had won this round.

Adlerangriff

In the second week of August the *Luftwaffe* launched Phase 2—*Adlerangriff*, or Eagle Attack—the aim of which was to destroy Fighter Command on the ground and in the air. Massed bomber raids in daylight, with a strong fighter escort, would be used to cause maximum destruction.

The basic bomber element was the *Kette* of three aircraft in V formation, with the wingmen stepped back from the leader and slightly higher or lower depending on the visibility from the cockpit, which varied with type. When flying in *Staffel* strength, either all *Ketten* flew in line astern (the *Staffelkolonne*) or the *Staffelwinkel* was adopted, in which all nine aircraft took up a large V formation.

In *Gruppe* strength, variations were possible. Widely used in the summer of 1940 was the *Gruppenkolonne aus Staffelwinkeln*, in which the three *Staffelwinkeln* flew in line astern. The *Stab*, usually a single *Kette*, flew at the front. The *Gruppenkolonne aus geschlossenen Staffelkeilen* was a valid alternative, in which each *Kette* in each *Staffel* flew in V formation, with the *Ketten* also in a V formation. Less often seen were the *Gruppenkeil*, consisting of *Staffelkolonnen* stepped to left and right of the leading formation, or any form of echelon by *Staffeln*.

When engaged by anti-aircraft fire, the formations opened out to present a more diffuse target, and began the 'Flak Waltz', a weave designed to ensure that the bombers were not there when the shells arrived. This could not be done on the bombing run as it spoiled the aim; at this point the bombers had to grin and bear it. When attacked by fighters, the opposite was true: formations closed as tightly as possible in order to mass their defensive fire. As previously mentioned, defensive armament was inadequate.

During the convoy battles *Luftwaffe* Intelligence had noted the fact that RAF fighters had a disconcerting habit of arriving promptly at the scene of the action. Monitoring British radio transmissions, they drew the obvious conclusion that the British had a sophisticated detection and control system and that the 100m towers along the coast were an integral part of this. Given that RAF fighters took twenty minutes to reach operational altitude, if the early warning system could be taken out Fighter Command would be immediately disadvantaged and the bombers would be storming in towards the coast before the alarm could be given.

Even at this early stage, the limitations of the Ju 87 had been recognised, and it was expected to be replaced by the Bf 210 fighter-bomber, or *Jabo*. To this end, an experimental unit, *Erprobungsgruppe 210*, had been formed a few weeks earlier to develop tactics. Commanded by Swiss-born Walter Rubensdörffer, it consisted of two *Staffeln* of Bf 110s and one of Bf 109s, the latter to provide fighter escort after dropping its bombs. Having cut its teeth on shipping attacks, it was tasked to hit the radar stations at Dover, Rye, Pevensey and Dunkirk (the last a little way inland in Kent) on 12 August.

German Bomber Order of Battle in the West, 13 August 1940

Unit	Type	Base	Commander/remarks
Luftflotte 2, commanded by Albert Kesselring			
EprGr 210	Bf 109/Bf 110	Calais-Marck	Walter Rubensdörffer*
II/LG 2	Bf 109[1]	St. Omer	Otto Weiss**
II/StG 1	Ju 87	Pas de Calais	Anton Keil
IV(St)/LG 1	Ju 87	Tramecourt[2]	Bernd von Brauchitsch
Stab/KG 1	He 111	Rosières-en-Santerre	*Obstlt* Exss
I/KG 1	He 111	Montdidier	*Major* Maier
II/KG 1	He 111	Montdidier	Benno Kosch*
III/KG 1	He 111	Rosières-en-Santerre	Willibald Fanelsa
Stab/KG 2	Do 17	Arras	Johannes Fink*
I/KG 2	Do 17	Epinoy	*Major* Gutzmann
II/KG 2	Do 17	Arras	Paul Weitkus*
III/KG 2	Do 17	Epinoy	Adolf Fuchs
Stab/KG 3	Do 17	Le Culot	Wolfgang von Chamier-Glisczinski*
I/KG 3	Do 17	Le Culot	Karl von Wechmar
II/KG 3	Do 17	Antwerp/Duerne	*Hpt* Pilger
III/KG 3	Do 17	St Trond	*Hpt* Rathmann
Stab/KG 4	He 111	Soesterberg	Hans-Joachim Rath*
I/KG 4	He 111	Soesterberg	*Hpt* Meissner
II/KG 4	He 111	Eindhoven	Gottlieb Wolff*
III/KG 4	Ju 88	Amsterdam/Schipol	Erich Bloedorn*
Stab/KG 53	He 111	Lille	*Obst* Stahl
I/KG 53	He 111	Lille	*Major* Kaufmann
II/KG 53	He 111	Lille	Reinhold Tamm
III/KG 53	He 111	Lille	*Major* Ritzscherle
Stab/KG 76	Do 17	Cormeilles-en-Vexin	Stefan Frölich*
I/KG 76	Do 17	Beauvais	*Hpt* Lindeiner
II/KG 76	Ju 88	Creil	*Major* Möricke
III/KG 76	Do 17	Cormeilles-en-Vexin	Theodor Schweizer
Luftflotte 3, commanded by Hugo Sperrle			
Stab/StG 1	Ju 87/Do 17	Angers	Walter Hagen**
I/StG 1	Ju 87	Angers	Paul-Werner Hozzel**
III/StG 1	Ju 87	Angers	Helmut Mahlke*
Stab/StG 2	Ju 87/Do 17	St Malo	Oskar Dinort**
I/StG 2	Ju 87	St Malo	Hubertus Hitschhold**
II/StG 2	Ju 87	Lannion	Walter Enneccerus*
I/StG 3	Ju 87	Caen	Walther Sigel**

continued

Stab/StG 77	Ju 87/Do 17	Caen	Clemens *Graf* von Schönborn-Weisentheid*
I/StG 77	Ju 87	Caen	Herbert Meisel
II/StG 77	Ju 87	Caen	Alfons Orthofer*
III/StG 77	Ju 87	Caen	Helmut Bode*
Stab/LG 1	Ju 88	Orléans/Bricy	Alfred Bülowius*
I/LG 1	Ju 88	Orléans/Bricy	Wilhelm Kern
II/LG 1	Ju 88	Orléans/Bricy	*Major* Debratz
III/LG 1	Ju 88	Orléans/Bricy	Ernst Bormann**
Stab/KG 27	He 111	Tours	*Obst* Behrendt
I/KG 27	He 111	Tours	*Major* Ulbrich
II/KG 27	He 111	Dinard	*Major* Schlichting[3]
III/KG 27	He 111	Rennes	*Freiherr* Speck von Sternberg
Stab/KG 51	Ju 88	Orly	Johann-Volkmar Fisser[4]
I/KG 51	Ju 88	Melun Villaroche	*Major* Schulze-Heyn
II/KG 51	Ju 88	Orly	*Major* Winkler
III/KG 51	Ju 88	Etampes	Walter Marienfeld*
Stab/KG 54	Ju 88	Evreux	Otto Höhne*
I/KG 54	Ju 88	Evreux	*Hpt* Heydebreck
II/KG 54	Ju 88	St André	*Obstlt* Köster
Stab/KG 55	He 111	Villacoublay	Alois Stoeckl*[5]
I/KG 55	He 111	Dreux	*Major* Korte[6]
II/KG 55	He 111	Chartres	*Major* von Lackemeier
III/KG 55	He 111	Villacoublay	*Major* Schlemell
KGr 100	He 111	Vannes	Kurd Aschenbrenner
Luftflotte 5, commanded by Hans-Jurgen Stumpff			
Stab/KG 26	He 111	Stavanger	Robert Fuchs*
I/KG 26	He 111	Stavanger	Hermann Busch
III/KG 26	He 111	Stavanger	Viktor von Lossberg*
Stab/KG 30	Ju 88	Aalborg	Walter Loebel*
I/KG 30	Ju 88	Aalborg	Fritz Doench*
III/KG 30	Ju 88	Aalborg	Gerhard Kollewe

Ranks are given only where forenames are not known.

* denotes the award of the *Ritterkreuz*, either previous to this date or afterwards. ** denotes the *Ritterkreuz* and *Eichenlaub*.

[1] This unit was equipped with Bf 109 Jabos in place of the Hs 123. It reverted to the latter on the Russian Front in 1941. [2] Ironically, this was near the site of the English victory against heavy odds at Agincourt in 1415. [3] Schlichting was shot down and taken prisoner on 12 August; he had not yet been officially replaced. [4] Fisser was shot down and killed on 12 August. [5] Alois Stoeckl was killed on 14 August. He was replaced by *Major* Korte of *I Gruppe*, who [6] was replaced as *Kommandeur* by Friedrich Kless*.

The *Jabo*s streaked down in shallow diving attacks and planted their bombs. The huge towers were seen to sway, but none was destroyed. However, all except Dover were off the air for several hours, although rapid repairs put the other three back on line during the afternoon. *EprGr 210* suffered no losses.

Towards noon a huge raid—almost 100 Ju 88s of *KG 51*, with a massive fighter escort—approached the Hampshire/Sussex coast. Most of the aircraft attacked Portsmouth, but two *Staffeln* split off and made a steep diving attack on the radar station at Ventnor on the Isle of Wight. This time damage was severe, and Ventnor radar was out of action for weeks. *KG 51* lost ten aircraft, eight to fighters, including their *Kommodore*, *Dr* Fisser, and another three damaged.

Another intelligence failure now occurred. Monitoring soon revealed that Pevensey, Rye and Dunkirk were back on the air, while transmissions apparently from Ventnor were also picked up. The RAF rushed a mobile station to the Isle of Wight, and while this only partially plugged the gap in the radar cover, to the *Luftwaffe* signals organisation it appeared that Ventnor was still fully functional. The conclusion was that the radar sites were almost impossible to knock out for any appreciable length of time, and further attacks on them became sporadic.

August 12 also saw the initial attacks on RAF airfields. Hawkinge and Manston were both forward airfields on the coast. At the latter, *EprGr 210* was once more to the fore, backed by Dorniers from *KG 2*. The raid was not very effective: only one aircraft was destroyed on the ground, and Manston was operational again within twenty-four hours.

The main airfield assault, launched over the next few days, was a fiasco thanks to wrong targeting. On 13 August Johannes Fink led 74 Dorniers of *KG 2* against the naval base at Sheerness and the Coastal Command airfield at Eastchurch. By complete coincidence, Spitfires of two squadrons were present on the ground, and *KG 2* claimed ten destroyed, although the true figure was one. The cost was high—five Dorniers lost and five more damaged.

In mid-afternoon, a multi-pronged raid was launched. About 40 Ju 88s of *KG 54* set off for Odiham and Farnborough, neither of them fighter airfields. A combination of clouds and fighter harassment ensured that their targets were not reached. About 80 Ju 88s of *LG 1*, with *III/LG 1* led by future

77

Ritterkreuz and *Eichenlaub* winner Ernst Bormann, headed for Southampton, where they caused heavy damage to the docks but, unbelievably, missed the vital Spitfire factory at Woolston. Two *Staffeln* broke away and headed for the fighter airfield at Middle Wallop. They failed to find it and bombed Andover instead, another non-fighter airfield.

Further west were 27 Stukas of *II/StG 2* led by *Ritterkreuz* holder Walter Enneccerus, followed by 52 Stukas of *StG 77* led by another *Ritterkreuz* holder, *Graf* von Schönborn-Wiesentheid. *II/StG 2* headed for Middle Wallop but was roughly handled by Spitfires, one *Staffel* losing six out of nine Stukas. *StG 77* failed to find the fighter airfield at Warmwell and dropped bombs at random over Dorset. Further to the east, *II/StG 1* failed to find Rochester and scattered its bombs across half of Kent, while *IV(St)/LG 1* attacked Detling, causing much damage. Again, neither was a fighter airfield.

The price of this catalogue of errors was high: five Do 17s, one He 111, five Ju 88s and six Ju 87s failed to return, while many more sustained severe damage. The escort fighters also suffered, eight Bf 110s and five Bf 109s being lost. By contrast, thirteen RAF fighters were lost, including the one on the ground at Eastchurch. The fabled Teutonic efficiency had been found sadly wanting.

Attacks on the following day were of lesser intensity. Manston was raided by *EprGr 210*, which lost two Bf 110s to ground fire in the process. Further west, three Heinkels of *Stab/KG 55* raided Middle Wallop but lost their *Kommodore*, *Ritterkreuz* holder Alois Stoeckl, to defending Spitfires.

A series of heavy raids was scheduled for 15 August. In the late morning more than 40 Stukas from *IV(St)/LG 1* and *II/StG 1* raided the forward airfields at Hawkinge and Lympne. While they caused serious damage, no fighters had been caught on the ground. Meanwhile *Luftflotte 5*, based in Scandinavia, entered the battle for the first (and last) time. German Intelligence, misled by the exaggerated victory claims of *Luftwaffe* fighter pilots, had concluded that almost all RAF fighters were now concentrated in the south, leaving the north of England vulnerable. More than 60 Heinkels of *KG 26* set out from Stavanger to attack targets in the Newcastle area. They were escorted by the Bf 110s of *I/ZG 76*. Further south, about 50 unescorted Ju 88s from *KG 30* took off from Aalborg and headed for the bomber base at Driffield.

KG 26 was intercepted by elements of several fighter squadrons in quick succession. The Bf 110s were unable to protect the bombers and lost seven of their number. Eight Heinkels were shot down, and with most bombs jettisoned into the sea the raid was a total failure. *KG 30* achieved surprise at Driffield, plummeting from the sky to destroy ten Whitley bombers and damaging the station buildings. RAF bomber ace Leonard Cheshire, who was present at the time, called it a fine achievement. Be that as it may, it was too costly to be repeated. Seven Ju 88s were lost, all to fighters, while three more crash-landed on the continent with battle damage. No British fighters were lost in either action.

In the south, the main attack was launched in the early afternoon. *EprGr 210* raided the fighter airfield at Martlesham Heath, putting it out of action for forty-eight hours but again failing to catch any fighters on the ground. Meanwhile the Dorniers of *KG 3*, led by Wolfgang von Chamier-Glisczinski, thundered in over the Kent coast. *I* and *II Gruppen* attacked Rochester, badly damaging the Short Brothers aircraft factory and the Pobjoy engine works. At the former, deliveries of the Stirling heavy bomber were significantly delayed, but, again, this was no part of the plan to reduce Fighter Command. *III Gruppe* once again turned its attention to Eastchurch. Two Dorniers were lost to fighters and another six damaged, this light rate of loss being due to the presence of a strong escort.

Further west, about 60 Ju 88s of *I* and *II/LG 1* set out for Middle Wallop and Worthy Down (the latter again not a fighter airfield) with a strong Bf 110 escort. Little damage was caused at either, while Odiham, about 30km to the north-east, was attacked in error. Intercepted, the Germans lost eight Ju 88s, five of them from Joachim Helbig's *4th Staffel*. Helbig himself barely escaped: he owed his survival to his gunner, who directed evasive action. His aircraft took 130 hits but still flew.

The final large raid took place in the early evening, when a force of Dorniers headed for Biggin Hill and *EprGr 210* went for Kenley. This time the *Luftwaffe* had its priorities right: both were Fighter Command sector stations. However, once again it all went pear-shaped. Harassed by fighters, the Dorniers bombed West Malling, which was not yet operational, while Rubensdörffer led his *Gruppe* against Croydon. This was fatal in more ways than one: first,

Croydon was within the prohibited Greater London area; secondly, the unit was intercepted over the target and suffered horrific casualties. Seven of the fifteen Bf 110s were shot down, including Rubensdörffer's.

The assault continued unabated on 16 August, but on the following day there was little activity. So far the *Adlerangriff* had been a catalogue of missed opportunities leavened with the odd outright disaster. However, the *Luftwaffe*'s mood was buoyant: if it was not destroying Fighter Command on the ground, it was inflicting a great deal of damage in the air, according to the inflated victory claims.

On 18 August the *Luftwaffe* had its target priorities almost right. A morning raid was scheduled against the fighter sector stations at Biggin Hill and Kenley. At noon, a massive force of Stukas would be launched against airfields at Thorney Island (Coastal Command), Ford and Gosport (Fleet Air Arm) and the radar station at Poling. Late in the afternoon, large raids would be directed at the fighter sector stations at Hornchurch and North Weald. All would have massive fighter escort.

Sixty Heinkels of *KG 1* were assigned to bomb Biggin Hill from high altitude in three waves, while 48 Dorniers and Junkers 88s of *KG 76* would attack Kenley. The latter would, however, be a little more complicated. First, twelve Ju 88s of *II Gruppe* would carry out a dive bombing attack on the hangars and airfield buildings. They would be followed after five minutes by 27 Dorniers of *I* and *III Gruppen*, bombing from high altitude. With confusion on the ground at its height, nine Dorniers of *9 Staffel* would sneak in at low level to demolish anything still left standing. But complex plans rarely survive contact with the executants, let alone the enemy! All depended on exact timing.

First off were the Heinkels of *KG 1*. They picked up their fighter escort at the coast and set course. *KG 76* had more difficulty. Cloud over the Pas de Calais hampered their rendezvous with the fighters; the Ju 88s in particular were delayed. When they finally started out, the Dorniers were already six minutes behind schedule, and the 88s were astern instead of in front. The Heinkels, notwithstanding their early start, brought up the rear.

Meanwhile, far to the south-west, the Dorniers of *9/KG 76* were skimming the Channel to stay under the electronic eyes of the British radar. *9 Staffel* was one of the few specialist low-level attack units, and the Dorniers were fitted with a 20mm cannon for strafing. Each carried twenty 50kg bombs, which could be dropped from as low as 15m.

As was often the case at this time, the *Staffelkapitän* was an observer, responsible for the tricky low-level navigation. But although they had evaded the radar, the aircraft had been spotted and tracked by the Observer Corps, and when they arrived at Kenley the defenders were ready and waiting. Worse still, the delayed main force had not yet arrived.

In the teeth of the defences, the attack was pressed home. Three hangars were hit, and bombs were seen bouncing down the runway 'like rubber balls'. Five Dorniers were hit almost immediately; in one the pilot was mortally wounded, and the situation was only saved by the observer, Wilhelm-Friedrich Illg, who grabbed the control column and pulled the Dornier away from the ground. Having removed the pilot from his seat, Illg took over, jinked to evade ground fire and turned on course for France. He eventually reached St Omer, and on the fourth attempt made a wheels-down landing. He was awarded the *Ritterkreuz* for his feat, although this was surprising, considering that, like most observers of the period, Illg had been a pilot before becoming an observer, in which capacity he was of course the aircraft commander. He had little time in which to savour his moment of glory, for on 1 September, flying with Mathias Maassen, another survivor of the Kenley raid, his aircraft was shot down near Dungeness and he was taken prisoner.

At last the survivors were clear of the airfield and able to turn for home, only to find the fighters waiting. Two ditched in the Channel, two crash-landed in France, and Illg, as related, landed normally although away from base. Wilhelm Raab landed at Amiens with a wounded navigator and later became one of only two pilots of *9/KG 76* to return to Cormeilles-en-Vexin that day.

High above, the rest of the Dorniers were just arriving. Attacked head-on by Hurricanes, several of them jinked out of the line of fire. This spoiled their bomb run; some chose alternative targets, whilst others did not bomb at all. The Ju 88s of *II Gruppe* were unable to dive bomb as briefed—smoke from three burning hangars was masking much of the airfield. Instead they attacked their alternative target, West Malling.

Apart from *9 Staffel*, which was nearly wiped out, *KG 76* lost two Dorniers from the high-level force and three damaged. *II/KG 76* lost two Ju 88s plus one damaged. All the victims fell to fighters.

Meanwhile *KG 1* had bombed Biggin Hill, but the aim was inaccurate and little damage was done. They encountered little opposition: *KG 76* had attracted almost all the fighters and lost just one Heinkel while another was damaged. Six fighters had been destroyed on the ground at Kenley, but none at Biggin Hill. It was a poor return.

To the west, a massive force of Stukas had assembled. It crossed the Channel *en masse* with its fighter escort before splitting into its component parts to attack individual targets. *I/StG 77*, comprising 28 Stukas, was assigned to Thorney Island, *II/StG 77*, with 28 Stukas, was to raid Ford, while *III/StG 77*, with 31 Stukas, was to attack Poling radar. The fourth unit involved, *I/StG 3* with 22 Stukas, headed for Gosport. Of the unit leaders, Walter Sigel was already a *Ritterkreuz* holder; others who would soon join him were Helmut Bode and Alfons Orthofer. Each Ju 87 carried a single 250kg and four 50kg bombs. Off Selsey Bill, the formation split into its component *Gruppen*, each of which headed for its target.

As we have noted, in most Stuka outfits the aircraft dived in line astern, all down the same 'chute', which made the task of the anti-aircraft gunners easier. Helmut Bode's *I/StG 3* attacked in *Ketten* to divide the defensive fire. Once established in the dive, Bode sprayed the target with his two fixed machine guns to distract the gunners; after he had pulled out, his radio operator fired also, to protect the following aircraft.

While diving, the Stukas were relatively immune from attack, as the fighters built up so much speed in the dive that they almost invariably overshot without being able to bring their guns to bear. The most dangerous moments were before the dive or after the pull-out. Caught then, Stukas were easy targets.

Kurt Scheffel, a frail and inoffensive man when the author met him in 1979 but who was destined to survive several hundred sorties on the Russian Front with *I/StG 77*, was soon in trouble. Stuka radio operators joked that they were living protection for their pilots. The joke turned grim just before the dive, when Scheffel's aircraft was hit by fighters, killing the radio operator and wounding him. His reflector sight smashed, he dived, aiming with his auxiliary ring-and-bead sight.

The aircraft having pulled out, all formation cohesion was lost. At full throttle Scheffel worked his way to the front of the gaggle where other aircraft could cover his undefended rear. With his left arm numb and his right hand dripping blood, he managed to nurse his Stuka back to base, but on arrival he was too weak from loss of blood to leave the cockpit. His aircraft had survived 84 hits!

He was lucky: his *Gruppe* lost ten aircraft, including that of the *Kommandeur*, Herbert Meisel. One returned damaged beyond repair with a dead radio operator; four more returned damaged, two with dead radio operators. The luckiest man of the day was radio operator Karl Maier, who received no fewer than eight bullet wounds, none of which was fatal. Or perhaps his pilot was even luckier!

The other *Gruppen* fared better. *II/StG 77* lost five Stukas and *II/StG 77* just two and two damaged. Helmut Bode's *I/StG 3*, well to the east of the main action, escaped without loss. But the overall losses were unsustainable, and from this day the Stukas were out of the battle.

The final raid of the day was mounted against Hornchurch and North Weald by 57 Dorniers of *KG 2* and 51 Heinkels of *KG 53*. Intercepted short of the target, the Heinkels lost four aircraft, including that of Reinhold Tamm, the *Kommandeur II/KG 53*, and one damaged. *KG 2* fared better, with one damaged. At this point the British weather intervened. Solid cloud cover at low altitude socked in both fighter stations, and the raiders, unable to see their targets, turned back.

By now *Luftwaffe* combat losses were averaging an unacceptable 49 aircraft a day, not counting 17 August, on which there was no real action. The German High Command insisted that the bombers be given close escort. While the *Jadgflieger* did not like this, the fact remains that in the final two weeks of August combat attrition fell by 60 per cent. Bf 109 losses remained constant at an average of eleven per day, but bomber and Bf 110 losses fell to ten, rather than 38 per day as previously. Interestingly, RAF fighter losses remained constant at nineteen.

Six days of poor weather followed, then once again the *Luftwaffe* began to launch mass raids, some aimed at airfields and others at ports and aircraft factories. Often a little more subtlety was employed. Bomber formations arrived over the Pas de Calais and circled for up to an hour in full view of British radar, only setting out for the target when their escort fighters arrived.

The hope was that the RAF squadrons would be scrambled too early, and be low on fuel when the time came to engage. While this was rarely the case, it had a knock-on effect. Held back, the fighters were scrambled only when the controller was certain that a raid was under way, and this left them desperately seeking altitude. Another ploy was to send out several raids on a wide front simultaneously, using dog-leg routes to cause confusion. Yet again, dummy raids were sent out, then withdrawn.

Raids on the fighter airfields, particularly those in south-eastern England, were having a cumulative effect. Apart from the destruction of *matériel*, many RAF pilots were nearing exhaustion. But, to *Luftwaffe* Intelligence, this was not obvious. The attainment of air superiority in time for the projected invasion seemed no nearer, and time was running out. Dissatisfaction with progress led to the main attacks being switched to London, and most of the Bf 109s were re-deployed to *Luftflotte 2* to increase the fighter escort available. This was Phase 4.

Bombs on London

It began in the late afternoon of 7 September. No fewer than 348 bombers drawn from five *Geschwader*, escorted by 617 fighters (mainly Bf 109s), set off for the capital. Subtlety was thrown to the winds: this attack was a sledge-hammer! The choice of London was also a surprise to the defenders: expecting the massive column of bombers to split up and attack individual targets, the defending fighters were positioned to cover the sector stations, and places like the Thameshaven oil refinery.

As a result, the juggernaut, headed by Johannes Fink with *KG 2*, reached the London dock area almost unopposed and bombed, causing heavy damage. By the time Fighter Command reacted, the bombers were on their way home, their losses negligible. Over the next few days further attacks were made on the metropolis, and while cloud hampered the bombing it hindered interception equally. Optimistic as ever, *Luftwaffe* Intelligence concluded from the lack of opposition that Fighter Command was on the verge of defeat—down to its 'last 50 Spitfires'.

With this in mind, all that was needed now was to bring about a large fighter battle, in which numbers would count. Two raids on the capital were planned for 15 September. The first would arrive just before midday. It consisted of 27

Do 17s drawn from *I* and *III/KG 76* and led by the *Kommandeur* of the latter, Slovenian-born *Ritterkreuz* holder Alois Lindmayr. He was an observer rather than a pilot, but this was the norm at the time.

Losses had prevented a single *Gruppe* from fielding a full formation of nine *Ketten*, and nineteen Dorniers of *III/KG 76* had been supplemented by eight more from *I/KG 76*. The two units joined up over Amiens, but were then forced to penetrate thick cloud. As observer Theodor Rehm recalled:

> . . . visibility was so bad that one could only see the leader's plane a few metres away. In our bomber four pairs of eyes strained to keep the aircraft in sight as its ghostly shape disappeared and reappeared in the alternating darkness and light. One moment it was clearly visible, menacingly large and near; then suddenly it would disappear from view, in the same place but surrounded by billowing vapour . . .

When they emerged from the clag at 3,500m, Lindmayr's aircraft orbited for ten minutes to allow the others to join up. But two aircraft had lost contact and returned to base. The remaining 25 Dorniers rumbled on towards the Pas de Calais, where they were scheduled to rendezvous with their fighter escort. This consisted of a *Gruppe* of Bf 109s as close escort, another as distant escort and a third freelancing ahead—about 120 fighters in all. The imbalance between bombers and fighters provided a vital clue: the Dorniers, not to put too fine a point on it, were bait!

As the Dorniers left the French coast at about 4,000m, two more formations of Bf 109s, each about twenty strong, took off. Both were from *LG 1*, and one of them had bombs slung under the fuselage. This was *II/LG 2*, led by *Ritterkreuz* holder and future *Eichenlaub* winner Otto Weiss, who had converted from the Hs 123 to the Bf 109 but who was fated to revert to the elderly biplane for the invasion of the Soviet Union in nine months' time. They climbed to about 6,000m and set course along the same track as the Dorniers, overtaking them fast.

British fighters were soon on the scene, but many were quickly engaged with the escorting 109s. Then two squadrons of Hurricanes attacked the bombers from head-on. Dornier pilot Wilhelm Raab, a survivor of the low-level attack on Kenley less than a month earlier, commented:

> They came in fast, getting bigger and bigger. As usual when under attack from fighters, we closed into tight formation to concentrate our defensive fire. It was very frightening: in the glass noses of our Dorniers there was not even a molehill to hide behind!

The Dorniers escaped serious damage and continued on their way. However, by the time they reached the London suburbs the 109 escort, low on fuel after fighting off the interceptors, had turned for home. Now the composite *Gruppe* of *KG 76* was in real trouble. On the bombing run, with elements of at least three British squadrons already in the vicinity, it was suddenly faced with the five-squadron Duxford Wing—56 fighters in perfect formation. Someone in Wilhelm Raab's Dornier—he was never quite sure who—quipped: 'Here come those last 50 Spitfires!' As an example of German gallows humour, this is hard to beat, yet it was less funny at the time. But twenty 50kg bombs from each aircraft were already going down, aimed at a complex of rail junctions south of Battersea power station. Whilst the railways were hard hit, inevitably some bombs went astray and struck houses in the vicinity. The modern term is 'collateral damage'.

The *Jabo*s were not engaged. Fighter Command standing orders were to ignore fighters if possible and concentrate on bombers. It was not spotted that the 109s were carrying bombs, and they were able to line up on their targets unimpeded. Aiming through their reflector sights in a 45-degree dive, they released their bombs at about 5,000m. Accuracy with this mode of delivery, from this altitude, was poor, and virtually no military damage was caused. But they suffered no losses.

The same could not be said for *KG 76*. After bombing it reversed course by turning to port, but some of its aircraft were already in trouble. Hopelessly outnumbered, it should have been annihilated, but fifteen Dorniers—all that remained in formation—managed to beat a fighting retreat, although almost all suffered some degree of damage. Six of the 25—or 24 per cent—were down, including Wilhelm Raab's, and another four, damaged and separated, managed to limp home. It was a tremendous achievement by Alois Lindmayr.

Even as the last Dorniers crossed out, the next attack was airborne over France. Having made rendezvous with their escorts, this fresh force, consisting of elements of four *Kampfgeschwader*, formed up and set course for London. On crossing the coast at Dungeness, the aircraft took up a formation of three columns on a 10km frontage. In the centre were 24 Heinkels of *I* and *II/ KG 53*, whose target was the Royal Victoria Dock. The port column consisted of 25 Dorniers of *III/KG 2*, with a further eighteen Dorniers of *II/KG 2* some five kilometres astern. Their target was the Surrey Commercial Dock. The starboard column comprised nineteen Dorniers of *II/KG 3*, bound for the Royal Victoria Dock, while five kilometres astern came 28 Heinkels of *I* and *II/KG 26*, briefed to attack the West India Dock. These carried 1,000kg bombs. It was a far more destructive force than the first raid, and its fighter escort was huge—no fewer than 361 fighters. If all went as planned, Fighter Command was in for a rough afternoon.

Matters did not go as planned. Unlike the noon action, in which the defending fighters were largely prevented from getting at the bombers, the three columns on a wide frontage proved vulnerable. Still on the approach, four bombers went down while seven were damaged, dropped out of formation and turned back. They arrived only to find the assigned objectives hidden under cloud, and bombed targets of opportunity. Virtually no military damage was caused. The bombers were harried all the way back to the coast, but losses were sustainable. *KG 2* lost eight Dorniers destroyed and five damaged, while *KG 3* lost six Dorniers and four damaged. *KG 26* got away more lightly, losing one Heinkel and three damaged while *KG 53* lost six Heinkels and four damaged. For the damage inflicted on the target, this was a poor return.

Two small raids were mounted on Portland and Southampton, the latter by *EprGr 210*, which missed the Spitfire factory at Woolston completely. Given that the landmarks for this were clear—the Itchen estuary and the floating bridge—*Jabo* bombing inaccuracy while using 45-degree diving attacks is the only excuse.

If there was one thing that the actions on 15 September proved, it was that Fighter Command was far from a spent force. This being the case, a seaborne invasion, never more than barely credible, moved into the realm of impossibility and was postponed indefinitely just days later. Even so, the daylight bombing campaign was not yet over. Once again *Luftwaffe* attention was turned to RAF airfields and aircraft factories. On 27 September Bf 110 *Jabos* of *V/ LG 1* and *II/ZG 76* swanned about over Kent and Sussex with no apparent objective other than to distract Fighter Command. They lost eight of their number. This demonstration was followed by the Ju 88s of *I* and *II/KG 77* which, unescorted owing to a failure to rendezvous with the 109s, lost twelve aircraft shot down.

Further west, the indefatigable *EprGr 210 Jabos* headed for an aircraft factory north of Bristol. Intercepted, they lost four Bf 110s, including that of *Kommandeur* Martin Lütz and *Staffelkapitän* Wilhelm-Friedrich Rössiger, both of whom were posthumously awarded the *Ritterkreuz* four days later. Promotion prospects with *EprGr 210* were always good! Acting *Kommandeur* (the fourth) Werner Weimann was lost on 5 October, while Otto Hintze, *Staffelkapitän 3/EprGr 210*, was shot down and taken prisoner on 29 October. Hintze received the *Ritterkreuz* while in captivity.

Massed daylight bomber raids virtually ceased in October as the autumn weather set in. Most attacks were flown by Bf 109 *Jabos*, which, whilst they largely evaded interception, caused little damage. The *Luftwaffe*, despite the 'lightning speed and undreamed-of might' promised by Hermann Goering, had met its first defeat.

The Night Blitz

Luftwaffe bombers, like their RAF counterparts over Germany, desynchronised their engines at night to give a *rhurr-rhurr-rhurr* noise intended to mislead sound locators. In practice, it had two effects. It made life uncomfortable on board the bombers, while it left those on the ground in no doubt of the nationality of those flying above.

As a four-year-old living in Hampshire, the author found this disconcerting. One knew that 'Jerry' was up there, and often felt that he was seeking one personally. But few bombs fell in the locality, despite the proximity of a huge army camp. Only rarely did the family seek shelter: usually we sat around the kitchen table, listening to the engine noises and the banging of nearby Bofors guns and watching the skin on our cocoa crinkle! Incidentally, bombs are often described as whistling down. They don't whistle; they scream! City dwellers had things much worse. In North London, a family of three girls and their mother dived under the kitchen table whenever they heard bombs coming down close at hand. The tension was, however, broken on one occasion when one of the girls announced that she had just sat in the dog's dinner!

It is a common misconception that night raiding only began when it appeared that the daylight assault was faltering. In fact, night raids commenced as early as June 1940, and gradually increased in strength. The first major raid was by Heinkels of *KG 4* on 18/19 June. It was carried out at the full moon, at an altitude low enough to be able to identify targets clearly. Five bombers were lost to night fighters, including that of *Freiherr* Dietrich von Massenbach, *Kommandeur II/KG 4*, shot down over Newcastle. A veteran of Poland and Norway, he baled out and was taken prisoner. He was awarded the *Ritterkreuz* on 27 August.

This loss rate was exceptional: only eleven aircraft were lost to combat causes in the entire month. While it is certain that the 'cat's-eye' night fighters had been lucky on this occasion, it equally showed that conditions conducive to accurate bombing at night—i.e. clear skies, a bright moon and a moderate altitude—were also favourable to the defenders.

Most raids at this time were harassing attacks; for example, four Dorniers from *KüFlGr 606* attacked the Rolls-Royce works in Glasgow at dawn on 18 July, at low level and in neat line astern. But within a week there was an ominous portent for the future when a Do 17 of *2/KG 2* was shot down into the Channel by a Blenheim equipped with air interception (AI) radar. Many months would elapse before the AI night fighter became a real threat to bombers, but eventually it proved the major hazard.

The main problem with night bombing, however, was finding and identifying the target. Suitable moon conditions were only available for a few days of each month, and these were often negated by the vagaries of the British weather. Nor did the navigational failings of *Luftwaffe* aircrew help: targets were often missed even in daylight. How much more difficult was it, then, to find a target at night?

Minelaying sorties were to a degree easier, in that the coastline showed up well on all except the darkest nights. On 22 July Hajo Herrmann, by now *Staffelkapitän 7/KG 4*, was, with four of his *Staffel*, tasked to lay mines in Plymouth Sound. Under the wings of each aircraft was a pair of 500kg magnetic mines. These had to be dropped at no more than 310kph and an altitude of no more than 100m. To avoid detection, he crossed the coast to attack from the most unexpected direction—inland. The plan was to descend from 5,000m, throttled back in a semi-stalled condition to minimise engine noise. The crews would then drop their mines, open the throttles and escape out to sea.

Arriving over Dartmoor, Herrmann could see Plymouth Sound clearly, lit by the half moon. Dive brakes open and engines idling, his Ju 88 descended at an angle of 45 degrees, nose-up to give an angle of attack just sufficient to maintain controlled flight. The nose-up angle was nearly his undoing: pre-occupied with searching ahead, he failed to notice until the last moment that he was heading straight for a barrage balloon. When he finally spotted it, it was too late: at such a low speed the controls were sluggish. Unable to man-oeuvre, he literally sat on top of the balloon, which sank rapidly under the weight of the aircraft. This situation could not last. The Junkers was not pre-cisely balanced on the balloon, and, fully stalled, fell off to one side. Herrmann recalled:

> . . . I noticed that the British searchlights were shining from above—we had fallen off the balloon and now we were upside down with virtually no forward speed, and going down out of control. I felt as though I was playing a piano which was falling from a five-storey building!

Herrmann slammed the throttles wide open and closed the dive brakes, but with less than 1,500m of altitude to play with the situation was critical. With

The Lorenz beam.

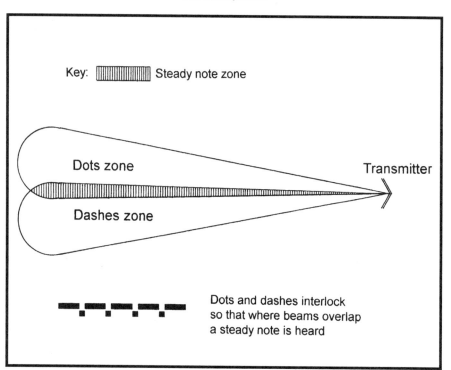

the controls unresponsive, he gave the order to bale out. Even as the escape hatch was jettisoned, flying speed was reached and he managed to pull out. By now he was coned by searchlights, while the anti-aircraft guns shot at him from all angles. Dropping his mines, he escaped untouched.

German Blind Bombing Systems

Even before the war, German scientists were working on methods of finding targets in darkness or bad weather. Two entered service at an early date—*Knickebein*, the 'magic crow' of legend, and *X-Gerät*. The former was very simple, and for this reason it could be used by any crew trained in the Lorenz blind landing system, and without any specialised equipment. The latter was much more complex, and needed special equipment and special training to use, but it was far more accurate.

Knickebein consisted of two transmitters which sent out beams that diverged slightly but overlapped in the middle. That on the left transmitted dots, that on

The Knickebein *bombing system.*

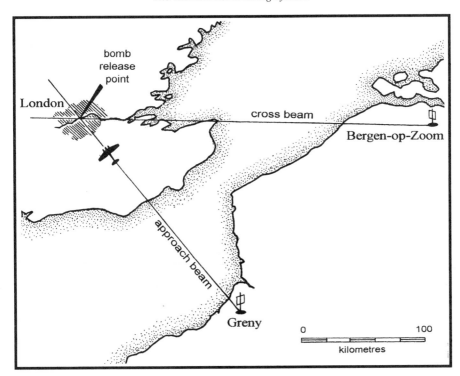

91

the right dashes; in the central overlap zone, dots and dashes merged into a steady note, and if the aircraft flew down the steady note zone it would be heading directly for the target. Ranging information was provided by another beam which crossed the first over the target. Accuracy was modified by range: up to about 400km could be achieved, but as the steady-note zone was one-third of a degree wide the lateral error was quite significant—1.6km at a range of 290km. Another problem was that at extreme ranges the bomber had to fly at more than 6,000m to receive the beam, and altitude degrades bombing accuracy.

Three factors eventually combined to discredit *Knickebein*. First, its accuracy was insufficient to allow anything but area attacks. Secondly, the RAF soon discovered it, and instituted countermeasures. While these were not always effective, the fact that they existed did not exactly inspire confidence in the system. Thirdly, the fact that the beams were known to the RAF gave rise to unease among the bomber crewmen. As Otto von Ballasko, a Heinkel pilot with *III/KG 1*, later commented:

> For all we knew, the night fighters might be concentrating all the way along the beam to the target; more and more crews began to use the *Knickebein* beams only for range, and kept out of them on the run up to the target.

This did nothing for bombing accuracy: when the users start to distrust a system, its value is instantly degraded.

X-Gerät was a far more sophisticated system. Like *Knickebein*, it had an approach beam, but this was crossed by three others. Initially the bomber flew to one side of the constant-note area. As the first cross-beam was passed, 30km short of the target, it lined up in the centre, making due allowance for crosswinds. The second cross-beam was 20km short of the target; as this was passed the observer pressed a switch which started a clock, having first set the altitude. As the third cross-beam was passed, just 5km from the target, another switch was thrown, starting another clock. The two clocks accurately measured speed over the ground. The bombs were then released automatically over the target. Maximum range was just under 300km, and theoretical accuracy about 300m. Fortunately for the British, the system was also susceptible to countermeasures.

X-Gerät was highly advanced for the period, but it demanded extremely precise flying over the final 50km and a practised observer to operate the

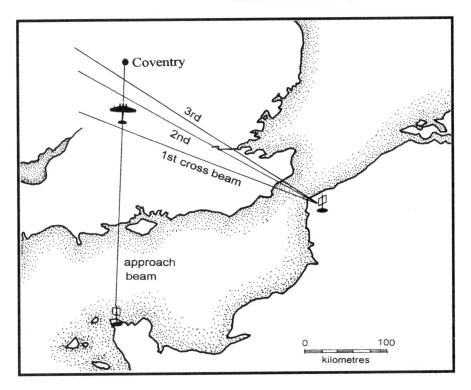

The X-Gerät *bombing system.*

system with precision. The unit chosen was *KGr 100*, which as *Ln 100* had carried out precision attacks against Polish targets, although results could not be ascertained at the time. Since then it had flown as an ordinary line unit against Norway and practised with *X-Gerät* over London, albeit without bombs, prior to the fall of France. *KGr 100* was an élite unit, its pilots selected for their blind-flying skills and its observers for their ability to handle complex electronic systems. At this point, the *Kommandeur* was Kurd Aschenbrenner, an administrator and signals expert who, contrary to many accounts, rarely flew.

An even more technically advanced system was *Y-Gerät*, also used by *KGr 100*, which was brought into service in August 1940. This used a single transmitter with a complicated signal which was automatically processed on board the bombers. Essentially it was similar to *X-Gerät*, but with no ranging cross-beams. Instead, the bomber re-radiated the signal back to the ground station, which by measuring the time lapse computed the range very accurately

93

and actually gave the signal to drop the bombs. Unfortunately for the *Luftwaffe*, like so much state-of-the-art technology, it proved to be very unreliable.

The other *Luftwaffe* aid to navigation was a network of radio beacons, each with an indentifiable signal. Cross-bearings on two or more would give the bomber its precise location. Here again British countermeasures intervened with masking beacons, or 'Meacons', which reproduced the original signals. Many German bombers were led astray by these, and more than one was fooled into landing in England. On 14/15 February 1941 Heinkel pilot Hans Thurner, of *KG 55*, was even stated to have touched down on three English airfields in the same sortie. On each occasion he discovered his mistake in the nick of time, opened the throttles and made a hasty departure, eventually returning to base. He was awarded the *Ritterkreuz* on 6 August 1941. One of the few bomber pilots to fly entirely in the West, as *Kommandeur I/KG 6* (Ju 188) he failed to return on 11 June 1944. He was awarded *Eichenlaub* posthumously on 20 September 1944.

The Y-Gerät *bombing system.*

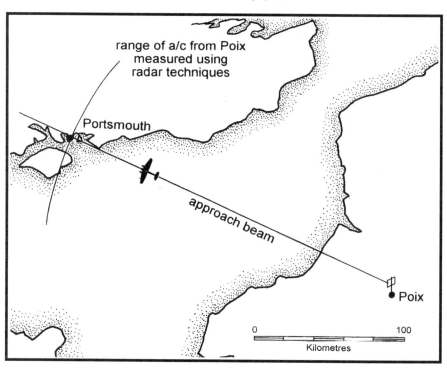

Flying from Vannes in Brittany, *KGr 100* mounted its first operation over Britain on 13/14 August 1940. The 'shadow' Spitfire factory at Castle Bromwich was hit, although not seriously, and so was the Dunlop Rubber Works. Significantly, the Bristol Aeroplane Company works at Filton was bombed through solid cloud on 19/20 August, causing a fair amount of damage. Night and cloud were no longer sufficient protection.

The first really large *Luftwaffe* night attack of the war was made on the Liverpool docks on 28/29 August, but the bombing was scattered and caused little damage. Attacks continued for the following three nights, but even with the participation of *KGr 100* they were ineffective. Many bombs fell on a decoy site.

Decoy sites were a major part of the British air defences, and consisted of four basic types. The first was the 'K' site, which replicated an airfield in the vicinity, with 'buildings', mown 'runways' and dummy aircraft. As a daylight decoy, it was less than effective; in fact an apocryphal story goes that a German aircraft once dropped a wooden bomb on a 'K' site. On the other hand, the occasional RAF bomber returning from Germany, unsure of its position, took them for real and lobbed in!

Night decoy, or 'Q', sites simulated the working lights of an airfield, including switch-off when the *Luftwaffe* was in the vicinity, leaving just a couple of lights 'accidentally' on. They were very effective, attracting 359 of the 717 bomber attacks launched at their parent (real) airfields.

Next came the 'QL' decoy sites, simulating marshalling yards, industrial complexes etc, which were much more sophisticated. Tram flashers and railway signals blinked on and off. For steelworks, orange lights shining on to sand looked like furnace glows, and many other variations were used.

Then there was the 'QF' site, which replicated fires three or four miles away from the actual target. These were lit as soon as the real target came under attack, and the race was then on to extinguish fires at the latter before the second wave of bombers arrived. Oil refineries presented a particularly intractable problem. The prevention of fires at oil refineries had long been studied; not so that of simulating them. The problems were eventually solved, but with oil consumption approaching 2,500 Imperial gallons per hour they were expensive.

The biggest and best decoy was the 'Starfish', instituted after the Coventry raid in mid-November 1940 and intended to resemble a burning city under attack. A number of methods were used. The 'Grid Fire' burned with a steady yellow flame, while 'Boiler Fires' simulated explosions on the ground. 'Basket Fires' and 'Coal Fires' represented burning buildings. It was all very complicated, but could hardly be otherwise.

The first 'Starfish' drew 59 bombs intended for Bristol on 2/3 December 1940; the most successful lured more than 200 bombs and parachute mines aimed at Portsmouth on 17/18 April 1941. Ju 88 pilot Peter Stahl of *6/KG 30* took part in this raid:

> The town and port of Portsmouth are covered by 3–4/10ths cloud, in addition to a mighty smoke cloud from the fires down below. All this greatly reduces ground visibility in the target area and I am hard put to find my way between the big dummy conflagrations and the real fires.

A very experienced pilot who obviously knew that the 'Starfish' was there, he still met with difficulties.

Many pilots maintained that they could always tell the difference between decoys and the real targets, but could they really? In all, decoys attracted 730 attacks during the war; these ranged in size from single aircraft to mass raids.

The huge daylight raid on London on 7 September 1940 was followed up at night. The bomber crews had no difficulty in finding their target: fires already burning could be seen from many miles away. Night after night for the next two months, often flying two and sometimes three sorties each, the bombers returned to the capital. At night, formation flying was not possible: the bombers departed their bases at about four-minute intervals, giving a spacing of roughly 19km between individual aircraft. This was known as a 'crocodile'. Decoys were useless in this situation: even with no fires on the ground, the serpentine course of the River Thames stood out clearly on all but the cloudiest nights.

Luftwaffe raids at this time were often described as 'terror attacks', intended to break the will of the British to resist. In theory, bomber pilots tried always to attack legitimate military objectives, and prided themselves on their accuracy. But, like their RAF counterparts, they could not overcome the fact that bombing was a very imprecise art, even in daylight and clear conditions.

Ugly and angular, the Ju 87 dive bomber, commonly known as the Stuka, was able to plant its bombs with greater precision than any other type. It spearheaded the armoured columns in the invasion of Poland, the West and the Soviet Union and achieved devastating results against British ships in the Mediterranean. Its first reverse came in the Battle of Britain, when it was badly mauled by British fighters. By 1944, it was far too vulnerable to anti-aircraft fire, and production ceased. This is a Ju 87R, a long-range anti-shipping variant with extra fuel in the wings and 300-litre drop tanks beneath them. (Bruce Robertson)

The Heinkel He 111H was the backbone of the Kampfflieger *in the early years of the war but by 1943 was rapidly becoming obsolete. This early model refuels prior to a raid against England. The fully glazed nose is evident, but its asymmetric shape is less so from this angle. (Bruce Robertson)*

This He 111H-5 of Stab III/KG 26 *was shot down on the night of 10 April 1941 by a Defiant night fighter. It crashed and burned out near Seaford in Sussex. (Bruce Robertson)*

The Henschel Hs 123B was the only dedicated attack aircraft in Luftwaffe service at the start of the war. Despite its antiquated appearance, it gave sterling service over Poland and France, and in the early months of the invasion of the Soviet Union. (Bruce Robertson)

The Heinkel He 115 was mainly used for minelaying in the early years of the war, but was also an effective torpedo bomber. It took part in a series of attacks on the ill-fated convoy PQ 17. Its 'boots' made it slow and lumbering, and if enemy fighters were present it was a sitting duck. That apart, so useful was it that production was restarted in 1943. (Bruce Robertson)

Not all bombs dropped went off. This German SC 500 penetrated the dome of the church at Mosta, on Malta, and landed in front of the altar. It is seen here with the team of Royal Engineers that defused it. (Bruce Robertson)

The Dornier Do 217E entered service in 1941 with II/KG 40 *in the anti-shipping role, and* II *and* III/KG 2 *as a bomber. It took part in the Baedeker Raids, and later in Operation* 'Steinbock'. *(Bruce Robertson)*

Not all Kampfflieger *were heroes. This Do 217M of KG 2 was assigned to raid the London Docks on the night of 23/24 February 1944 but was damaged by a 'Z' rocket battery over Ealing, whereupon the crew baled out. Unmanned, it flew on as far as Chesterton, Cambridgeshire, before making a fairly smooth wheels-up landing. (Bruce Robertson)*

The Focke-Wulf FW 200C caused untold damage to Allied shipping in the Atlantic, but there were never enough of them to be really effective. Moreover, it was not really strong enough to withstand the stresses and strains of operations. (Bruce Robertson)

The Junkers Ju 188A was basically a very much improved Ju 88, and was used extensively in Operation 'Steinbock'. The aircraft seen here belonged to 2/KG 6, and is being loaded with two torpedoes. (Bruce Robertson)

With coupled engines driving two huge four-bladed propellers, the Heinkel He 177A was the nearest the Luftwaffe ever got to having a true strategic bomber. It was endlessly delayed by engine fires caused by the unconventional layout, and by the time the problems were solved it was too late. (Bruce Robertson)

The near-triangular fuselage section of the Henschel Hs 129B, adopted to minimise frontal area to improve survivability, is clearly seen from this angle. It was the first of the 'big gun' anti-tank aircraft, but its flying qualities were poor and its engines unreliable. (Bruce Robertson)

The Junkers Ju 87G was essentially the D model fitted with a 37mm cannon pod under each wing, which ruled out a steep diving attack. As a tank-buster it was lethal in the hands of an expert, but the pods adversely affected handling, and it was no aircraft for a beginner. (Bruce Robertson)

The Focke-Wulf FW 190 started to replace the Ju 87 in 1943. It was less accurate but far more survivable owing to its greater speed, and two dedicated attack variants were produced. This FW 190F-8 has a dust filter on the port side of the engine. (Bruce Robertson)

One of the largest bombs used by the Luftwaffe *was the 1,800kg Satan. This example was left behind during the retreat from Cyrenaica. (Bruce Robertson)*

A replacement for the elderly Bf 110, the Messerschmitt Me 410 was built in several variants, only a few of which were fast light bombers. Sheer speed made it a difficult opponent for British Mosquito night fighters. (Bruce Robertson)

The final offensive role of the Heinkel He 111H was as a carrier of the air-launched Fi 103 'Doodlebug', one of which is seen under the wing of this KG 53 aircraft. Just visible is the umbilical which starts the pulse-jet engine. (Bruce Robertson)

The Arado Ar 234 was the world's first operational jet bomber. It was normally twin-engined, but this experimental four-engined variant reveals in detail the launching trolley and triple skid undercarriage featured on all early aircraft.

The trolley and skid arrangement proved too unwieldy for operational use, and the final variant of the Ar 234 had a conventional tricycle undercarriage. The projection above the cabin is a periscopic bomb sight for use in shallow diving attacks. (Bruce Robertson)

The Messerschmitt Me 262A was adapted as a fighter-bomber to become the Sturmvogel, *but speed and manoeuvrability were degraded by external loads, while bombing accuracy was hard to obtain, even in shallow diving attacks at low level. (Bruce Robertson)*

Ritterkreuz *and* Eichenlaub *holder Hans-Georg Bätcher rather sheepishly celebrates his 500th sortie. He was lucky to make it: he was shot down over France on 5 June 1940 and taken prisoner, but released at the Armistice. Later that year he was fortunate to survive an encounter with a British night fighter. He flew a total of 658 sorties on all fronts, and ended flying Ar 234 and Me 262 jets. (Alfred Price)*

(Above left) In a full and varied career in which he rose to high command, Werner Baumbach received the Ritterkreuz *with* Eichenlaub *and* Schwerten. *He flew mainly the Ju 88 with* KG 30.
(Above right) Ritterkreuz *holder Walter Bradel rose from* Staffelkapitän *to* Kommodore *of KG 2. He was killed when his Do 217 crashed on landing at Amsterdam on 5 May 1943, after raiding Norwich. (Alfred Price).*

Ritterkreuz, Eichenlaub *and* Schwerten *holder and former Ju 88 bomber pilot Hans-Joachim Herrmann accompanies* Reichsmarschall *Hermann Goering on an inspection of* Wilde Sau *night-fighter pilots. (Alfred Price).*

How it often ended; full military honours for Walter Bradel and his crew in May 1943. (Alfred Price).

There is a time and place for everything, and taking happy snaps when you are down in the desert with hundreds of miles to walk to Benghazi would not seem to be either: Martin ('Iron Gustav') Harlinghausen, right, wearing his Ritterkreuz and Eichenlaub, seen after his grand tour of the Suez Canal. He ran out of fuel and only reached safety after an epic five days. Harlinghausen was the great anti-shipping specialist, and flew as an observer. On the left is his regular pilot, Robert Kowaleski. (Alfred Price)

(Left) Karl-Heinrich Höfer, seen here as Kommandeur II/KG 55, flew on both the Western and Eastern Fronts. He was awarded the Ritterkreuz in May 1943 and the Eichenlaub in November 1944, mainly for actions in the East. He survived the war. (Alfred Price)

(Below) Bernhard Jope, arguably the most distinguished Condor pilot with KG 40. He was later Kommandeur III/KG 30 and led the attack which sank the Italian battleship Roma. Here he receives the Eichenlaub to his Ritterkreuz from the Führer on 24 March 1944. To Jope's left is Hans-Georg Bätcher. (Alfred Price)

(Above left) Ritterkreuz *holder Robert Kowaleski, who regularly flew with Martin Harlinghausen as his observer, with whom he perfected the 'Swedish Turnip' attack against shipping. At first a staff officer, he was later* Kommandeur II/KG 26 and III/KG 40. *He became* Kommodore KG 76 *in February 1944. (Alfred Price)*

(Above right) Ritterkreuz *holder Viktor von Lossberg (right) was* Kommandeur III/KG 26 *in Norway in 1940. He was operating from a frozen lake when the ice started to thaw; one Heinkel was lost. Quickly ordering his men to jettison their bombs on to the ice to lighten the aircraft, he succeeded in getting the rest off safely. (Alfred Price)*

(Above left) Dieter Lukesch was an Austrian pilot with 7/KG 76 (Do 17) in the first year of the war, and was twice shot down behind enemy lines, but returned safely. After the Battle of Britain he converted to the Ju 88 and flew in the night Blitz. By October 1944, as Staffelkapitän 9/KG 76, *he was awarded the* Eichenlaub *to the* Ritterkreuz. *(Alfred Price)*

(Above right) Helmut Mahlke had a rugged war. Kommandeur III/StG 1 *for the Battle of Britain, he was badly shot up over Malta in February 1941, then in the East was shot down in flames three times in the first few days, being severely injured the final time. He was awarded the* Ritterkreuz, *having flown 145 sorties. (Alfred Price)*

(Above left) Volprecht Riedesel Freiherr *zu Eisenbach flew mainly the Ju 88 on the Eastern and Italian Fronts, but as* Kommodore KG 54 *converted to the Me 262 jet when the unit became* KG(J) 54 *late in 1944. He was awarded the* Eichenlaub *to his* Ritterkreuz *in January 1945 but was shot down and killed by Mustangs on 9 February. (Alfred Price)*

(Above right) Horst Rudat was awarded the Ritterkreuz *on 24 March 1943 after intensive operations on the Eastern Front.* Staffelkapitän 2/KG 55 *(He 111), he flew relief sorties into the Stalingrad pocket and on one occasion managed to airlift 27 soldiers out—which must have been very cramped. In 1944 he led a* Mistel Staffel *of* KG 101 *in France and at the end of the war was* Kommandeur II/KG 200. *(Alfred Price)*

(Left) Hans-Ulrich Rudel, seen in the cockpit of his Stuka, probably in 1942. He went on to become the most decorated soldier of the Third Reich, and the only recipient of the Golden Oakleaves. (Alfred Price)

The accuracy of daylight level bombing using the German Lotfe 7D tacho-metric sight would put 50 per cent of individually aimed bombs within 91m of the centre of the target from an altitude of 3,000m. At double this altitude, the error became something in excess of 400m. This was in clear conditions; in poor visibility the error could increase by 250 per cent. However, only rarely were bombs dropped individually. The normal procedure was to drop them in a stick with spacings preset from 10m to 100m. Twenty 50kg bombs could thus extend in a line varying between 200m and nearly 2km long, which took care of some of the longitudinal inaccuracies.

At night, bombing accuracy using normal methods was very poor, although, as we have seen, *X-Gerät* could give much better results if not subjected to countermeasures. Its main value was to ensure that the attack started off in more or less the right place. But that still left the non-specialist units to put down their bombs in the areas where fires had been started. Once again, inher-ent inaccuracy was a major problem.

Being shot at did nothing to improve matters: as a rule of thumb, the aver-age miss distance recorded on the training range triples when the crew is actu-ally under fire. Inevitably, most bombs missed their assigned targets, and many caused heavy damage in civilian areas.

Two German weapons were inherently inaccurate. Incendiaries tended to scatter when dropped, and were easily blown off course by the wind. Then there was the land mine. Developed as a naval weapon, this had greater de-structive power than any conventional German bomb of the early war period and was widely used against inland targets. Prior to release, the bomber had to throttle right back and reduce speed, as the mine had to descend under a para-chute. Dropped from four or even five kilometres high, however accurate the initial aim the weapon could (and often did) drift a long way off course before it hit the ground.

The Firelighters

Given half-way decent visibility, coastal targets were easy to find. Inland tar-gets were a different matter. These could only realistically be found by spe-cially equipped units. By default, *KGr 100*, using *X-Gerät*, became the first, but not the only, German target-marking outfit. Unlike the later RAF Path-

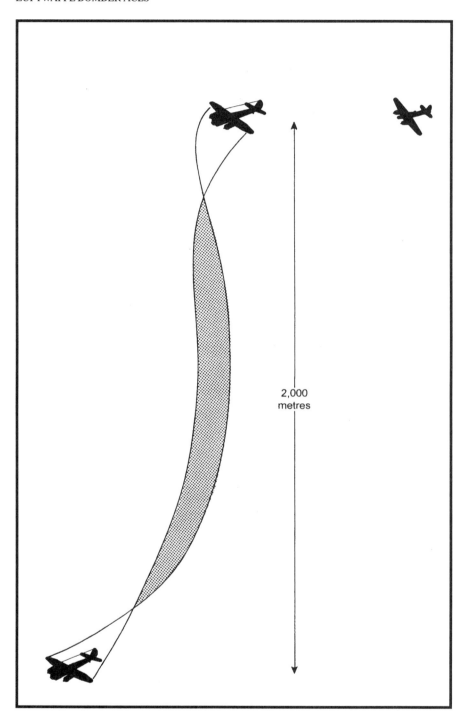

Fighter evasion with a Junkers Ju 88.

finders, *KGr 100* made little use of flares and none of pyrotechnics. Nor did it concentrate its efforts at the beginning of an attack. Instead it dropped a combination of high-explosive and incendiary bombs over an extended period to start fires, which in turn would lead other bombers to the objective.

The first major attack in the firelighting role was made by *KGr 100* using *X-Gerät* on Coventry on 14/15 November 1940. Yet although the fires raised could be seen from France, almost one-fifth of the aircraft despatched failed to reach their target. This is totally inexplicable.

That on Coventry was the first of many such raids. The second target-marking unit was *III/KG 26*, also with Heinkels, which used *Y-Gerät*, difficulties with which have been previously mentioned. When the weather was unsuitable for a mass raid, both units carried out precision attacks.

Matters would have gone ill for the British had these been allowed to flourish unchecked, but here three factors intervened. The first was *X-Gerät* and *Knickebein* jamming: not that either was ever totally effective, but jamming caused a great deal of confusion. The second was the 'Meacons', which fouled up the navigational beacons. The third was the advent of a truly effective night fighter, led to its target by ground control and using AI radar for the terminal portion of the interception. During 1940 the weather had accounted for more losses than the British defences. For example, one of the most distinguished German bomber pilots of the war, Werner Baumbach of *KG 30*, had crashed twice while landing in poor visibility, on 16 October and 24 November, but was each time unhurt. But, as 1941 progressed, British night fighters became the main enemy.

Tactics Against the Night Fighters

In the day battles of the summer of 1940, German bombers often returned safely with up to 200 hits from rifle-calibre machine guns. This was made possible by a combination of armour protection and self-sealing fuel tanks. The main armament of the latest RAF night fighter, the Beaufighter, consisted of four 20mm Hispano cannon, just a few hits from which could tear a bomber apart.

The object of the exercise was, from the German point of view, to spot the night fighter first, but this was far from easy. Bombers took to flying just above, or just below, the cloud base, to take refuge if they were intercepted. Speed was important, to reduce the time that the bomber was at risk over the British Isles, but in one recorded instance a Heinkel was intercepted flying barely above the stall. The Beaufighter pilot throttled right back but was unable to stay behind it. This of course could only work on a very dark night, with minimal visual distance; on a clear night, the bomber would have been a turkey. As the fighter pilot commented, 'He made our task almost impossible.'

In the hands of an experienced pilot, agility played its part. Despite being a bomber, the Ju 88 could perform an upward roll with ease if unladen. Even with a bomb load on board, it could take extreme evasive action. On 13 March 1941 Peter Stahl was heading for Hull with a pair of mines. It was a bright moonlit night. When one of his crew reported a night fighter astern, he reacted instantly:

> Without further ado I pull *Cäsar* [his Ju 88] into a steep half-roll to port and let it fall upside down into the night. Surely, nobody could follow that! I have just levelled off when Hein comes over the intercom again, repeating his warning. The devil! Once more we shoot like a stone into the pitch blackness below. And then a third time!

On the third occasion, by now down to 800m, he managed to shake off his pursuer. With two tonnes of mines aboard, it was a remarkable achievement.

On the following night he revealed another trick. On the return leg he deliberately chose to make a long detour, simply to keep the moon at an angle to one side. The direct route would have placed the moon almost directly ahead, to a stalking night fighter's advantage.

Not all were so lucky, nor so experienced and cunning. Bomber losses to night fighters in January 1941 were a mere 0.02 per cent, with three bombers shot down. By May of that year this had increased to 3.93 per cent, with losses of 96. While this was not yet unsustainable, it was a indicator for the future.

Casualties for *KGr 100* from January 1941 to 27 July, when the unit was deployed to the Eastern Front, are fairly typical. In this period, eighteen aircraft were lost—more than 50 per cent of establishment. Of these, ten are known to have fallen to night fighters, a further seven to unknown causes and one to an operational accident. Eleven were damaged in the same period, four by night fighters, two by anti-aircraft fire, three in operational accidents and two to unrecorded causes.

Most of the destruction took place in the final three months. Horst Goetz is recorded as saying to new crews joining the *Gruppe*, no doubt with tongue firmly in cheek: 'Do not tell us your names. In two weeks you will be dead, and we shall have remembered your names for nothing!'

One memorable event. Hans-Georg Bätcher had joined *1/KGr 100* on 1 July, having earlier been shot down over France and taken prisoner. On the night of 9/10 July his Heinkel was attacked by a night fighter over the Midlands and badly shot up. Having jettisoned his bombs, he sought refuge in the clouds far below. His flight mechanic was dead, his radio operator badly wounded. His port motor had stopped, his autopilot, compass and trimming were all out of action and his tail was badly damaged. Unable to maintain a straight course, he held his crippled Heinkel in a gentle turn to starboard as long as possible, then reefed it round to resume a new heading to port of where he actually wanted to go. After describing a series of ellipses, he finally coaxed his aircraft to Cherbourg, where he belly-landed on the runway. It was an incredible piece of flying.

Bätcher, who was awarded the *Ritterkreuz* in 1942 and the *Eichenlaub* in 1944, was an outstanding bomber pilot. On 15 July 1941 he was appointed *Staffelkapitän 1/KGr 100*, replacing Hermann Schmidt, another future *Ritterkreuz* recipient.

117

# 6. CAMPAIGNS IN THE SOUTH

To paraphrase Robbie Burns, 'The best laid plans of mice, men, and *Führers*, gang oft agley!' And so it proved. Hitler's game plan from mid-1940 was clear. With Poland, Denmark, Norway, the Low Countries and France subjugated, Britain was to be forced out of the war either by threats or conquest, leaving the Third Reich free to attack the Soviet Union in May 1941. The *Blitzkreig* tactics which had proved so successful against Poland and in the West would then sweep all before them, and result in a victory in the East before winter. This would give Hitler hegemony over most of Europe, with the *Lebensraum* that he had always demanded—a German Empire stretching eastward to the Urals, to say nothing of control of the mineral riches of the area.

Two things now interfered with his plans. The first was the refusal of the island nation to be cowed, which had led to the first defeat for the previously all-conquering *Luftwaffe*; the second was the overweening ambition of the leader of his ally in the Rome–Berlin Axis—*Il Duce*, Benito Mussolini.

Mussolini, the self-styled modern Caesar, wanted an Italian Empire to match the Roman Empire of old. He already controlled Libya and Abyssinia (now Ethiopia) in north and east Africa, and Albania in the Balkans, but wanted much more. A jackal following the lion's kill for pickings, he brought Italy into the war in June 1940 by invading the south of France at a time when France was clearly beaten. The downside of this was that it left Italian forces facing the British in Africa at two points, the borders between Libya and Egypt, and those between Abyssinia and Sudan, of which only the former concerns us.

By December 1940 the Italians were on the verge of defeat. Their army had been routed and chased out of Cyrenaica, while the Royal Navy dominated the Mediterranean. Malta, a few miles south of Sicily, was ideally placed to interdict Italian supply routes to North Africa by sea and by air. To assist, the *Luftwaffe* despatched their anti-shipping experts, *Fliegerkorps X*, under Chief of Staff Martin Harlinghausen, from Norway to Sicily, in December 1940. His initial strike force consisted of *II/KG 26* and *2/KG 4*, both with Heinkels. These were quickly supplemented by two *Gruppen* of *LG 1* with Ju 88s and two Stuka *Gruppen, I/StG 1* commanded by Walter Enneccerus and *II/StG 2* under Paul-Werner Hozzel, both holders of the *Ritterkreuz*. These last were the primary attack units. While Malta was important, the main target was the aircraft carrier *Illustrious*, which had launched a devastating strike against the *Supermarina* in Taranto harbour shortly beforehand. It was estimated that four direct hits would sink *Illustrious*. To this end, the two *Gruppen* practised dive bombing a floating mock-up. It was a large target, 230m long by 28m wide—not easy to miss, especially with no one shooting back!

The chance came on 10 January 1941 in the Sicilian Narrows. Italian torpedo bombers lured the defending fighters away and shortly afterwards about 40 Stukas struck, using a combination of 250kg general-purpose and 500kg armour-piercing bombs. A few Stukas went for the two escorting battleships to draw their fire.

British carriers were unique in having an armoured flight deck about 90mm thick. While this raised the centre of gravity, reducing their seaworthiness, it also meant that the vulnerable hangar deck, with its aircraft, fuel and munitions, was better protected than that of any other carriers in the world. This was to save *Illustrious*, though only just. As the Stukas attacked, Swordfish pilot Charles Lamb was about to land-on, unaware that anything was wrong:

> . . . a strange aircraft came into view, flying from port to starboard, right in front of me, across the flight deck . . . As I pressed the trigger of my Vickers gun, the Stuka was right ahead in my sights, but it dipped as though in salute and dropped an enormous great bomb right down the after lift well, which was still gaping. The bomb looked like a GPO pillar-box painted black. By the flames which shot out of the hole in the deck, I realised that it had rolled off the lift and exploded in the hangar. Then the lift itself burst out of the deck, all 300 tons of it, and shot a few feet into the air and sank back into the lift-well on its side, like a great wedge-shaped hunk of cheese.

Five more direct hits were scored, but only one other caused critical damage. The attacks were made by *Ketten*, synchronised from different directions. The majority were from astern, a few degrees off the direct line. Lamb, his Swordfish badly damaged by Stuka guns, ditched near a destroyer and was picked up.

Having survived another attack, and yet another direct hit, *Illustrious* limped into Malta. Her ordeal was not yet over, as Stuka and Ju 88 attacks during the next few days caused further damage. She finally escaped to Alexandria, and from there to the United States for a much-needed refit. The Stukas had not yet finished with the Royal Navy. On 11 January *I/StG 2*, led by Enneccerus, encountered two cruisers and two destroyers. The subsequent attack damaged HMS *Gloucester* and sank HMS *Southampton*.

Attention was then turned to Malta. First in action were the Ju 88s of Joachim Helbig's *II/LG 1*, which had also taken part in the attacks on *Illustrious*. It was joined in February by the Stukas of Helmut Mahlke's *III/StG 1*. Mahlke himself had a very fortunate escape on 26 February. A direct hit by anti-aircraft fire tore a huge hole in his starboard wing. As he wobbled shakily back out to sea, he was attacked by a Hurricane, but this was repelled by his radio operator. Other arrivals in that month were the Ju 88s of Hajo Hermann's *9/KG 30*, which preceded the other *Staffeln* in the *Gruppe*. Their first sortie against Malta, flown with Helbig's *Gruppe*, was described in the Prologue.

The next sortie was to Tobruk, to attack warships. The aircraft missed the target completely, dropped their bombs on a target of opportunity, then, plagued by having eaten too many oranges before take-off, landed at an Italian airfield in Libya—to answer the call of nature!

North and East Africa were not the only Italian follies of the period. Having annexed Albania in 1939, *Il Duce* overreached himself once more by invading Greece on 28 October 1940, only to meet fierce resistance which stopped his army in its tracks. British reaction was immediate: Crete was occupied, and a few RAF squadrons were sent to the mainland to support the outnumbered and ill-equipped Hellenic Air Force.

Hitler saw this as a threat to his forthcoming invasion of the Soviet Union. If British troops arrived on the Greek mainland they could pose problems for his southern flank. Moreover, RAF bombers would then be within striking distance of the vital Romanian oilfields at Ploesti. A German invasion of Greece was now inevitable.

At the same time, it was considered essential to keep Italy in the war. To this end, the *Deutsches Afrika Korps*, commanded by Erwin Rommel, was despatched to Libya to bolster the Italians there. The latter resulted in one of the great epics of the war. Malta, the unsinkable aircraft carrier, was well placed to strike at Axis supply routes across the Mediterranean, and, as we shall see, failure to subjugate it later became a critical factor in the desert campaign.

Assault in the Balkans

Operation *'Marita'*, the attack on the Balkans, was originally scheduled for 1 April 1941. Yugoslavia had agreed to allow the German Army passage through its territory, and a two-pronged attack, through Yugoslavia and Bulgaria, was planned. At the last minute, the Yugoslavs changed sides. In the face of this altered situation, Hitler immediately delayed the impending attack on the Soviet Union in order to deal with it.

Like the Polish Air Force before it, the Yugoslav Air Force deployed to secondary airfields, only to find that barely half were operational, while inadequate communications reduced their effectiveness. Moreover, their positions were betrayed by a Croatian staff officer, and some 60 per cent of effectives were destroyed on the ground.

Units were transferred from the West for this campaign, although as it was spearheaded by the Stukas of *StG 3* and *StG 77*, assisted mainly by low-flying Dorniers of *KG 2* and *KG 3*, this did little to weaken the assault on Britain. Launched on 6 April, the main attack was directed against Belgrade, the targets in which were the Citadel, the Parliament buildings and the castle and barracks in the Topcider district. As the Panzers raced through the mountain passes, Yugoslav resistance collapsed and the *Wehrmacht* drove on into Greece.

As previously noted, Joachim Helbig's *II/LG 2* had been joined in Sicily by Hajo Herrmann's *9/KG 30*. Since then the other two *Staffeln* of *III/KG 30* had arrived, led by *Ritterkreuz* holder Arved Crüger. This *Gruppe* was to carry out what proved to be one of the most devastating attacks of the entire war.

On the night of 6/7 April the target was the Greek harbour at Piraeus, which was crammed with shipping. The assigned load was two mines, but Herrmann, always a law unto himself, added two 250kg bombs to the load carried by his

---

Bomber Units, Operation *'Marita'*, 5 April 1941

Unit	Type	Base
Stab, I, III/KG 2	Do 17	Austria
III/KG 3	Do 17/Ju 88	Austria
Stab, I,II,III/KG 51	Ju 88	Austria
II/KG 4	He 111	Austria
Stab, II/StG 3	Ju 87	Graz, Austria
Stab, I, III/StG 77	Ju 87	Arad, Romania
Stab, I, III/StG 2	Ju 87	Bulgaria
I/StG 3	Ju 87	Bulgaria
I/StG 1	Ju 87	Bulgaria
II(Schlacht)/LG 2	Bf 109E	Bulgaria
10(Schlacht/LG 2	Hs 123	Bulgaria

Note: *Schlacht/LG 2* had already started reverting to the Hs 123 from the Bf 109E *Jabo*.

Staffel. Crüger, making a last-minute inspection, ordered them to be taken off, adding the comment, 'And try and look a bit happier next time!' Herrmann gave the order, but, after Crüger had departed, managed to ensure that it was not obeyed.

The weather forecast was not good—heavy cloud over the Greek mountains. Crüger's solution was to climb over them. Herrmann preferred to approach beneath the cloud base, threading his way between the islands, in line astern at between five- and seven-kilometre intervals (just over one minute). At every turning point each bomber would fire a flare to guide the aircraft behind it. Accurate navigation was essential for the leader, but Herrmann had no worries on that score. His observer was the very experienced future *Ritterkreuz* winner Heinrich Schmetz, steering by compass and by stopwatch.

Well into the mission, great flashes were seen. The superstitious thought that these might be caused by the Olympian Gods occurred but was quickly rejected. It was in fact the 8th *Staffel*, flying higher and suffering icing, which had been forced to jettison its mines, which had exploded on impact. Herrmann was in many ways typical of the regular German officer in that his education had been classical rather than technical. The ratio was about nine in every ten. His classical background took over as he neared the target.

For the first time in my life I saw those places that we had discussed so often during our schooldays, from class to class, in history, legend and poem. There they all were—the battlefields of Leuktra and Platea. By the pale light of the moon I saw Marathon and Athens. Phidias, Plato and Aristotle all lived and worked there.

Sterner realities soon asserted themselves. The harbour entrance was narrow, while the mines could only be dropped from low level and a speed of no more than 300kph. As at Plymouth almost a year earlier, Herrmann elected to attack from the landward side, and he throttled back to a little above the stall at about 3,000m. With dive brakes deployed, he hauled hard back on the stick. Buffeting violently, the Junkers, by now semi-stalled, fell steeply, nose-up, towards the entrance channel. Levelling out at 300m, Schmetz dropped the mines, then tore at full throttle out of the cage!

Back at altitude, Herrmann circled to distract the defences while the remainder of his *Staffel* attacked. His two 250kg bombs remained. Two orbits were made while Schmetz calculated the wind speed and heading. Selecting what appeared to be the largest ship in the harbour below, Herrmann sneaked

Hajo Herrmann's flight, 6/7 April 1941.

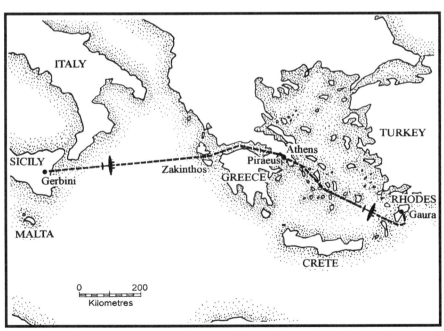

123

Bomber Units, Operation 'Mercury', 20 May 1941		
Unit	**Type**	**Base**
Stab, I and III/KG 2	Do 17	Menidi
I and II/LG 1	Ju 88	Eleusis
II/KG 26	He 111	Eleusis
Stab and II/StG 1	Ju 87	Argos
I/StG 3	Ju 87	Argos
StG 77	Ju 87	Argos
Stab and I/StG 2	Do 17/Ju 87	Molaoi
III/StG 2	Ju 87	Scarpanto

in at 1,000m, then throttled back to no more than 250kph. An upward lurch announced that the Schmetz had released the bombs and Herrmann pivoted around his port wing tip to observe the result.

It was rather more than he expected. A tremendous explosion lit up the area and violent turbulence tossed the heavy Junkers about like a toy. His target had been the ammunition ship *Clan Frazer*, which still had most of its cargo on board. It blew up with such ferocity that ten other ships were sunk and many more damaged, while Piraeus, by far the most important Greek port, was wrecked from end to end.

The fact that Herrmann's Ju 88 survived the blast was little short of miraculous. Only its tough structure, stressed for dive bombing, allied to a steep angle of bank which minimised its presented area, allowed it to stay in the air. However, it had not escaped unscathed. The port engine was damaged—whether by anti-aircraft fire, night fighters or flying debris was never established—and had to be shut down. With no chance of returning to Sicily, Herrmann headed for Rhodes, only to arrive in the middle of an air raid with fuel gauges reading zero. The landing could only be described as fraught.

Crete

Greece was quickly overwhelmed by the Germans, leaving the British-garrisoned island of Crete as the cork in the bottle. A seaborne invasion was projected, but no adequate troopships were available. The solution adopted was an airborne landing, using paratroops and gliders. Operation 'Mercury' commenced on 20 May.

The assault began on 20 May, led by the Dorniers of *I* and *II/KG 2* and the Heinkels of *II/KG 26*. They were followed by the Stukas of *StG 2*. For an air landing to succeed, the defences had to be suppressed, and to a degree this was a failure. While German airborne and mountain troops eventually captured the island, it was a Pyrrhic victory. Losses in men and transport aircraft were tremendous, and the German airborne forces were never again used in anger.

The real significance of the battle for Crete was, however, the confrontation between aircraft and ship which ensued. The Germans tried to reinforce their beleaguered airborne troops by sea, but the convoy was intercepted and broken up by British surface forces on 22 May. But this put the latter within bomber range, and they were attacked by the Ju 88s of *I/LG 1*, led by Kuno Hoffmann. The cruisers *Gloucester* and *Fiji* and the destroyer *Greyhound* were sunk, and the cruiser *Naiad* was badly damaged by a near miss. Dorniers from Herbert Rieckhoff's *KG 2* joined the fray, causing more damage to *Naiad*, while a direct hit was scored on the cruiser *Carlisle*. Later that day the battleship *Warspite* was damaged by a direct hit. *Fiji*'s end was unusual: she was sunk by two 250kg bombs from Bf 109 *Jabo*s of *I/LG 2*. In June Hoffmann was awarded the *Ritterkreuz*, mainly for this successful action, while in July Rieckhoff received the same award. Among the other pilots who took part was future *Ritterkreuz* winner Gerd Stamp.

On the next day three destroyers were caught by Stukas of Hubertus Hitschhold's *I/StG 2*, which sank *Kashmir* and *Kelly* with direct hits. At this point the only British carrier in the eastern Mediterranean, HMS *Formidable*, entered the lists, launching a strike against the *III/StG 2* airfield on the island of Scarpanto, east of Crete, on 26 May. The carrier was located quite fortuitously by *II/StG 2*, led by Walter Enneccerus. Based in North Africa, this unit was actually looking for troopships. Equally fortuitously, the carrier was caught recovering aircraft, and was in a poor position to launch fighters to defend herself. Two direct hits by 500kg armour-piercing bombs, and a near miss which caused underwater damage, put *Formidable* out of the fight. She followed *Illustrious* to the United States for a refit.

By 29 May British forces were evacuating Crete. With no air cover, the Royal Navy was vulnerable. Two more destroyers were lost to air attack, this time by *StG 77*, and two cruisers were badly damaged.

If the dive bombers seemed notoriously 'dead-eye' in these anti-shipping operations, one thing must be borne in mind. Taking into account the numbers involved, direct hits were scored by far less than one in ten of the bombs dropped—even against large targets like aircraft carriers!

Malta

With the fall of Crete, many *Luftwaffe* units were redeployed to the east, ready for the invasion of the Soviet Union in June. Others remained in North Africa to support the desert campaign. The *Regia Aeronautica* was primarily responsible for operations against Malta, with the *Luftwaffe* playing a stiffening role.

Raiding Malta gave little scope for subtlety and virtually none for diversionary tactics. The only targets were the three airfields, plus the emergency strip at Safi, and Grand Harbour. The airfields were connected with taxiways, which meant that unless all three runways could be put out of action at once the RAF could still operate. A modern parallel was the Gulf War of 1991, when it proved impossible completely to close down the huge Iraqi airfields.

The Maltese airfields were easy to see from the air on a clear day. They were ringed with blast pens, many of which were constructed from empty petrol cans filled with sand and stones. The local weather sand-blasted the paint from them, with the result that, from the air, the shiny metal stood out, looking, as one *Luftwaffe* pilot commented, 'like little strings of pearls'.

When the Blitz on Malta started in earnest, the Stukas were often allocated an individual pen as a targets. The only problem was what it contained. If it was empty when the attack came in, an alternative target had to be sought. But if there appeared to be an aircraft in it, was it a real aircraft, a decoy or something damaged beyond repair but used to attract bombs? There was no means of telling! In 1942 the emergency landing ground at Safi was used for decoys to the exclusion of all else.

Attacks on Malta began even before the Balkan campaign and, as we have seen, bombers based in Sicily were often diverted to targets in Greece. For some considerable time, Malta took a low priority. *III/KG 30*, having frequently mounted raids on Greece, now turned its attention to the island stronghold once more.

In the late spring of 1941 Arved Crüger had decamped to Capri to marry a glamorous film star, leaving Hajo Herrmann as Deputy *Kommandeur*. One of the first tasks for his *Gruppe* was to act as bait, to draw up the British fighters to be shot down by the *Jagdflieger*. He planned to approach the island from the north-west at between 5,000 and 6,000m, then level bomb Grand Harbour, where a cruiser and other warships were berthed. The altitude was on the high side for bombing accuracy, but as the bombers were primarily bait this hardly mattered. At least one of his aircraft was damaged by anti-aircraft fire, but all returned safely. Being bait was not to his taste, so he suggested that night raids on the fighter airfields would be more effective.

Approximately a dozen night raids were then flown, one of which, on 29 April, was of particular interest. The *Gruppe* was to attack from several directions by *Staffeln*, although not of course in close formation, throttled right back in a gentle glide (one of Herrmann's favourite ploys) at between 800 and 1,000m. This was far lower than could reasonably have been attempted in daylight. The anti-aircraft gunners on Malta were good: after all, they had had plenty of practice! To enable the Junkers pilots to see their targets, a flare-dropping Heinkel of *III/KG 4* was to illuminate the target from about 6,000m. Detected almost at once, the Heinkel was surrounded by anti-aircraft fire, but dropped its flares perfectly. *Stab* and *7/KG 30*, led by Herrmann, bombed by their light. The Heinkel turned away, then came back in for its second run. Its cockpit sparkling like a diamond in the glare of the searchlights, it was hit and a trail of fuel streamed back from one wing. Undaunted, the young pilot released the second string of flares, lighting up the target for *8/KG 30* to attack. By all the rules, he should then have turned for home, but no—losing height, he turned south into the darkness. By now down to below 3,000m and flying on one engine, the Heinkel pilot came in for his third and almost suicidal run, dropped his flares, then limped north, out to sea. *9/KG 30*, led by future *Ritterkreuz* winner Helmut Weinreich, then bombed. The only aircraft to be lost in this raid was the Heinkel, which crashed on the edge of its airfield at Comiso.

The pilot survived the crash, critically injured. His name is unknown, but as Herrmann, who on their first and only meeting at the briefing had been doubtful about him, recorded: 'He was my Unknown Warrior of the Second World War. It is very difficult to judge a man. Some men act big; some men are big.'

The record shows that the *Kampfflieger* were ineffective during the second half of 1941. RAF and Fleet Air Arm aircraft, and Royal Navy surface forces and submarines based on Malta, cut a deadly swathe through the Axis supply convoys to North Africa. In November 1940 Axis losses approached 60 per cent, and lack of supplies greatly hindered Rommel's campaign in the desert.

This could not be allowed to continue, and a sharp reaction took place in January 1942. Four Stuka *Gruppen* were sent to Sicily—the training *Gruppe* of *StG 1*, and *II* and *III/StG 3*, with *I/StG 3* staging through bound for North Africa. In addition, five Ju 88 *Gruppen* arrived—*I/KG 54*, *II* and *III/KG 77*, *KGr 606* and *KGr 806*, the last two of which were anti-shipping specialists. Lavishly supported by fighters, they quickly made Malta untenable for bomber and naval units; indeed, the cruiser *Penelope* suffered so much damage from bomb splinters that she became known as 'HMS Pepperpot'! Once more the Axis supply convoys could sail almost unmolested.

The reinforced *Kampfflieger* nearly, but not quite, achieved its aim of pounding Malta into surrender. It was not done without loss. Many distinguished German pilots and leaders went down over the island. Among them, recently appointed as *Kommodore KG 77*, was Arved Crüger, who fell over Malta in March 1942.

The RAF held off the attacks with large reinforcements of Spitfires. *Kampf-flieger* losses mounted, then, in May, urgent needs elsewhere saw the striking forces scattered once more. *II/StG 3* departed for the desert and *II* and *III/KG 77* headed for the Eastern Front, while *I/KG 54* left for Greece.

Just one last success was achieved against the Royal Navy. On 11 May four destroyers were attacked by Joachim Helbig's *I/LG 1*, which was now based on Crete. Only fourteen Ju 88s were serviceable, but these managed to sink one ship. A further attack by Gerhard Kollewe's *II/LG 1* achieved nothing. Then Helbig returned, with only seven aircraft, although these had picked crews. Among them were future *Ritterkreuz* winners Gerhard Brenner, Iro Ilk and Otto Leupert, all of whom scored direct hits (although not one of whom survived the war). Only one destroyer survived this attack.

Malta could now be reinforced at will. Once again it became a base for offensive action and Axis supply losses soared. In all *Luftflotte 2* could muster only eleven *Gruppen* of bombers, including the torpedo bombers of *KG 26* and the Stukas of *StG 3*, to cover the eastern Mediterranean from Greece and Crete, the Maltese Narrows from Sicily, and the Western Desert. Given that serviceability was rarely more than 50 per cent, it was a vast area.

Once more the supply situation in the desert became critical, and in September reinforcements started to arrive. It was too late. The unsinkable aircraft carrier was now fully operational, and by December the Axis forces in the desert were in full retreat following the Battle of El Alamein.

North Africa

The fast-moving ebb and flow of the war in the desert, with huge advances and retreats, ironically became known as the Benghazi Handicap! In fact, the changing fortunes of each side can to a fair degree be linked with the situation on Malta.

Luftwaffe units were first deployed to North Africa in January 1941. Compared to other theatres, the bombers and Stukas played a relatively minor role. One reason was the paucity of fixed targets. For example, given the flat and generally firm terrain, airfields could be set up almost anywhere, which meant that there was little point in bombing runways. Another was the numerically small force involved, which was spread over hundreds of miles of desert. The harsh climate reduced serviceability, while fuel, spares and ordnance shortages often limited the number of sorties that could be flown.

The port of Alexandria and the Suez Canal were just within reach for much of the time, but the raids that could be mounted against these were mere pinpricks. As was so often the case, the lack of a true long-range bomber handicapped the *Luftwaffe*, and the damage caused was hardly worth the effort and the losses. Future *Ritterkreuz* and *Eichenlaub* winner Georg Sattler of *LG 1* had a lucky escape on one of these raids in June 1942. His aircraft was attacked by a night fighter and an engine was set on fire. He was forced to ditch off Tobruk. Fortunately for him the latter was then in German hands, and he managed to swim ashore.

One interesting long-range raid was, however, mounted. On 21 January 1942 a Heinkel fitted with long-range tanks set out for a French base on Lake Chad used as a trans-Africa staging post by the Allies. This was a round trip of nearly 2,500 miles, and consequently the bomb load was minuscule. Almost inevitably the aircraft ran out of fuel on the return leg and landed in the desert. So remote was the spot that it was a week before a reconnaissance aircraft found it. A Ju 52 flew out with fuel and the Heinkel, piloted by Theo Blaich, returned safely to base.

Most of the Western Desert was ideal tank country—flat and with few obstacles. Unless supply dumps or road convoys could be identified, there were few opportunities for the Stukas to strike, and even fewer for the level bombers. Tanks, especially moving tanks, made poor targets, while the dust thrown up by their movement, made worse by the smoke of battle, exacerbated the problem of identification. There was, however, one notable exception—Bir Hacheim.

Occupied by the Free French under General Koenig, this was the southernmost of a line of fortified positions linked by minefields. On 3 June 1942 Walter Sigel's *StG 3* commenced the air bombardment. Little damage was done: most bombs buried themselves in the soft sand, which smothered their explosions. British fighters joined the fray, and *StG 3* lost fourteen aircraft in seven days. In all, more than 1,000 sorties were flown against Bir Hacheim, but even this was not enough. Two *Gruppen* of *LG 1* were ordered to assist. The next attack failed because smoke and dust obscured visibility, but finally, with Rommel's troops closing in, the fortress fell. The myth of Stuka invincibility had crumbled a little more.

Under desert conditions the *Jabo* was rather more useful. Spraying an area of desert with cannon and machine-gun fire was potentially far more effective against diffuse targets such as deployed infantry than dropping bombs on them, although bombs were routinely carried. Another advantage was that they could attack at high speed and low level, which improved the chances not only of surprise but also of survivability. Fast, low-flying aircraft were difficult to see from above by fighters, while they presented fleeting targets to anti-aircraft gunners.

Two *Jabostaffeln* were quickly on the scene in 1942, one each from *JG 53* and *JG 27* and both with Bf 109s. Their primary targets were Allied airfields.

Also available in this role were the Bf 110s of *III/ZG 26* and the 'solid nose' Ju 88C heavy fighters of *12/LG 1*.

In October the two Bf 109 *Staffeln* and aircraft of a third unit combined in Sicily to form a *Schlachtgruppe—I/SG 1*, equipped with the FW 190. This latter was a far more robust aircraft than the Bf 109 and better suited to the attack mission. *I/SG 1* went to North Africa in November. Meanwhile *III/ZG 1* started to re-equip with the Bf 210. A tricky aircraft to handle, the 210 was not a success and served with only a handful of units.

The only other new type to see service in North Africa was the Henschel Hs 129. Designed exclusively for the close air support mission, this aircraft had a heavily armoured cockpit with a pathetic view 'out of the window'. It was underpowered, not very manoeuvrable, and unreliable. The type served with a modest amount of success on the Eastern Front, but in North Africa it served only with *4* and *8(Panzer)/SG 2* and achieved little, mainly because of unserviceability.

Following the Battle of El Alamein, and Operation 'Torch', the Allied landing in Algeria, the North African campaign inexorably drew to a close. The *Luftwaffe* strike forces were very heavily outnumbered in the air, and most were withdrawn in spring 1943.

7. WAR IN THE EAST

Anyone who had read Hitler's manifesto *Mein Kampf*—it is misleading to call it a book—should have been able to forecast war between the Third Reich and the Soviet Union. Yet, when it came, the Soviet Union was caught largely unprepared. Stalin appears to have believed that it could not come so soon, with Britain still unconquered in the West. After all, *Mein Kampf* had specifically stated the dangers of war on two fronts.

The Soviet Air Force had commenced a massive modernisation programme in 1941 and was working on more than 200 airfields in the threatened area. Yet the signs were clear: *Luftwaffe* reconnaissance aircraft had overflown Soviet territory from October 1940, usually at high altitudes. The pressurised Ju 86P could reach 12,000m quite comfortably, making it virtually immune from interception, but even when one of these was forced down in Soviet territory by bad weather on 15 April 1941 the evidence was ignored.

Operation *'Barbarossa'*, the invasion of the Soviet Union, was launched on 22 June 1941. The primary *Luftwaffe* target was the huge Soviet Air Force, which outnumbered its German opponent many times over. The attack had necessarily to be on a wide front. In the far north was *Luftflotte 5*, based in Finland, although this was mainly responsible for covering Norway and Denmark, and as such, was a sideshow to *'Barbarossa'*. Further south was *Luftflotte 1*, essentially the northern front, with *Luftflotte 2* covering the centre. The southern front was the responsibility of *Luftflotte 4*.

The ground offensive was scheduled for dawn, to achieve maximum surprise, but unless other measures were taken the Soviet fighter bases well behind the front would be alerted in good time. To synchronise airfield attacks with the main offensive, a few picked crews from *KG 2* (Do 17s), *KG 3* (Ju 88s) and *KG 53* (He 111s) were sent off early. To avoid detection they flew as high as their bomb loads would allow, their routes as far as possible taking them over the sparsely inhabited Pripet Marshes. Once over Soviet territory they split into *Ketten* of three aircraft and searched for their targets. Throttling back, they quietly lost height and lined up for the bombing run. Timing their onslaught to the minute to coincide with the opening of the ground offensive, each *Kette* raced across its assigned Soviet airfield at low level, scattering hundreds of SD 2 fragmentation bombs in its wake. Surprise was total. While the destructive power of the SD 2 was small, the cumulative effect of hundreds of them scattered across an airfield threw the defenders into utter confusion. This was all that was needed—a delay until the main force of level bombers arrived overhead.

Two-thirds of the *Luftwaffe* strike force took part in the first wave of attacks, against 31 airfields. On many of these, Soviet aircraft were lined up wing tip to wing tip—a perfect target. The destruction was enormous. The Soviet Official History admitted losing 800 aircraft on the ground on that first day alone, although German claims were rather higher. Over the next few days the campaign to neutralise the Red Air Force in the battle area continued, and largely succeeded. Even the *Jabos* were involved: all Bf 109s of *JG 27* and many from other units carried racks which held 96 SD 2s. Walter Storp's *SKG 210* (previously *EprGr 210* but now a *Geschwader*, although with only two *Gruppen*) flew an average of 300 sorties per day for the first five days. It was beyond all doubt a *Luftwaffe* victory of the first magnitude, gained with minimal losses. In fact, a significant proportion of *Luftwaffe* losses was caused by faulty fragmentation bombs. Often the SD 2 and the larger SD 10 failed to release, then exploded while still attached to the aircraft.

The Stukas had taken little or no part in the airfield attacks: they flew up to eight sorties a day, and their primary task remained battlefield air interdiction, blasting a path for the advancing Panzers and disrupting Soviet reinforcements. By the fourth day they were joined by most of the *Kampfgruppen* in their task, although in the main these used their longer range and heavier bomb loads in areas the Stukas could not reach.

With the Panzers pushing on, the front was extremely fluid. This occasionally led to awkward situations, such as the time when *II(Schlacht)/LG 2* (Otto Weiss) had to defend its own base from Soviet attack, and occasional 'friendly

Bomber and Stuka Order of Battle, Eastern Front, 24 June 1941

Unit	Type	Decorated Commanders
Luftflotte 5		
IV/LG 1	Ju 87	Arnulf Blasig*
Luftflotte 1		
II/KG 1	Ju 88	Herbert Lorch*
III/KG 1	Ju 88	
Stab/KG 76	Ju 88	*Dr* Ernst Bormann**
I/KG 76	Ju 88	Ludwig Schulz**
II/KG 76	Ju 88	*Freiherr* Volprecht von und zu Eisenbach Riedesel**
III/KG 76	Ju 88	Alois Lindmayr*
Stab/KG 77	Ju 88	Johann Raithel*
I/KG 77	Ju 88	Joachim Poetter*
II/KG 77	Ju 88	Dietrich Peltz***
III/KG 77	Ju 88	Heinz Richter*
KGr 806	Ju 88	Hans Emig*
Luftflotte 2		
II(Schlacht)/LG 2	Bf 109/Hs 123	Otto Weiss**
Stab/KG 2	Do 17	Herbert Rieckhoff*
I/KG 2	Do 17	
III/KG 2	Do 17	
Stab/KG 3	Ju 88/Do 17	
I/KG 3	Ju 88	
II/KG 3	Ju 88	Peter-Paul Breu*
III/KG 3	Do 17	
II/KG 4	He 111	*Dr* Gottlieb Wolff*
Stab/KG 53	He 111	Paul Weitkus*
I/KG 53	He 111	
II/KG 53	He 111	
III/KG 53	He 111	
Stab/SKG 210	Bf 110	Walter Storp**
I/SKG 210	Bf 110	Wilhelm Stricker*
II/SKG 210	Bf 110	Rolf Kaldrack**
Stab/StG 1	Ju 87/Bf 110	Walter Hagen**
II/StG 1	Ju 87	Johann Zemsky**
III/StG 1	Ju 87	Helmut Mahlke*
Stab/StG 2	Ju 87/Bf 110	Oskar Dinort**
I/StG 2	Ju 87	Hubertus Hitschhold**
III/StG 2	Ju 87	Heinrich Brücker*

continued

Stab/StG 77	Ju 87/Bf 110	Clemens *Graf* von Schönborn-Wiesentheid*
I/StG 77	Ju 87	Helmut Bruck**
II/StG 77	Ju 87	Alfons Orthover*
III/StG 77	Ju 87	Helmut Bode*
Luftflotte 4		
I/LG 2	Bf 109	
Stab/KG 27	He 111	
I/KG 27	He 111	Joachim Petzold*
II/KG 27	He 111	Reinhard Gunzel**
III/KG 27	He 111	
Stab/KG 51	Ju 88	
I/KG 51	Ju 88	
II/KG 51	Ju 88	
III/KG 51	Ju 88	
Stab/KG 54	Ju 88	Walter Marienfeld*
I/KG 54	Ju 88	
II/KG 54	Ju 88	
Stab/KG 55	He 111	Benno Kosch*
I/KG 55	He 111	
II/KG 55	He 111	*Dr* Ernst Kühl*
III/KG 55	He 111	
7/LG 2	Bf 110	

*Ritterkreuz; **with Eichenlaub; ***Eichenlaub and Schwerten. Many of these awards were made after 22 June 1941.

fire' incidents were inevitable. This problem has never been satisfactorily solved: all too many occurred in the Gulf War of 1991.

Inexorably the German advance continued, with encircling movements to cut off and destroy whole Soviet armies. Here the main differences between the campaign in France and the war in the East first manifested themselves. The distances were far greater, and every kilometre of advance widened the front still more. The army was ever more thinly stretched, and made increasing demands on the *Kampfflieger* to plug the gaps. The *Luftwaffe* became ever more subservient to the needs of the Army.

The comprehensive network of metalled roads of France was now just a distant memory. In the East the routes were rarely more than dirt tracks. In the open steppes, the Soviet Army used both verges, effectively resulting in a road 100m wide! Bombing them was futile: it merely resulted in a few pot holes, which were quickly filled. The one *Luftwaffe* advantage was that huge Soviet columns were sometimes caught on these wide 'roads', and great execution was then done.

As in France, the short-legged Stukas continually moved forward to stay within range of the front, flying up to eight sorties a day. This put a tremendous strain on the supply organisation to provide fuel, ordnance and spares in sufficient quantities. The *Kampfgruppen* were still based way back and, as the distance to the target areas increased, were forced to reduce bomb loads for extra fuel. Then, with the coming of the autumn rains, the dirt roads turned to mud. This not only exacerbated the supply situation; the Stukas bogged down on their temporary airstrips. Often they could only taxi if the wheel fairings were first removed.

The vast distances involved put a premium on rail transport for the Soviets. Not only supplies, but tanks and guns had to be got to the front. At this point the railway specialist *Eisenbahn Staffeln* started to emerge, although these were not formalised until December 1942. The tactics were pioneered in Poland in 1939. Close to the front, the bombers, usually a *Kette* of three and often operating with a fighter escort, bombed from medium altitude, attacking at a shallow angle and releasing the bombs in a closely spaced stick, usually at 10m intervals. This gave a good chance of achieving at least one cut per stick.

Far better results could be achieved on deep-penetration flights. These flights were usually undertaken by single bombers which crossed the battle area at a relatively safe altitude and headed for the interior, for areas where anti-aircraft fire or fighters were unlikely to be encountered. Once there, they descended to between 300 and 500m, following the tracks. Having taken drift sights to establish the direction and strength of the wind, they released their bombs singly. With a load of twenty 50kg bombs, several cuts could theoretically be made over a considerable distance, closing the line for far longer than a single cut would have done. This was a classic example of economy of force.

One of the problems encountered was that sometimes the bombs bounced off the track. This was largely overcome by using special bombs with spikes in the nose, which dug into the ground and arrested their onward movement. These had to be dropped from 50m in a shallow dive. Of course, if a train was encountered it was attacked, making the sortie one of armed reconnaissance. Bridges were generally avoided, as these were usually heavily defended, and a single bomber would be extremely lucky even to hit it, let alone drop a span.

Remarkably, few large-scale raids were mounted against Soviet goods yards—the one place where locomotives and rolling stock could have been destroyed in quantity. However many tanks the factories were producing, they were of little value if they could not have been brought to the front. So what was achieved? By 13 November 1941, 3,579 railway interdiction sorties were flown, claiming 1,736 track cuts (which sounds disappointing), 159 trains and 304 locomotives destroyed and 1,584 trains and 103 locomotives damaged.

Bridges were the province of the Stukas. Notoriously hard to hit, and even harder to destroy, bridges demanded precision attacks by sufficient aircraft not only to give a chance of scoring enough hits to cut them, but also to suppress the gun defences while doing so. The main problem was that there were not enough Stukas to fulfil all the demands made upon them. Rarely were there more than 300 dive bombers operational at any one time.

As the campaign drew on, three factors emerged. The first was Soviet anti-aircraft fire, which, having improved with practice, made low-altitude attacks extremely risky, forcing the *Kampfflieger* ever higher while making the life expectancy of the *Stukaflieger* very problematical. The second was the enormous amount of *matériel* that the Soviets managed to produce. It was at this point that the lack of a truly strategic German bomber began to be felt—something that could carry a heavy load against Soviet production centres. Thirdly, whilst various encircling movements were made, the three main German lines of advance became evident—towards Leningrad in the north, towards Moscow in the centre and towards Stalingrad in the south. An ominous twist to this was that the further east the advance, the wider the front. 'Front' was actually a misnomer: from this time on it was a series of troop concentrations surrounded by wide open spaces. This had its advantages for shot-down German flyers seeking to return to friendly territory, provided only that they could keep going long enough.

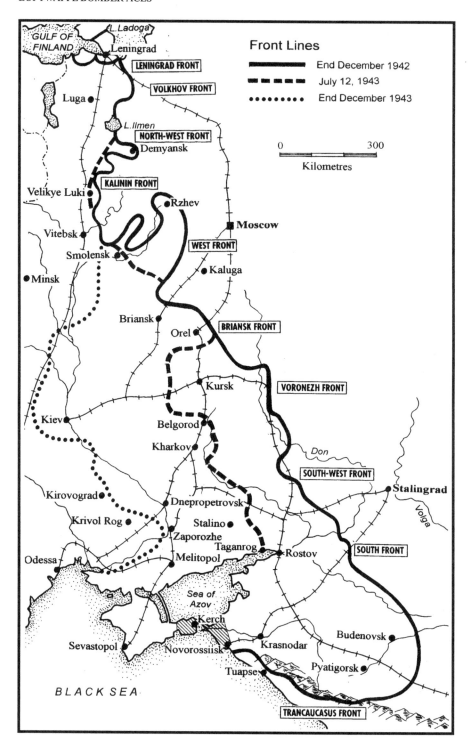

Leningrad, 1941

The primary importance of Leningrad was the harbour of Kronstadt, the base of the Soviet Baltic Fleet. The latter consisted of two battleships, two cruisers, thirteen destroyers and 42 submarines. As such it posed a considerable threat to German supply routes to the northern front. The main protagonist in the attack on Leningrad was Oskar Dinort's *StG 2*, and it was in this series of raids that the most decorated *Luftwaffe* flyer of the war first rose to prominence.

Hans-Ulrich Rudel commenced the war as an observer with a reconnaissance *Staffel* in Poland, although he had previously trained as a Stuka pilot. The son of a priest, he was teetotal and an exercise freak, which had not exactly made him popular. He re-joined the Stukas in France in 1940 but did not fly operationally. He was transferred to *I/StG 2* in the Balkans, but prejudice by his seniors kept him from operations over Greece and Crete.

His first operational sortie came in the East with *1/StG 2*, commanded by Ernst-Siegfried Steen. By sheer chance, both were transferred to *III/StG 2* shortly afterwards, Steen as *Kommandeur*. On 21 September the *Gruppe* attacked once more, this time carrying large armour-piercing bombs. With Rudel flying No 2 to Steen, they commenced their dive from 3,000m. Suddenly Steen's Stuka accelerated, leaving Rudel far behind. Rudel retracted his dive brakes to catch up, then started to overshoot. He recalled:

> I streak past him within a hair's breadth. Is this an omen of success? The ship is centred plumb in the middle of my sights. My Ju 87 keeps perfectly steady as I dive; she does not swerve an inch. I have the feeling that to miss is now impossible . . . Now I press the bomb release switch on my stick and pull with all my strength. Can I still manage to pull out? I doubt it, for I am diving without brakes and the height at which I have released my bomb is not more than 300m.

Rudel lost consciousness in the pull-out, recovering his vision to find himself skimming very low over the water. Astern, the battleship *Marat* had blown up. High above, *Kommodore* Oskar Dinort radioed congratulations. For this, and for his earlier precision attacks on bridges, Rudel was awarded the *Ritterkreuz*.

Two days later Steen was gone. Attacking the cruiser *Kirov*, his Stuka took a direct hit from anti-aircraft fire and crashed into the sea. With him went

Alfred Scharnovski, Rudel's regular radio operator. Steen received a posthumous *Ritterkreuz*.

The March to the East

Although besieged, the city of Leningrad held out. With the Soviet Baltic Fleet neutralised, it became a sideshow. Further south, the advance continued. The German Army reached the very gates of Moscow towards the end of the year, but, slowed by mud, then stopped in its tracks by the Russian winter, it fell back.

Moscow was first bombed on 22 July. The force of 127 aircraft consisted of Heinkels drawn from *KG 53*, *KG 55*, *III/KG 26* and *KGr 100*, the last two temporarily transferred from the West, and Ju 88s from *KG 3* and *KG 54*. As they overflew the capital, 300 searchlights lit up the sky, dazzling them. This was accompanied by an intense anti-aircraft barrage. The result was that concentration was not achieved, and the 104 tonnes of high-explosive bombs and 46,000 incendiaries were scattered over a wide area, causing little damage.

On the following night 115 bombers raided Moscow, but only 100 on the next. Gradually the impetus fell away, and of the 76 attacks made on the Russian capital in 1941 more than three-quarters involved ten bombers or fewer. *KGr 100* was pulled back to Germany in November and became *I/KG 100*; also withdrawn was *III/KG 26*, which became *II/KG 100*.

In the south, progress had been equally rapid. The dual objective was to seize the grainfields of the Ukraine and the oilfields of the Caucasus. The Soviet naval base at Odessa was bypassed (it was later evacuated), then the Crimea was to be overrun, thus neutralising the main Soviet Navy bases in the Black Sea. This last, however, was easier said than done.

The two main air units in this theatre were *III/KG 27*, which soon started to lay mines off the Soviet ports, and *I/StG 77* commanded by Ali Orthover, which was rushed down from the north to support the advance. The *Gruppe* soon put its Crete experience to good use in sinking several warships. The Crimea fell, all except for the modern fortress of Sevastopol in the west and the Kerch peninsula in the east. But, as winter tightened its grip, the southern front stabilised.

The Road to Stalingrad

The year 1942 saw *Luftwaffe* air operations continue much as before, with units allocated to the various armies. This was probably an error: *General der Flieger* Paul Deichmann has since stated that the level bombers should have been amalgamated under a central command in order to achieve concentration of force at critical spots. Certainly this would have allowed mass raids to be carried out, and these would have been far more destructive than the nibbling attacks that actually took place. As it was, the army commanders were reluctant to relinquish overall control of their air assets. In quiet sectors—and there were several of them—the *Kampfflieger* could easily have been underemployed. This would have shown up on the returns to the High Command, which would therefore have been likely to switch bomber units to areas where they could be more effectively used.

To avoid this, the sortie rate was effectively massaged by using the *Kampfflieger* and *Stukaflieger* for operations which were not really militarily necessary. On paper this demonstrated to HQ how essential it was that they remained where they were; in practice many aviators and aircraft were lost to no good purpose. However, in crisis situations units were transferred to other commands, with North Africa the main beneficiary.

The German offensive resumed in the late spring of 1942, but most of the effort was now in the south. The main thrusts were towards Stalingrad, both as an important communications centre and to secure the northern flank of the armies pushing towards the Caucasian oilfields, with Baku on the Caspian Sea as the final objective .

In the Crimea, the Kerch peninsula was taken between 7 and 15 May after hard fighting. *StG 77* was in the forefront. Among its casualties was *Ritterkreuz* holder Johann Waldhauser, who fell to anti-aircraft fire on 13 May on his 312th sortie. The *Geschwader* was then switched north to hold a Soviet counter-attack near Kharkov.

It remained to reduce the Sevastopol fortress, and this was a very tough nut. With *StG 77* once more back in the Crimea, aided among other units by *I/StG 1* under *Ritterkreuz* winner Alfred Druschel, who was later awarded the *Eichenlaub* and *Schwerten*, the main attack began on 7 June after a few days spent softening up the surrounding area. The air attack was intense: a total of

390 aircraft flew 23,751 sorties, and 20,500 tonnes of bombs were dropped, in less than four weeks. Only 31 aircraft were lost. Very heavy bombs, the SC 1400 and SC 1800, were needed against part of the fortifications, such as the Maxim Gorky heavy gun cupolas. Sevastopol finally surrendered on 4 July.

The summer of 1942 passed with air operations much as before. German troops in the south-west had almost reached the Chechen capital of Grozny, while in Stalingrad they were engaged in house-to-house fighting. Recently returned from the front after a bout of jaundice, Hans-Ulrich Rudel took command of his old *Staffel* in *III/StG 2* in time to take part. Accuracy was essential. He recalled:

> We have to drop our bombs with painstaking accuracy, because our own soldiers are only a few metres away in another cellar behind the debris of another wall. On our photographic maps of the city every house is distinguishable. Each pilot is given his target precisely marked with a red arrow.

This would have been a tall order even with modern precision-guided weapons. *General* Wolfram von Richthofen noted sourly in his diary that his Stukas were now dropping bombs within grenade-throwing range!

Meanwhile the level bombers were also engaged in *Gruppe* strength, but confined to interdicting river traffic and silencing artillery batteries on the west bank of the Volga. Then came the Soviet counter-attack, sweeping aside the weak forces south and north of the beleaguered city. By 23 November the German Sixth Army at Stalingrad was encircled. *StG 2*, by now reduced to less than one-third of establishment, was caught in the trap, but for a short while was still able to fly defensive sorties. Then, as stocks of fuel and ordnance diminished, it was evacuated, leaving only *6 Staffel*, commanded by Heinz Jungklausen, to carry on the fight for a while longer before evacuating westwards. He was awarded the *Ritterkreuz* in October 1943.

Hardly had he re-joined what remained of his *Geschwader* than its airfield was nearly overrun by a Soviet cavalry unit, backed by a few tanks, which had penetrated one of the huge holes in the front. With no ground troops present, the *Stukaflieger* had to defend itself with a non-stop series of sorties. Rudel flew no fewer than seventeen times on that day!

Epic though it was, the doomed attempt to supply the Sixth Army by air lies outside the scope of this present work. Just one point was relevant. In an ominous portent for the future, some *Kampfgruppen* were used to supplement the transport fleet, which represented a further diminution of bomber strength. In all, 165 He 111s and seven He 177s were lost in the airlift, not counting 'real' transports. Even the long-range FW 200 Condors of *KG 40* were put at risk.

The Tide Turns

At the end of 1942 the Soviets struck again, this time in the Caucasus. The German armies beat a hasty retreat and just managed to get their heads out of the noose before Stalingrad fell on 2 February 1943. A toehold was maintained on the Kuban peninsula, across the narrows of the Sea of Azov from the Kerch peninsula in the Crimea. Nor was that all. In the north, the seventeen-month siege of Leningrad was finally lifted, while another thrust was aimed towards Kharkov. The tide had turned. From now on it would ebb relentlessly westwards.

Tank busting had been proving an increasing problem for the *Luftwaffe*. As previously noted, tanks were particularly difficult to destroy from the air. When in 1941 and 1942 the Army had been advancing, mobility kills had been enough as the stationary steel monsters could be quickly overrun by the ground forces. On the retreat this was not the case, as tracks and bogeys could be quickly repaired. At the same time, the excellent T-34/76 was pouring off the Soviet production lines. A new answer was needed.

Guns were far more accurate than bombs, but could an aircraft carry a gun potent enough to pierce the armour of a tank? From the front there was little chance, unless a lucky shot penetrated a vision slit. Side armour was rather thinner, but was still a difficult proposition. But the rear, where the engine and fuel were located? Tank engines are necessarily powerful, they create a lot of heat, and cooling them is a problem. Consequently the motor compartment armour had to be relatively thin; it was also perforated for ventilation. The rear decking was the most vulnerable area, and therefore the preferred target.

Two dedicated German anti-tank aircraft entered service at about this time. The first was the Henschel Hs 129B, which we have already seen in North Africa. Initially the main armament of this aircraft was a 30mm MK 103, with

Kursk: *Luftwaffe*[1] Bomber and Attack Order of Battle

Unit	Type	Notable commanders
Luftflotte 6		
Stab/KG 1	Ju 88	Heinrich Lau*
I/KG 1	Ju 88	
III/KG 1	Ju 88	
Stab/KG 3	Ju 88	
I/KG 3	Ju 88	
II/KG 3	Ju 88	Peter-Paul Breu*
III/KG 3	Ju 88	
Stab/KG 4	He 111	Dr Gottlieb Wolff*
II/KG 4	He 111	
III/KG 4	He 111	Reinhard Graubner*
II/KG 51	Ju 88	Herbert Voss*
Stab/SG 1	FW 190	Alfred Druschel***
I/SG 1	FW 190/Hs 129	Georg Dörffel**
II/SG 1	FW 190/Hs 129	
Stab/StG 1	Bf 110	Gustav Pressler**
II/StG 1	Ju 87	
III/StG 1	Ju 87	Friedrich Lang***
IV(Pz)/SG 9	Hs 129	Bruno Meyer*
Luftflotte 4		
Stab/KG 27	He 111	*Freiherr* Hans-Henning von Beust**
I/KG 27	He 111	Joachim Petzold*
III/KG 27	He 111	
14(Eis)/KG 27	He 111	
III/KG 51	Ju 88	
Stab/KG 55	He 111	Dr Ernst Kühl**
I/KG 55	He 111	
II/KG 55	He 111	
III/KG 55	He 111	Willi Antrup**
I/KG 100	He 111	
Stab/StG 2	Ju 88	Dr Ernst Kupfer***
I/StG 2	Ju 87	Karl Henze*
II/StG 2	Ju 87	Bruno Dilley**
III/StG 2		Friedrich Lang***
Stab/SG 77	Ju 88	Helmut Bruck**
I/StG 77	Ju 87	Werner Roell*
II/StG 77	Ju 87	Alexander Gläser**
III/StG 77	Ju 87	
PzJagdStaffel/JG 51	Hs 129	

* *Ritterkreuz*, ** *Eichenlaub*, *** *Schwerten*. [1] Romanian and Hungarian units also took part.

armour-piercing ammunition. By the midsummer of 1943, five *Staffeln* of Hs 129Bs were operational on the Eastern Front. These were *4* and *8/SG 1*, *4* and *8/SG 2* and the *Panzerjäger Staffel* of *JG 51*. In October that year these units were amalgamated to form the five-*Staffel IV/SG 9*.

The second was the Ju 87G, armed with two 37mm Flak 18 cannon carried underwing in pods. The weight of these adversely affected performance and handling; nor was a steep dive to attack the thin top armour possible. Rudel took the first Ju 87G to the Crimea in May 1943, but on his first sortie he was hit by anti-aircraft fire and forced to return without attacking.

Tactics for the Ju 87G were quickly evolved. The best attack angle was from the rear, either at ground level or in a shallow dive, firing at close range in order to obtain the necessary accuracy. This left the tank-busters dangerously exposed to anti-aircraft fire. The solution was for the gun-armed Stukas to operate in conjunction with conventional bomb-armed birds, the main function of which was to suppress the defences.

The Battle of Kursk, which commenced on 5 July 1943, was the last major German attempt to regain the initiative on the Eastern Front. Although primarily a tank battle, in which the numbers involved far exceeded anything before or since, air power was heavily engaged. It was actually a double battle. The Soviet Army occupied a huge salient around Kursk, while the German Army occupied a similar salient around Orel to the north of Kursk. The German plan was to pinch out the Soviet salient around Kursk, using the Orel salient as the northern wing of the pincers. But the Germans delayed too long, and the Soviets not only reinforced the Kursk area but deployed to pinch out the Orel salient. The result was a horrific slugging match.

The level bombers were scheduled to take off at dawn, to attack concentrations of Soviet troops. They were to have strong fighter escort. But, at the last minute, a huge Soviet formation was detected, coming straight at the five crowded *Luftwaffe* airfields around Kharkov. The bombers were held on the ground while the fighters scrambled to deal with the threat. Fortunately they succeeded in breaking up the massive raid, otherwise the planned offensive would have stalled at the first hurdle.

As was by now traditional, while the level bombers hammered the rear areas, the Stukas and Henschels were thrown into the cauldron of the massive tank battle. Rudel was quickly in action. On his first sortie he destroyed four tanks, and later that day another eight. Twice in the next few days the tank under attack exploded in his face, forcing him to fly through a curtain of fire. He survived on both occasions, albeit with scorched paint and many splinter holes in his aircraft.

As usual, flank protection for the onrushing Panzers was provided from the air. On 8 July patrolling Hs 129s of *IV(Pz)/SG 9* sighted a large Soviet all-arms force approaching the open flank. *Kommandeur* Bruno Meyer at once called for reinforcements. He was soon joined by the rest of his *Gruppe. IV(Pz)/ SG 9* was a large *Gruppe*, with four *Staffeln* of sixteen aircraft each. They had recently arrived from Germany, and serviceability was high.

Meyer had received the *Ritterkreuz* for an action near Vitebsk in 1941. Flying antiquated Hs 123 biplanes, his *Staffel, II/LG 2*, had encountered a force of Soviet tanks attacking a German unit. The aircraft had already dropped their bombs, and all that was left was rifle-calibre machine guns—and bluff. When dived at full throttle with the engine over-revving, the *'Ein-Zwei-Drei'* made a noise like artillery fire. Amazingly it worked! Convinced they were under attack from a superior force, the 47 Soviet tanks panicked and drove into a marsh.

Now Meyer led his men into the attack with a really lethal machine. Among his *Staffelkapitäne* was future *Ritterkreuz* winner Franz Oswald, eventually credited with about 44 tanks destroyed. Coming from abeam and from the rear to confuse the defenders, they fired four or five 30mm shells on each pass. Within minutes several tanks were on fire. At the same time FW 190s of Alfred Druschel's *SG 1* roared in to scatter fragmentation bombs on the Soviet infantry. Druschel already held the *Ritterkreuz* with *Eichenlaub* and *Schwerten*. The attack was halted.

The Panzers failed to encircle Kursk for lack of reserves. Then, on 11 July, the Soviet armies launched their counterstroke at Orel. Threatened with a double encirclement, the Panzers ceased their offensive, and only repeated attacks by the Stukas of Ernst Kupfer's *StG 2* and the Hs 129s of Bruno Meyer's *IV(Pz)/ SG 9* enabled them to avoid a disaster bigger even than that at Stalingrad.

It was not done without loss. Walther Krauss, *Kommandeur III/StG 2*, was killed by a bomb from a night nuisance-raiding Po-2 near Orel on 16/17 July

1943. He was awarded the *Eichenlaub* posthumously on 3 January 1944. Egbert Jaekel, *Ritterkreuz* holder and *Staffelkapitän 2/StG 2*, had always maintained that his Stuka was particularly fast and never hesitated to attack Soviet fighters. On 17 July he did it once too often and was shot down and killed by an La-5. It was his 983rd sortie. Four days later *Ritterkreuz* holder Willi Hörner, *Staffelkapitän 7/StG 2*, was hit by anti-aircraft fire and was killed in a crash-landing near Orel. These were but a few of the losses.

The Long Road Back

From this point on, *Luftwaffe* actions on the Eastern Front were largely confined to holding back the Bolshevik hordes, whose advance was limited only by logistics. On relatively few occasions could they take the offensive, and in little over a year they were reduced to defending the Reich. At this point the once almost omnipotent Stukas became little more than cannon fodder for the anti-aircraft gun defences.

They were largely replaced by FW 190F and G *Jabos*, which carried 250 or 500kg bombs. Attacks would be made in shallow dives from 2,000m down to about 5–10m above ground level, at a speed of about 500kph, the bombs being released when the target disappeared under the nose. Against soft targets, bomblet containers (the modern term is CBUs) were used.

By 1944 US Army Air Forces daylight raids on the German homeland were becoming severe. An obvious ploy on the part of the German fighters was to intercept them on the homeward leg. To avoid this, the USAAF began the so-called shuttle missions, often turning south after bombing to land in Italy or North Africa. On 21 June 1944 a shuttle mission landed at Poltava and Mirgorod in Russia. It had been followed from Germany by a Ju 88 of a reconnaissance unit, which took photographs of them on the ground. That night a large raid was mounted against the Soviet bases. Led by Willi Antrup, *Kommodore KG 53*, it consisted of about 200 Heinkels from *KG 4, KG 27, KG 53* and *KG 55*, with *KG 4* dropping flares. Poor weather conditions caused the attack on Mirgorod to be abandoned but the other raid was devastating. Of the 72 B-17s, only two survived unscathed, while 44 were completely destroyed. In addition, five American and Soviet fighters were destroyed and 28 others damaged. Nearly half a million gallons of fuel were set on fire. It must, however, be said that if the *Luftwaffe* had possessed a strategic bomber with a payload perhaps four times that of the He 111, the destruction could have been almost total. When, on the following night, the *Kampfflieger* raided Mirgorod, the birds had flown. This was the last major German bomber raid of the war, for which Antrup was awarded the *Eichenlaub* on 18 November.

In the final months of 1944 most *Luftwaffe* bomber units were disbanded, and many bomber pilots transferred to fighters. This was a tremendous advantage for the *Nachtjagdflieger*, as the bomber pilots were generally experienced in night and instrument flying, although less so for the day fighters. A classic example was *Prinz* Heinrich zu Sayn Wittgenstein, who transferred from bombers and claimed 83 night victories before falling to an RAF night fighter.

In last few months of the war the He 177 was used on the Eastern Front and for the first time pattern bombing was used. Horst von Riesen, by now *Kommodore KG 1*, led his *Geschwader* against the railway centre of Velikye Luki, some 480km west of Moscow. It must have been an impressive sight—a *Stab* of four aircraft followed by three *Gruppen* of 27 aircraft in vics at about 6,000m. But the time for *Luftwaffe* strategic missions was past: most targets were well out of range. Quite apart from any other considerations, fuel was by now so short that such missions were out of the question. Von Riesen was then ordered to send his huge bombers out on anti-tank sorties. After losing several aircraft, with no commensurate return in tanks destroyed, the order was rescinded.

The *Luftwaffe* had never really had a strategic role: by the time it became possible, lack of fuel prevented it.

8. THE STRATEGIC WAR AT SEA

As we have seen in previous chapters, the *Luftwaffe* expended a great deal of effort in anti-shipping operations in the early years of the war—attacks on the Polish fleet in harbour; attacks off Norway and in the North Sea and the English Channel; minelaying off British ports; operations in the Mediterranean, particularly off Crete; and attacks on the Eastern Front at Kronstadt, in the Black Sea and in the Caspian Sea. But these were all primarily tactical.

One definition of the difference between tactical and strategic has already been given, but there is an analogy which is much more graphic. With a milch cow as an example, tactical operations are aimed at knocking over the bucket of milk; strategic operations consist of making the cow unable to yield by cutting off its food source! As a land-based power, the Third Reich operated on interior lines during the Second World War, which gave it unrivalled opportunities for strategic operations by interdicting supply routes, thus starving the various cows.

Most important of all was the sea blockade of the British Isles, which by the late spring of 1943 came close to severing the transatlantic supply routes which kept the island nation in the war. This was prosecuted by a few dozen U-boats with little assistance from the air. Had a truly long-range reconnaissance bomber been available to the *Luftwaffe*, the pendulum could have swung in favour of Germany. As it was, advances in technology succeeded in countering the U-boat menace.

It was in the best interests of the Allies to keep the Soviet Union in the war, and to this end huge amounts of *matériel* were shipped to Murmansk. The interdiction of these convoys was of great importance, but, again, only tactical aircraft were available to do it. In any case, this could only have been effective had it been coupled with a long-range bomber force able to carry out heavy attacks on the centres of Soviet war production, and such a bomber force did not exist.

On a lesser scale, there was a half-hearted attempt to block the Suez Canal which carried supplies to the Empire forces in North Africa. Then came attacks on the supply routes to the Allied landings in Algeria in 1942–43, but in both cases it was a matter of too little too late. When in 1943 Italy changed sides, a damaging attack was launched on the Italian Fleet as it sailed for Malta. This last blurred the dividing line between strategic and tactical, but as it was aimed at keeping the Italian Navy out of the war it is arguable that it was the former.

The Battle of the Atlantic

At sea, the primary German weapon was the U-boat. Although generally described as a submarine, it was actually a submersible, operating on the surface for most of the time and submerging only when it was necessary to remain unseen. Operating in 'wolfpacks', U-boats were very effective once in contact with a convoy, but their greatest problem was locating it.

The Atlantic Ocean is huge, and even in good visual conditions search range was little more than 10km. Rumbling along on the surface at about 14 knots, a U-boat could search an area of only about 6,000 square kilometres in twelve hours. While this may sound a lot, it was a mere bagatelle in the vast wastes of the ocean. Just occasionally, German Intelligence would be able to decipher the Allied codes and predict where a convoy would be at a given time. But if this was more than 900km away a U-boat stood little chance of catching up, even at maximum speed, within twenty-four hours.

The answer had to be air reconnaissance. The FW 200 Condor, cruising at 335kph at 600m for four hours, could cover 67,000 square kilometres of sea— more than eleven times the search area of a single U-boat in twenty-four. Given several Condors, the advantages were obvious.

The Condor had been designed as a civilian airliner. It was not stressed for military operations, and many modifications were needed before its entry into *Luftwaffe* service. The first military production variant was the FW 200C-1. The fuselage and wings were beefed up with various structural tucks and gussets, and stronger main gear legs with twin wheels were fitted. Extra fuel

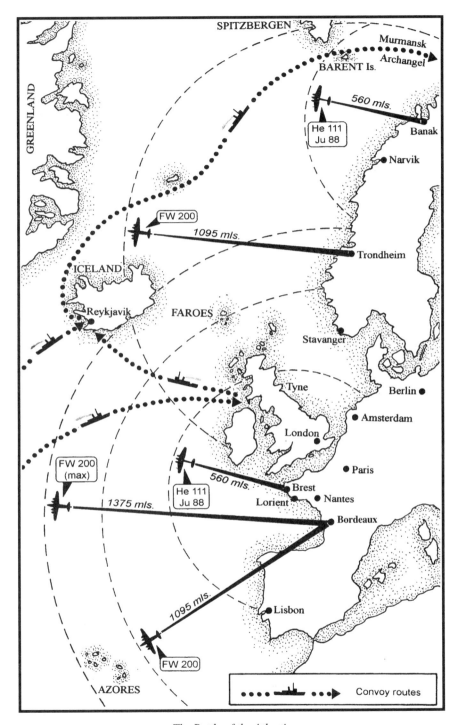

The Battle of the Atlantic

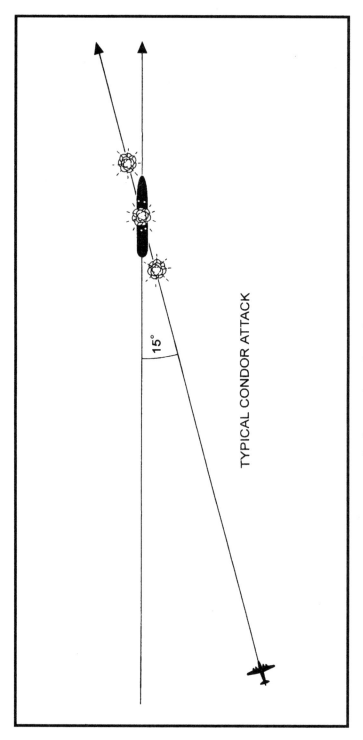

TYPICAL CONDOR ATTACK

15°

Single-aircraft attacks on shipping.

tanks occupied the former passenger cabin in the fuselage, and a large ventral gondola, slightly offset to starboard, housed a forward-firing 20mm MG FF cannon and a rearward-firing, pintle-mounted 7.9mm MG 15 machine gun. A second MG 15 was located in a dorsal position aft. These weapons gave only a limited amount of protection against fighter attack, but, operating far out over the ocean, the Condor was not expected to encounter enemy fighters on a regular basis. The main purpose of the weaponry, particularly the cannon, was to keep the heads of the ship's gunners down during an attack.

The mission was armed reconnaissance: having first located enemy ships and reported their position, the Condor would then attack them, especially if they were sailing singly without escorts. Consequently, provision was made to carry four 250kg bombs, two under the wings outboard of the engines and two beneath the inboard engine nacelles.

The first *Fernaufklärungstaffel* (long range reconnaissance *Staffel*) in the *Luftwaffe, 1(F)/120,* was established on 1 October 1939 at Bremen under the command of Edgar Petersen, a former long-distance airline pilot. Initially its main task was to fly long-range weather reconnaissance sorties. European weather comes in from the west, and data from far out over the Atlantic was essential to the 'weather frogs' in preparing their forecasts. A secondary task was to support the U-boat campaign, although in the early stages of the war this was accorded a low priority.

The first Condor operational sorties were flown on 8 April 1940—reconnaissance over the North Sea—and three days later the aircraft carried out the long-range bombing mission against Narvik described in an earlier chapter. Later that month the unit was redesignated *1/KG 40*. Deployed to Gardermoen in Norway, Condors ranged as far afield as Greenland and Jan Mayen Island.

When, on 10 May, the campaign against the West started, the Condors returned to Germany and were tasked with mining the approaches to British harbours, with a 1,000kg magnetic mine under each outboard wing station. This was not a good idea. The Condor was underpowered at the best of times, and the extra weight and drag of two large mines made matters worse. Speed was reduced to a little over 190kph, at which the Condor wallowed and lurched through the air, barely under control. Losses approached an unacceptable 20 per cent, and after a month minelaying sorties were discontinued. Meanwhile two more *Staffeln* had been formed. On the fall of France in June 1940, *1* and *2/KG 40* were deployed to Bordeaux on the Biscay coast while *3/KG 40* was based at Cognac. They became a *Gruppe—I/KG 40*. From their new bases, Condors could range out well past the Azores and as far as Iceland.

Over the Atlantic

From Bordeaux, the Condors took up their original mission, armed maritime reconnaissance. At this time the British convoy system had not been fully implemented and single ships or stragglers could often be found. Over the next few months many small freighters were hit by Condors in the Western Approaches, although not all were sunk.

The usual method of attack was to come in from astern at a very fine angle and just above masthead height, shooting with the 20mm cannon to suppress the defences, then release all the bombs in a stick. This gave the best chance of scoring direct hits. While a Condor at such close range was a very inviting target, few were lost. Armament on small vessels was minimal, and often had a very limited field of fire.

Two *Ritterkreuze* were awarded to members of *I/KG 40* during 1940: Bernhard Jope of *2/KG 40* received the first on 30 September while *Kommandeur* Edgar Petersen received his on 21 October.

On 26 October 1940 Bernhard Jope of *2/KG 40* was on patrol off the Irish coast in poor visibility when he spotted a very large ship travelling at high speed. It was the 43,000-tonne liner *Empress of Britain*. Attacking from dead astern from about 150m altitude, Jope released one bomb. It hit amidships and started a fire. Circling to port, he came in from astern again, screened by the smoke from the fire caused by the first bomb. While the smoke may have hindered the ship's gunners, it also hindered Jope's bomb aimer. The second bomb missed, and Jope, his aircraft slightly damaged by return fire, circled, then came in from ahead, where visibility was better. This time he released two bombs. Both hit, but one failed to explode and rolled overboard. The other struck near the stern and started another serious fire.

By now out of ordnance, Jope circled the stricken liner before heading back to Bordeaux while radioing the position of his victim. Burning and abandoned, the *Empress of Britain* refused to sink and, with a skeleton crew aboard, was taken in tow. Two days later a U-boat sank her with torpedoes.

This action pointed the way to closer co-operation with the U-boats. As *Grossadmiral* Dönitz stated on 30 December: 'Just let me have a minimum of twenty FW 200s solely for reconnaissance purposes, and U-boat successes will go up!' He was being optimistic. The Condor was a rather fragile, 'this side up' aeroplane and was largely unsuited to the rigours of military operations. In consequence, serviceability was low: at any one time, only between a quarter and a third of the two dozen or so aircraft on strength were available. This was far too few to make continuous shadowing of convoys possible.

A typical event occurred on 16 January 1941. A Condor flown by *Hauptmann* Verlohr, *Staffelkapitän* of *1/KG 40*, sighted and attacked a convoy west of Ireland. He sank two ships, then remained in contact for several hours until low fuel forced him to break off. In all that time, no other Condor was able to reach the convoy, nor any U-boat. Next morning contact could not be regained. The same thing happened on three more days in January. Unless many more aircraft could be made available, the task was hopeless.

Even as the *Jagdflieger* were honoured for their victory scores, so anti-shipping pilots built up a score of tonnage sunk—as did U-boat commanders. This probably had much to do with the fact that, as in the air, overclaiming was rife, not in numbers but in tonnage, despite the fact that the flyers of *KG 40* had been drilled in ship recognition. A classic example took place on 9 February 1941. The Condors were supposed to locate convoys and, after attacking, shadow them while waiting for the U-boats to arrive. This usually failed because the time that the Condor could remain on station was far too short to allow the U-boats to close. The obvious answer, a relay of Condors, was impracticable due to low aircraft availability. On this occasion a U-boat had located a convoy and shadowed it, sending position reports by radio. Provided the U-boat could make contact in the first place, this was in some ways preferable. The U-boat could remain on station for days if need be, while the response time of the Condors was a matter of hours.

Five Condors of *2/KG 40* set out from Bordeaux to intercept the convoy, which was inbound from Gibraltar. The pilots were all experienced: *Staffelkapitän* Fritz Fliegel, Hans Bucholz and Heinrich Schlosser were all awarded

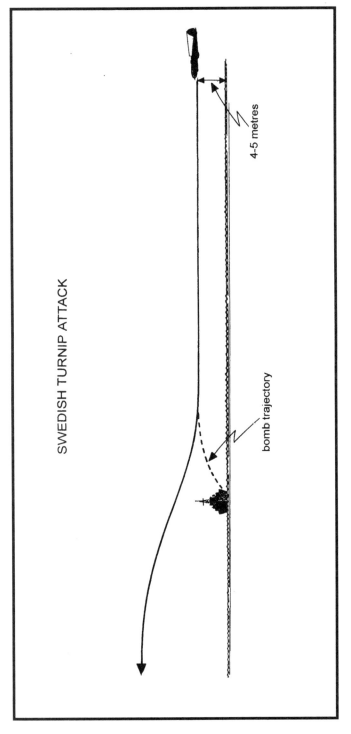

SWEDISH TURNIP ATTACK

4-5 metres

bomb trajectory

The 'Swedish Turnip' attack.

the *Ritterkreuz* later in the year. The other two pilots were *Ritterkreuz* holder Bernhard Jope and *Oberleutnant* Adam. Adam was forced to break off and return to base when his fuel tanks were holed, fortunately without a fire starting. The others pressed home their attacks, claiming six ships sunk with a total tonnage of nearly 30,000. In fact, five ships went down at the time, the total tonnage of which was 9,250, and a sixth much later. The fact remains that it was a successful action, even if the reported tonnage was tripled. Meanwhile *KG 40* had been expanded to a full *Geschwader*, with Petersen as *Kommodore* from 1 March. *II/KG 40*, equipped with Do 217s and He 111s, was based in Holland, while *III/KG 40* was at Bordeaux, with He 111s pending re-equipment with Condors.

At this point the High Command started to take the Atlantic campaign really seriously. In March Martin Harlinghausen was appointed *Fliegerführer Atlantik*, to concentrate all anti-shipping operations. In addition to *KG 40*, he commanded *1* and *3/Aufklärungsgruppe 123* with Bf 110s and Ju 88s, based at Lannion in Brittany, *KGr 606* with Ju 88s, and *KüflGr 106* with a mix of Ju 88s and He 115s.

Harlinghausen, widely known as 'Iron Gustav', had commanded the He 59s of *AS/88* in the Spanish Civil War, where he had developed the 'Swedish Turnip' attack. Whereas Condors attacked down the line of the ship in a shallow dive, the 'Swedish Turnip' attack was made from abeam, where the ship presented the largest area, and was intended to score hits on or below the waterline. The attack run was made at a height of 45m and a speed of about 290kph. The bombs took just three seconds to reach the surface from this height, and travelled a forward distance of about 240m.

Altimeters at this time were barometric and were notoriously unreliable at low altitudes. This called for extremely precise judgement on the part of the pilot, who, in addition to estimating the correct lead against a moving target, also had to avoid flying into the water or getting too high. The task of the observer/bomb aimer was equally onerous: he had to judge the exact range and moment at which to release the bombs. Too early, and the bombs, which were time-fuzed with a typical delay of eight seconds, could bounce off the surface of the water to an altitude even greater than that of the aircraft; too late, and at best they would cause damage to the superstructure if they did not miss altogether.

For 'Swedish Turnip' attacks the bombs had to fall flat if the correct trajectory was to be achieved. For this reason the nose-up carriage in the internal bay of the He 111 was unsuitable and the weapons were carried on underwing racks. So adept did 'Iron Gustav' become that on at least three occasions in 1940 he succeeded in sinking two ships in a single sortie by using alternate racks—the classic 'left and right'.

The ultra-low-level attack had its advantages. The bomber was difficult to spot against the sea, while the target ship stood out against the horizon—even, given halfway decent visibility, at night.

Other Spanish Civil War veterans had used the 'Swedish Turnip', including Walter Storp, but Harlinghausen became the leading exponent of this attack. This was unusual in that he was not a member of an operational unit; in fact, he was Chief of Staff of *Fliegerkorps X*. A believer in leading from the front, he had flown as an observer in He 115s on reconnaissance missions, then He 111s of the *Fliegerkorps X Stab*—a unique German innovation. He was awarded the *Ritterkreuz* on 4 May 1940 and the *Eichenlaub* on 30 January 1941. His usual pilot was Robert Kowalewski, his staff operations officer, with whom he developed a close understanding. Kowalewski was awarded the *Ritterkreuz* on 24 November 1940.

Desert Diversion

Harlinghausen and Kowalewski had flown a sortie of a totally different nature in January 1941. The twin keys to the desert war were Malta, which we have already examined, and the Suez Canal, through which supplies reached the British. At this point *Fliegerkorps X* was deployed to the Mediterranean.

A single understrength *Gruppe* of anti-shipping specialists, *II/KG 26*, was deployed to Benghazi, some 1,200km from the Canal, right at the limit of the range of the Heinkel 111, but no other base was available at the time. A landing accident reduced the fourteen Heinkels to eleven, while three of the remainder were earmarked for reconnaissance.

On 17 January a British convoy was noted about to enter the Suez Canal from the south. That night the eight strike aircraft were sent off at half-hourly intervals. Because only the most economical cruise settings and careful trimming would suffice, Harlinghausen decided to lead the raid in person. Four hours after take-off, the aircraft arrived at the southern end of the Canal, then flew northwards along it, but found nothing. Harlinghausen radioed instructions to the following aircraft to seek alternative targets, then turned southwards once more. Having attacked a ferry, they then discovered the convoy, dispersed and anchored in the Great Bitter Lake.

The 'weather frog' had forecast adverse winds for the return flight, with the most advantageous altitude 3,500m. Unfortunately he was wrong: the headwind proved to be double that forecast, about 120kph. With no landmarks to guide them, the Heinkels plodded westwards. One after the other, seven ran out of fuel and force-landed in the desert. The sole survivor had become aware of the strength of the headwinds and had returned at low level, reaching base on the last of his fuel.

Worst off were Harlinghausen and Kowalewski, who came down about 280km east of Benghazi. Believing themselves to be much nearer, they set fire to their Heinkel and started to walk. They were not located and picked up until four days later. However, they fared better than three other crews, who were taken prisoner.

Not for the last time the *Luftwaffe* regretted the lack of a strategic bomber force. This attempt at carrying out a strategic mission with tactical bombers that were totally inadequate in numbers can only be described as a fiasco. Later in the war other raids were launched at the Suez Canal area, but with little success.

Fliegerführer Atlantik

In the early years of the war it was calculated by the *Luftwaffe* that 30,000 tonnes of shipping were sunk for each aircraft lost. But as 1941 progressed more warships escorting the convoys, and heavier defensive armament on the merchantmen, made low-level attacks ever less profitable. Even ships sailing singly posed a risk to a low-level attacker.

Just before sunrise on 21 May young Hans Buchholz, proudly wearing his new *Ritterkreuz*, encountered the SS *Umgeni*. A fast ship, she was steaming unescorted some 480km off south-western Ireland. Bucholz descended to low level to remain unseen, but a sharp-eyed lookout had spotted him and raised the alarm. He thundered in from the starboard beam in a 'Swedish Turnip' attack, strafing with his 20mm cannon as he came.

The ship's guns opened up and a 12pdr shell appeared to hit the Condor. No bombs were dropped on the first pass, and the Condor roared overhead, hard hit, with three of its four engines on fire. Despite this, it turned back as if to re-attack before splashing into the sea at a flat angle, then sinking. Five crewmen were rescued by *Umgeni*, but Bucholz and his observer had been killed.

Shortly afterwards, Harlinghausen was forced to forbid the low-level attack which he had pioneered as the losses had become unsustainable. *KG 40* was reduced to high-level attacks, for which the bomb sighting system was inadequate, or reconnaissance and shadowing, remaining outside the range of anti-aircraft fire. It was, however, difficult to maintain contact with a convoy for more than a day, which was generally insufficient to home the U-boats. Matters were rapidly made worse by the presence of fighters, at first carried by catapult-equipped merchantmen, then later by escort carriers. These made prolonged shadowing a very hazardous business.

Yet another threat was posed by Allied long-range anti-submarine aircraft, which engaged the Condors if they found them. These battles of the heavy-weights were conducted like naval engagements of the Napoleonic era, each side seeking an altitude advantage instead of the wind gage and formating on the other, exchanging broadsides. Nelson would have approved!

The Allied aircraft, with their power-operated gun turrets, often had the advantage, although much depended on relative performance, which enabled the attacker to hold its position. The battles of the giants could go either way. On 17 July 1941 an RAF Whitley with one engine shot out was forced to ditch near the convoy it was protecting, having first compelled the Condor to abandon its shadowing. Fortresses and Liberators were a different matter. These could not only outperform the Condors; they out-gunned them. On at least two occasions Condors were shot down by Liberators, which exploited their superior performance to take the upper position and out-gun them. In an action on 27 July 1943, a Liberator of the USAAF shot down a Condor but sustained mortal damage itself in the engagement. While for the most part these clashes were inconclusive, the fragile Condors were usually driven off.

From the summer of 1941 the *Luftwaffe* campaign over the Atlantic became unravelled. *Kommodore* Edgar Petersen moved to the Mediterranean in August with a detachment of six Condors and nine He 111s of *KG 40*, but within days he was relieved of his command and appointed Director of Research for the He 177. Also in August, Robert Kowaleski, by that time *Kommandeur* of *II/KG 26* (He 111) was appointed *Kommandeur* of *III/KG 40* (FW 200), a position he held for the next two years.

Shortly after this Harlinghausen found trouble. Still leading from the front, in November he attacked a large transport in the Irish Sea. His Heinkel was badly damaged. His pilot, *Oberfeldwebel* Ducha, managed to nurse it across Wales and Cornwall, only to ditch off Brittany. Rescued by fishermen, 'Iron Gustav' had sustained severe injuries, and he spent the next three months in hospital.

Arctic Operations

Supply convoys to Murmansk, carrying war materials to the hard-pressed Soviets, started in August 1941. From the outset, aircraft carriers were provided to give fighter cover, while their torpedo bombers constituted a threat to German surface units. For the remainder of the year they encountered little or no opposition and passed virtually unmolested. When, with the onset of winter, the German land offensive stalled, these took on a new importance. Six Condors of *7/KG 40* were deployed to Stavanger in Norway to reconnoitre for the *Kreigsmarine*, but initial results were poor.

In 1942 a *Luftwaffe* strike force was gradually assembled in northern Norway. First to arrive were the Ju 88s of Hajo Herrmann's *III/KG 30* and the torpedo-carrying He 115 floatplanes of *1/KüFlGr 406*. But in the perpetual gloom of winter in the Arctic Circle, little could be done operationally. In any case, more reinforcements were to come.

In January 1942 Martin Harlinghausen, a strong advocate of the torpedo and now recovered from his injuries, was appointed *Kommodore KG 26*. This was a unique feature of the *Luftwaffe*: high-ranking staff officers were sometimes sent to operational commands. Perhaps the most extreme case had been 'Smiling Albert' Kesselring, a prewar Chief of Staff of the entire *Luftwaffe*, who had then commanded *Luftflotte 2* in 1940.

'Iron Gustav''s *Geschwader* had been training at the torpedo establishment at Grosseto in Italy, but then almost immediately *6 Staffel* was sent to the Crimea for anti-shipping operations. *I/KG 26* (He 111) and *III/KG 26* (Ju 88) completed their torpedo training and deployed to Norway in March.

161

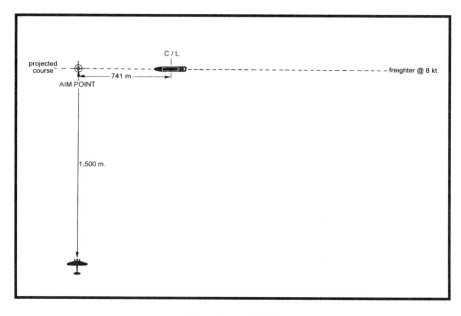

Torpedo attack (1).

Torpedo bombing was an art. The approach was made at low level and moderate speed from abeam, to give the greatest possible target, releasing the weapon at a range of about 1,500m. Once in the water, the torpedo was slow moving and took up to three minutes to cover the intervening distance. Against a freighter, travelling at typically eight knots, the aiming point had to be almost 400m ahead of the target, although the length of the vessel gave a fair margin for error. This notwithstanding, judgement of range and lead was critical. Another potential, if less serious, source of error was lining up the attack exactly from the beam. Of course, destroyers moving at three times the speed of a freighter, exacerbated the aiming problems manyfold.

Much depended on attacking unobserved. If the attack was seen coming in, the ship would attempt to 'comb' the torpedo tracks by turning hard into them, rather in the manner that a fighter would evade attack by another fighter. This not only ruined the original attack computation; it provided a much smaller head-on rather than a beam-on target. To overcome this, a method known as the 'Golden Comb' was devised. Several *Ketten* would attack from the beam, drop their torpedoes, then turn away. Perhaps a minute or so later, one or two more *Ketten* would attack from a 90-degree angle to the original course of the

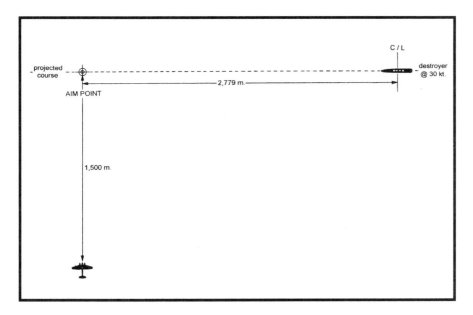

Torpedo attack (2).

convoy, either from ahead or astern. As the ships turned to comb the torpedoes from the initial attack, they would thus present their beams to the new one. However, the 'Golden Comb' attack demanded extremely precise timing. Another factor was that the ships could not only turn into the initial attack; it was in some ways more effective to turn away from it. Unless the second *Ketten* had guessed right, they were badly placed for a beam attack against the new heading. Given these imponderables, the 'Golden Comb' attack, although great in theory, was rarely successful. Nor was it a good idea in the presence of Allied carrier fighters. The *Luftwaffe* had been influenced by the success of Japanese Navy torpedo attacks, and to a lesser degree by those of the *Regia Aeronautica*. What they had overlooked was that the Japanese 'Long Lance' torpedo was a much faster, much longer-ranged and far more effective weapon.

Against the Murmansk convoys the weather was a factor. Low cloud prevented level bombing and severely hampered dive bombing. At least torpedo attacks could be carried out beneath the low cloud base, always assuming that visibility and sea state permitted.

Convoy PQ.12 had been located south of Jan Mayen Island on 5 March 1942. Snowstorms prevented air attack, and a *Kriegsmarine* force, which in-

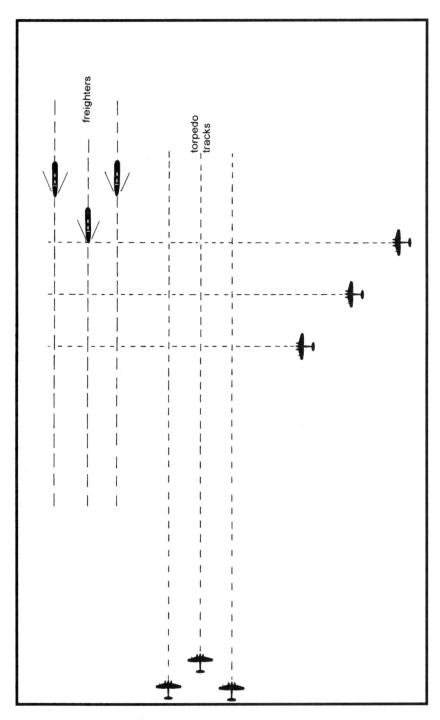

The 'Golden Comb'.

cluded the battleship *Tirpitz*, succeeded in sinking a solitary freighter that had straggled.

Hajo Herrmann's *III/KG 30* assiduously practised steep and shallow dive attacks at this time. But the enemy was not the only danger. As he commented:

> The distances we flew over the sea were long, and the water was very cold—approximately zero degrees Centigrade. Anyone who fell into it froze to death, even if he were able to get into his dinghy straight away. Moisture on the body and a stiff breeze of between minus 10 and minus 30 degrees Centigrade killed within 20 minutes . . .

At this time the *Luftwaffe* had developed a towed device called *Ente* to deter fighter attacks from astern, but Herrmann was unable to secure a supply of these. Instead he used something both available and affordable—toilet rolls. Thrown out, these quickly unwound in the slipstream, resembling some form of lethal entanglement. Whether these were actually used in combat does not seem to have been recorded, but it is probable that the gunners responsible would have been far more occupied in taking aim than with throwing innocuous rolls of paper.

Ideally the Murmansk convoys would have kept out of range of the shore-based bombers, but even at the height of summer they were limited by the southern fringe of the Arctic pack ice. They assembled at Reykjavik in Iceland, within reconnaissance range of the Condors of *KG 40*. Spies on the ground kept watch on their movements.

Winter in the Arctic consisted of almost perpetual night, coupled with fog and blizzards. Once a Murmansk convoy was under way, it was difficult, and sometimes impossible, to locate. Between late March and the middle of May about 100 sorties were flown against four convoys. PQ.13 was scattered by bad weather and lost two freighters to *III/KG 30*. In truly appalling weather PQ.14 lost no ships to air attack, but sixteen of the original 24 were damaged by ice in thick fog and were forced to return to Reykjavik. PQ.15 lost three ships to torpedo aircraft between 26 April and 7 May. About ten aircraft were lost. This was not good news, but as the hours of daylight lengthened and the weather improved the scene was set for an epic confrontation.

Convoy PQ.16 was attacked over six days in late May and in the course of 311 sorties lost ten ships. German losses were negligible, amounting to just three aircraft. After a hiatus in June, in which twenty-four hours of daylight were available, came the ill-fated PQ.17. This sailed on 27 June 1942 in thick fog—so thick, in fact, that a Condor of *3/KG 40* almost collided with one of the escorting cruisers in an attempt to maintain contact. In vain—the convoy was swallowed up in the clag. Four days later, with the convoy already past Jan Mayen Island, the fog cleared and U-boats gained contact. A U-boat attack on 2 July was beaten off by the escort, but by now PQ.17 had come within range of land-based bombers.

First to attack, at dusk that evening, were eight He 115 floatplanes of *1/ KüFlGr 406*, each armed with a single torpedo. They were met by a wall of anti-aircraft fire which forced *Staffelkapitän* Herbert Vater to jettison his tin fish and alight on the water, from where he was rescued by a fellow *Staffel* member. No hits were scored.

The weather then worsened and contact was lost, not to be regained until the early morning of 4 July, when *1/KüFlGr 906*, also with He 115s, made a surprise attack, hitting, but not sinking, an American Liberty ship. This was later finished off by a U-boat. Despite clear skies, the next attack was delayed

The fate of convoy PQ.17.

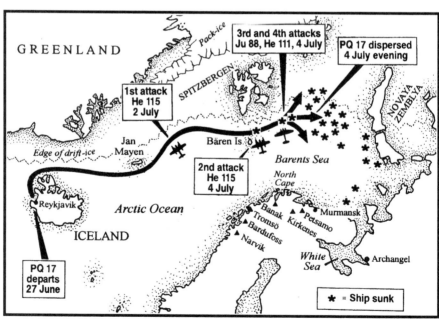

until that evening, when a *Staffel* of *KG 30* failed to score. An hour later 25 torpedo-carrying He 111s of *I/KG 26* put in an appearance. These carried out 'Golden Comb' attacks from several directions, sinking one freighter and damaging another and a tanker. The damaged freighter was later finished off by a U-boat. The SS *Navarino* fell to Konrad Hennemann, who was shot down and killed by anti-aircraft fire seconds later. Credited with sinking unidentified American cruisers in a low-level attack only the day before, he was awarded a posthumous *Ritterkreuz*. At this point the British Admiralty made a grave mistake. Believing that powerful *Kriegsmarine* surface forces were closing on the convoy, they ordered it to scatter.

So far, the German bomber pilots had been held at bay by the powerful combined defences of the convoy; scattered, the convoy became a collection of isolated and relatively defenceless targets. First into the attack, on 5 July, was *KG 30*, now three *Gruppen* strong, led by *Kommodore* Erich Bloedorn. In addition to Herrmann, the *Kommandeure* were Konrad Kahl and Erich Stoffregen, both of whom were awarded the *Ritterkreuz* shortly afterwards. They sank six vessels and badly damaged many more. In all, 24 ships were sunk, eight by air attack alone and a further seven shared with U-boats. The loss to the Soviet war effort was tremendous—3,350 vehicles, 430 tanks and 210 aircraft.

Not until September did PQ.18 sail for Murmansk. Located off Jan Mayen Island, it was first attacked by *KG 30*. The Ju 88s failed to score any hits and were pursued by Fleet Air Arm Sea Hurricanes. This left the way clear for the He 111s of *I/KG 26*, led by their new *Kommandeur* Werner Klümper, a Spanish Civil War veteran. Astern of them came a single *Staffel* of *III/KG 26*, led by *Kommandeur* Klaus Nocken. From 30 torpedoes launched, eight ships went to the bottom. No Heinkels were lost, although six were very heavily damaged.

On the following day *I/KG 26* was ordered to concentrate on sinking the aircraft carrier HMS *Avenger*. Klümper led his 22 remaining Heinkels into the attack, only to be intercepted by the defending Sea Hurricanes. Braving not only the fighters but also a storm of anti-aircraft fire, he went in, but only two aircraft managed to launch their torpedoes and the carrier combed these with ease. Five aircraft went down and a further nine were written off on their return. On the next day the weather socked in, preventing further air attacks. *I/KG 26* had been decimated for what amounted to a relatively small return.

With the onset of winter, effective operations became nearly impossible and most units were withdrawn to the south. *I/KG 26* flew torpedo attacks in the Mediterranean with a great deal of success, although *Kommandeur* Klaus Nocken was shot down five times before relinquishing command in February 1944. Air interdiction of the Murmansk convoys lapsed, and after the end of 1942 no ships were lost to air attack until 1945.

Guided Missiles

Germany entered the field of guided missiles as early as October 1914. Flight-testing a biplane glider torpedo intended to be launched at warships from a Zeppelin began in January 1915 using command guidance. Development was, however, protracted, and the war ended before the device could enter service.

Intense anti-aircraft fire had by 1942 made low-level bombing attacks on shipping a costly undertaking, while, despite optimistic claims for the Lotfe 7D bomb sight, hitting a moving ship from 5km up was not really a viable proposition. The only stand-off weapon at first available was the torpedo, and this was not only far from easy to use with any accuracy: it brought the launching aircraft well inside the reach of the defensive fire. *Luftwaffe* figures gave a success rate of under 25 per cent, and this was probably optimistic. What was really needed was a weapon which could be launched from well outside the range of AA fire and be steered on to its target. Two such weapons made their débuts in August 1943—the powered Henschel Hs 293 and the unpowered Fritz X.

The Hs 293 was like a small aeroplane with stubby wings, built around the warhead of an SC 500 light-case bomb, which meant that it was of limited use against heavily armoured warships. It was launched from high altitude and had a maximum range of 18km, although this was only usable in clear visibility. Just after launch, the underslung liquid fuel rocket motor lit up and accelerated the missile on its way for a few seconds. A bright flare in the rear allowed the observer to maintain visual contact with the Hs 293, controlling it with a joystick, the movements of which transmitted radio commands. The use of eighteen different channels allowed up to eighteen aircraft to launch at the same time without cross-interference.

Fritz X looked much more like a missile, with fixed cruciform winglets forward and a complex system of control spoilers aft. An armour-piercing

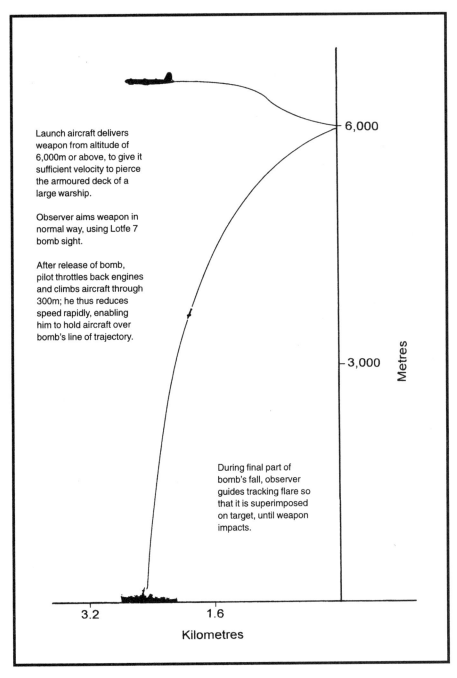

Typical attack using a Fritz X guided bomb.

169

warhead filled with 300kg of Amatol made it well suited to attacking large warships. A heavy weapon (1,570kg), it was unpowered, and its horizontal range was only about 5km. Like the Hs 293, it was radio command-guided, and carried a flare in the tail. Operational usage differed, however: Fritz X was aimed like a normal bomb, after which the parent aircraft climbed steeply to dump speed, forcing the missile out in front so that the observer could track it. Course corrections were made only in the final stages of flight.

In July 1943 specialist units were assigned to carry the new weapons. *II/KG 100* was equipped with the Do 217E, modified to carry an Hs 293 under each wing panel, while *III/KG 100* flew the Do 217K-2, with a Fritz X under each inner wing panel. The K-2 was a high-altitude variant with a greatly extended wingspan. Training complete, *II/KG 100* moved to Cognac, from where it could cover Biscay and the Western Approaches, while *III/KG 100* went to Marseilles, from where it could range out into the Mediterranean.

The combat début of the Hs 293 took place on 25 August 1943 when twelve Do 217Es of *II/KG 100*, led by Heinz Molinus, attacked a group of British U-boat hunters near Biscay. Several missiles malfunctioned, and the only damage caused was by a single near miss. Two days later the *Gruppe* struck again, at a similar target in the same area. This was more successful: two direct hits sank a corvette and damaged a destroyer, while a second corvette was damaged by near misses. The next *II/KG 100* attack took place on 4 October off the North African coast, when one freighter was sunk and three more damaged. The cost was high: one Dornier was shot down, while four others crashed on landing. Molinus was among the fatalities.

Also equipped to carry the Hs 293 were the He 177A-5s of *II/KG 40*, formerly *I/KG 50*, which arrived at Bordeaux on 25 October. Only one major attack was attempted, against a convoy on 21 November, but this was thwarted by bad visibility. Transferred to the Mediterranean soon afterwards, the *Gruppe* attacked a convoy off the Algerian coast on 26 November, sinking a troopship. Again the cost was high: four out of the fourteen Heinkels were shot down, including that of *Kommandeur* and *Ritterkreuz* holder Rudolf Mons, and two more crashed on landing. A few Condors of *III/KG 40* were modified to carry two Hs 293s but were completely unsuccessful with this weapon, which badly degraded aircraft performance. On 28 December 1943 a Condor

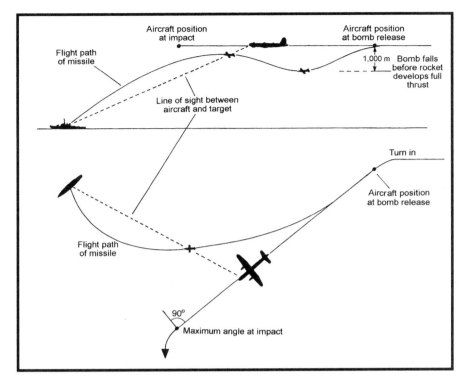

Typical attack with an Hs 293 glider bomb.

thus laden was intercepted and forced down by a lumbering RAF Sunderland flying boat!

The combat début of Fritz X took place on 9 September 1943. Italy was on the point of changing sides and *III/KG 100*, led by Bernhard Jope, was on standby to intervene if the Italian Fleet left port. When the word came, eleven Do 217K-2s took off and slowly climbed to 6,000m. At that altitude, individual ships were not recognisable, so the Dorniers aimed at the largest of them. Two hits were scored on the battleship *Roma*, sinking her, and one on the battleship *Italia*, which, although badly damaged, managed to reach Malta. Jope was at first unaware of the extent of his success. As he later commented:

> We did not see the *Roma* explode. That happened after we left. We saw the explosions as the bombs hit, but how often had we seen this before and then the ship managed to limp back into port?

Even as this action took place, the Allies landed at Salerno, south of Naples. This was just the sort of massive concentration of shipping to suit *III/KG 100*, but heavy fighter cover made the attack perilous. Despite this, Jope's Fritz X scored a direct hit on the battleship HMS *Warspite*. Two more direct hits came perilously close to sinking her, and other hits badly damaged two cruisers.

The landings at Anzio in January 1944 provoked an even stronger German reaction, with *KG 40* and *KG 100* joining forces. The Achilles' heel of both weapons was, however, the guidance system. By now the Allies had introduced jamming, and this, coupled with strong fighter defences, rendered the attacks ineffective. Of the warships present, only a cruiser and a destroyer were sunk while bomber losses were high. The day of the *Luftwaffe* guided anti-ship missile had been all too brief.

# 9. WESTERN FRONT, JULY 1941–MAY 1944

With most German bomber units transferred to the Eastern Front, the scale of attacks against targets in the British Isles was greatly reduced. Raids of about 80 aircraft were launched twice against Birmingham and once against London in July and August, but after this inland targets were, with the exception of Manchester, which was attacked by about 40 bombers on 12 October, relatively neglected. A few damaging raids were mounted against ports on the north-east coast, while minelaying continued much as before.

The reduction in *Luftwaffe* night activity coincided with an accession of strength to the British defences. Ground radar coverage greatly increased, and ever more radar-equipped night fighters entered service. With fewer bombers pitted against more fighters, the risks increased. Clear moonlit skies were no longer the advantage that they once had been, and the *Kampfflieger* increasingly sought the cover of darkness. This aided British electronic countermeasures, which scored several notable successes by misleading bombers as to their true location. Unable in dark and cloudy conditions to pinpoint their position by landmarks on the ground, a number of pilots landed on English soil in error—victories without a shot being fired.

In the first two months of 1942 the *Kampfflieger* flew a mere 68 sorties against inland targets—little more than one a day—although during this period 724 oversea sorties were mounted, many by *Luftflotte 5* in Scandinavia. Single bombers tried to take advantage of adverse weather to sneak inland in so-called *Piratenangriffe*, or pirate attacks. Not that these could have caused much physical damage, but the disruption to industry brought about by air raid warnings could have justified them. But radar-carrying Beaufighters made them hazardous: often scrambled during the day to search for raiders among tumbled cloudscapes, they became all-weather rather than night fighters.

These attacks were supplemented by daylight hit-and-run raids on coastal targets by the *Jabostaffeln* of *JG 2* and *JG 26*, using Bf 109Fs, each carrying a single 250kg bomb. The former concentrated on shipping, claiming twenty vessels sunk in the first half of 1942. The latter concentrated on industrial, utility and communications targets on the south coast of England.

Unlike in 1940, when they penetrated at high altitude and called whatever they hit 'the target', they now came in at low level, beneath the radar. Bombing accuracy remained a problem: the ingress at high speed and low level gave little time to spot and line up on the target, while light anti-aircraft fire proved a considerable distraction even when it missed.

As with the 'Swedish Turnip' attack, judging range accurately was crucial. If released too soon, the bombs, which were delay-fuzed, could easily hit the ground and bounce clean over the target. At least two schools were hit during this phase. It was a story as old as air warfare—missing valid military targets resulted in collateral damage; but as these attacks began to be regarded as reprisals for the RAF Bomber Command raids on the Fatherland, this was not taken too seriously.

The two *Jabostaffeln* were formalised on 10 March 1942 as *10(Jabo)/JG 2* and *10(Jabo)/JG 26*. Attacks normally consisted of a *Rotte* (pair) or up to two *Schwärme* (eight aircraft). By summer the units had re-equipped with the FW 190A, able to carry a much heavier bomb load—one 500kg beneath the fuselage and four 50kg bombs on underwing racks. Little military damage was caused: the main effect of the *Jabo* raids was to keep RAF resources tied down. This they succeeded in doing. Spitfires were simply not fast enough to catch the low-level raiders, and most casualties were caused by light anti-aircraft fire. During 1942 losses approached 5 per cent, while *10(Jabo)/JG 26* lost nine pilots killed and two taken prisoner—nearly 100 per cent of establishment. But when the extremely fast Typhoon entered service in numbers in early 1943, *Jabo* raids started to become really unprofitable. A raid on London on 20 January 1943 by about 30 *Jabos*, escorted by fighters, lost nine aircraft, three *Jabos* and six escorts.

In February 1943 *10(Jabo)/JG 26* was redesignated *10(Jabo)/ JG 54*, though not for long. A *Schnellkampfgruppe* (fast bomber unit), *III/SKG 10*, had been formed in the Mediterranean late in 1942. Two more *Gruppen* and a *Stab* were formed to bring it up to *Geschwader* strength, and these were deployed to northern France under the *Kommodore, Ritterkreuz* holder Günther Tonne. At this point, the two *Jabostaffeln* became *14* and *15/SKG 10* to form a new *IV Gruppe*, bringing the number of *Jabo*s ranged against Britain to 119.

In daylight, the method of attack used against targets near the coast was as follows. Strength was anything between a *Rotte* (pair) and four or even five *Schwärme* of four aircraft each. They approached low over the sea, approximately 10m in line abreast by *Schwärme*. As the coast was neared, each *Schwarm* switched to line astern and opened the throttles wide. As they crossed the coast they zoom-climbed to about 300m to allow the leaders to acquire their targets, and turned back seawards before attacking in a shallow dive. After bombing, they returned to sea level to escape at high speed.

SKG 10 flew both day and night sorties, but, while the damage caused was of little military significance, losses were high—the equivalent of two *Gruppen*. For example, the first night *Jabo* raid on London, on 16/17 April, carried out at high level, lost five out of 47 aircraft, or more than 10 per cent!

At night the fast FW 190s were difficult to catch. Those who took constant evasive action mainly survived, but the less experienced pilots relied on sheer speed for safety. Against experienced Mosquito night fighter crews, this was not enough. Night navigation proved a problem for *II/SKG 10*. Following a night raid on London on 16 April, two FW 190s mistook the landing lights at West Malling in Kent for their home base and landed. They were followed by a third, who had got lost, while a fourth crashed close by. Remarkably, the RAF countermeasures organisation played no part in this fiasco. Two other FW 190s failed to return, making this an expensive night for the *Luftwaffe*.

A crisis in the Mediterranean in June then caused *II* and *IV/SKG 10* to join *III Gruppe* in Sicily, leaving *I Gruppe*, commanded by future *Ritterkreuz* winner Kurt Dahlmann, to hold the ring. Their troubles were not over: on the night of 16/17 July two more FW 190s landed at West Malling in Kent.

Stratospheric Strikers

Like modern politicians, the Third Reich often preferred appearance to substance. Faced with increasingly heavy bombing raids on the Fatherland, they determined to demonstrate that they could strike back with impunity. The vehicle chosen was the Junkers Ju 86R, an ultra-high-altitude aircraft previously used (as the Ju 86P) for reconnaissance but modified to attain even greater heights while carrying a 250kg bomb. The bomb load was totally inadequate, as was the means. When the *Höhenkampfkommando* reached France in August 1942 it consisted of just two Ju 86Rs. As for accurate bomb aiming from 12km high, the means simply did not exist.

The first raid took place on 24 August. The pilot was Horst Goetz, whom we last met flying with *KGr 100*. After climbing for an hour over France, he arrived at 12,000m and, still climbing, set course for England. His target was the Army base at Aldershot, but his single small bomb landed at Camberley, several kilometres to the north. Shortly afterwards, the second Ju 86R aimed its bomb at Southampton. Several Spitfires tried, but failed, to intercept.

On the following day, Goetz was aloft again. With confidence born of the previous mission, the crew wandered across southern England, aiming to cause as much industrial disruption as possible, before lobbing their bomb in the general direction of Stansted. Comfortable in the pressurised cockpit, Goetz habitually flew in carpet slippers. A film buff, after shooting the view of south-eastern England laid out like a map below, he then pointed the camera at his feet to demonstrate.

Several more raids followed, of which the most destructive occurred when the single bomb landed in the centre of Bristol. For individual aircraft the air raid warning was not sounded, and unfortunately this led to severe casualties, with 48 dead and 26 seriously injured.

The stratospheric attacks came to an end on 12 September when a specially modified Spitfire IX intercepted Goetz at 12,800m, north of Southampton. The German pilot jettisoned his bomb, depressurised the cockpit and sought to climb away, heading back to France. The Spitfire followed with ease, only to have one cannon jam at the critical moment. Just one hit was scored, and Horst Goetz regained his base safely. As a propaganda weapon—and it was little more than this—the Ju 86R was finished, and the short-lived high-altitude campaign ended.

The Baedeker Raids

On the night of 28 March 1942, RAF Bomber Command launched a devastating fire raid on the old Hanseatic town of Lübeck. Incensed, Hitler ordered a series of revenge attacks against lightly defended towns and cities in England. These were to be terror attacks in the full sense of the word, aimed primarily at the civilian population. Shortly after they had commenced, he spoke of taking a *Baedeker's Guide* and crossing off each city as it was destroyed, thus giving this campaign its emotive name.

Once again, the means were inadequate. *KG 2*, equipped with Do 217s, had mounted what few nuisance raids had taken place prior to this, suffering operational attrition. It was supported by the Ju 88s of *KGr 106* and *KGr 606*. Also available were a few He 111s of *I/KG 100*.

On the night of 23 April about 40 bombers, mainly Do 217s of *KG 2*, set off for Exeter, but the sky was overcast and only one bomber hit the target. On the following night, conditions were better, and the *Kampfflieger* tried again. This time the attack was in two waves of about 25 aircraft, so widely separated in time that many crews flew in both. With no balloon barrage to counter, and minimal gun defences, many aircraft attacked from 1,500m, causing considerable damage. Four bombers were lost.

Some idea of the weakness of the bomber force in the West can be gained from the fact that on the next night, against Bath, using every serviceable bomber, even those with operational training *Gruppen*, and flying twice during the night, only 151 sorties could be mounted. Again, four bombers were lost.

This was the pattern of future Baedeker Raids. Weakly defended cities were attacked on moonlit nights from quite low altitudes, using *Knickebein* and *Y-Gerät* to find the target. Norwich (home of the Boulton & Paul aircraft factory), York, Canterbury and others were attacked; even Cowes on the Isle of Wight was targeted. It was not done without loss, and bomber strength was gradually eroded. By August the strength of the average raid was down to twenty aircraft, while the crew strength of *KG 2* was 26 per cent of what it had been at the start of the year. And this despite receiving replacements! The loss rate was unsustainable, and as the year wore on the Baedeker Raids petered out, leaving the *Jabo*s to hold the ring.

Angriffsführer England

Dietrich Peltz was appointed *Angriffsführer England* on 1 April 1943, his task to direct the air assault on Britain. He was very experienced, having commenced the war as a Stuka pilot and then converted to the Ju 88 in the summer of 1940. Awarded the *Ritterkreuz*, *Eichenlaub* and *Schwerten*, he had held a variety of commands before this latest appointment. He had of course no chance of achieving victory against 'England', but he took the view that, if a negotiated peace was possible, his operations might just be able to influence the terms.

Even before Peltz's appointment, the *Kampfflieger* in the West were slowly gathering strength. By mid-January both *KG 2* and *KG 6* each had about 60 bombers on strength and were re-equipping with improved models of the Do 217 and Ju 88. Attacks on London resumed on 17 January 1943, when 117 sorties were mounted against the docks. The heaviest raid on the capital for some twenty months, even this limited effort involved most crews flying twice. The damage was not serious, but six bombers were lost. It was more than six weeks before another such raid was carried out, with similar effect.

Further attacks were made against Southampton, Newcastle and Norwich in March, again with heavy losses. *KG 2* lost 26 bomber crews during the month, although some of these had been engaged on minelaying sorties. Raids on the Baedeker cities continued, still with disproportionate casualties compared with the damage inflicted.

When in June the crisis in the Mediterranean occurred, Peltz was also sent there, handing over command to Stefan Frölich. A previous *Kommodore* of *KG 76*, Frölich had been awarded the *Ritterkreuz* on 4 July 1940, at the age of 50. Now a *Generalmajor*, he briefly assumed command of *Fliegerkorps IX*. His tenure was marked by the increasing use of Pathfinders but lasted only until the return of Peltz on 3 September.

On 13 June SD 2 anti-personnel bombs were used against Grimsby in an attempt to hamper fire-fighting. These small (2kg) weapons had been used against the Soviet Union, but this was their first time against an British target. The SD 2 was released in a container which opened at a preset altitude, disgorging dozens of bomblets which spiralled down over the surrounding area. They became known as 'butterfly bombs' from their shape. To digress for a moment, one immediate effect was that Army officers visited almost every school in the country, showing models and warning pupils not to touch it if they saw one. This was potentially counterproductive. The universal reaction in the author's class was: 'Gee whizz; let's go and look for some!' Needless to say we didn't find any, but if we had we would probably have thrown stones at them to see what happened.

Pathfinders, in the form of *KGr 100*, were no new thing for the *Luftwaffe*, but whereas these had dropped incendiaries to start fires to guide the main force, it was now obvious that something better was needed. Lack of resources meant that the lavish scale of RAF Pathfinders over Germany could not be emulated, and the project started with a single *Staffel*, *15/KG 6* being re-designated *1/KG 66*. Training began in the summer of 1943 and strength was gradually increased to that of a *Gruppe*, although it was some considerable time before the unit became fully operational.

First in was the target-finder, who released flares. Two minutes later came the target-markers, who dropped up to eighteen coloured flares, which burned with a green, white, or yellow flame for about four minutes. Still later coloured marker bombs, often red, which burned on the ground, were used. Incendiaries were also dropped to start fires on the ground. These were followed after a further two minutes by a pair of illuminators, dropping more flares. It was a far cry in both effort and sophistication from what the RAF was doing nightly over Germany.

On 17 August 88 bombers raided Lincoln. Harassed inbound by guns and night fighters, they failed to land a single bomb on the city, losing eleven aircraft in the process. On the following day the Ju 188 made its operational début in the West when three aircraft of *1/KG 66* made a daring daylight attack on the city, using cloud cover to avoid interception. Once again, they did little damage. Another aircraft to make its operational début in the West at about this time was the Messerschmitt Me 410, which was used both as an intruder and as a fast bomber, in which latter role it was generally involved in harassing attacks. The first unit to operate the type was *II/KG 2*.

On 7 October the *Luftwaffe* first used *Düppel*, metallised strips which produced false echoes on British radar screens. This simple countermeasure had been known for some considerable time and the RAF had codenamed it 'Window'. The *Luftwaffe* had not used it because the RAF's advantage would be much greater than their own. Then, in July, Bomber Command had used 'Window' in the Battle of Hamburg and, with nothing to lose, the *Luftwaffe* now

Luftwaffe Order of Battle, Operation 'Steinbock', 20 January 1944

Unit	Type	Aircraft/ serviceable	Bomber Aces
Stab/KG 2	Do 217	3/3	*Kdre* Karl Kessel,* Ernst Andres,* Kurt Seyfarth*
I/KG 2	Do 217	35/35	Josef Steudel*
II/KG 2	Ju 188	35/31	Wolfgang Hankamer*
III/KG 2	Do 217	38/36	Peter Broich,* Alois Magg*
V/KG 2	Me 410	27/25	Rudolf Abrahamczik*
Stab/KG 6	Ju 88	3/3	*Kdre* Hermann Hogeback,*** Willi Dipberger,*[1] Günter Glasner,*[2] Willy Lehnert*[4]
II/KG 6	Ju 88	39/39	*Kdr* Hans Mader*
III/KG 6	Ju 88	41/37	*Kdr* Rudolf Puchinger,* Franz Gapp, * Hans Kirn*
II/KG 30	Ju 88	36/31	
I/KG 40	He 177	15/15	
Stab/KG 54	Ju 88	3/3	*Kdre Freiherr* Volprecht von und zu Eisenbach Riedesel*
I/KG 54	Ju 88	36/25	
II/KG 54	Ju 88	33/33	
I/KG 66	Ju 88/188	45/23	*Kdr* Hermann Schmidt*
Stab/KG 76	Ju 88	5/4	
I/KG 76	Ju 88	33/31	Alfred Enssle*
I/KG 100	He 177	31/27	Hans-Georg Bätcher,** Hans Hormann,*[1] *Dr* Herbert Klein*[3]
I/SKG 10	FW 190	25/20	*Kdr* Egon Thiem,* Otto Heinrich,* Kurt Dahlmann,** Norbert Schmitt,* Ernst von Weyrauch*

*Ritterkreuz; **Eichenlaub; *** Schwerten; [1] observer; [2] gunner; [3] radio operator.

introduced *Düppel* into service. On this occasion 35 bombers were inbound to Norwich, and in spite of the presence of night fighters only one aircraft was lost—a tremendous improvement. However, by now raids were few and far between.

It had become increasingly obvious that the Baedecker reprisal raids were costly failures. Then, on 3 December 1943, *Luftwaffe* Supreme Commander

Hermann Goering issued an operational order to the effect that attacks were to be stepped up.

Operation *'Steinbock'*

The highly optimistic aim of *'Steinbock'* was to avenge the so-called RAF terror attacks on German cities. As the Baedeker raids had failed to do this, the reasoning was that more force was needed. This was of course to completely ignore the fact that whatever the *Luftwaffe* could do, the combined bomber forces of the RAF and USAAF could pay them back one hundredfold. It also presupposed that the effete citizenry of England could sustain far less bombardment than the sturdy National Socialists of the Third Reich without revolting against the government.

Actually, Goering had a point. A ruthless and authoritarian dictatorship, backed by the *Gestapo* with its pervasive network of informers, was far better equipped to hold its citizens in subjugation than was any democratic government, even with the constraints of war. In more recent times, this was underlined by the Gulf War of 1991, when Saddam Hussein retained control of Iraq despite a massive military defeat. However, friend Hermann reckoned without the British national trait which is at once their greatest strength and their greatest weakness—they are stubborn!

For *'Steinbock'*, the offensive strength of *Luftflotte 3* was more than doubled. *Gruppen* were transferred from other theatres in conditions of great secrecy, while units already in place flew little. In consequence, serviceability was exceptionally high at the start of the campaign, whereas the norm was little more than 50 per cent.

In order to maximise the damage, the largest bombs available to the *Luftwaffe*, of 2,500kg, were to be used while stocks lasted, and smaller bombs used only to bring the bomb load up to the maximum. These were to be filled with the extremely powerful, if sensitive, 'England Mixture', consisting of Hexogen and Trialen. For fire-raising, the new AB 1000 container was used. This held up to 620 1kg incendiary bombs, dispensing them at intervals to spread them evenly over a large area.

The lack of navigational and bombing accuracy demonstrated in many of the Baedeker Raids was unaffordable. To improve matters, the Pathfinder

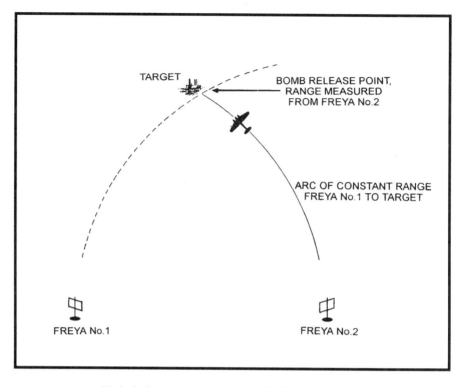

Method of operation of the Egon *blind bombing system.*

Gruppe I/KG 66 was equipped with *Egon*, a new system similar in concept to the British Oboe. The bomber, tracked by ground radar, flew a curving course at high altitude a constant distance to it. A second ground radar measured the range to the bomber and signalled the bomb release point. The maximum range of this system was about 275km, and the maximum obtainable accuracy about 200m, although this last was difficult to attain under operational conditions. A second gadget was *Truhe*, which aided navigation by monitoring signals from the British Gee navigational system. *Knickebein* and *Y-Gerät* were also used, in a hopeful attempt to conceal the new systems.

The first *'Steinbock'* raid took place on 21 January 1944, with 227 bombers. No longer was the 'Crocodile' used: the main force assembled into compact gaggles, crossing the coast of England between Hastings and Folkestone, and set course for London. As the bombers came within range of British radar they started to drop clouds of *Düppel*. Ahead of them were the Pathfinders of

I/KG 66, which, as they approached the city, dropped a string of white flares to indicate the correct course for the main force. The target area, with Waterloo Station at its centre, was then marked with green and white flares. The main force bombed, then escaped eastwards towards the North Sea. Returning to base, they refuelled and rearmed, then, minus seven of their original number, set out once more for the capital.

A raid of 447 sorties on the same night sounds impressive, but in fact little damage was done. Most bombs fell well outside the London area, with Kent getting more than its fair share, presumably on the approach. This appears to indicate poorly trained bomber crews and inadequate target-marking.

Despite the extensive use of *Düppel,* losses were heavy. British fighters and anti-aircraft guns accounted for 25 bombers, while another eighteen were lost for operational reasons, amounting to nearly 19 per cent of the aircraft taking part. At this rate, the *'Steinbock'* force would quickly have bled to death. Never again was a double raid mounted.

A raid by 285 bombers on 29 January caused considerably more damage, starting many fires, for fourteen losses—a more acceptable attrition rate. By then, however, the Allied landing at Anzio in Italy had caused four *Gruppen* of bombers, three of Ju 88s and one of He 177s to be transferred to the Mediterranean. This was a serious loss of strength.

Nine raids were made on London during February. The first four were largely ineffective but the remainder were fairly concentrated. A change in tactics became apparent. No longer did the bombers head straight for the target area; instead they flew past London, on at least one occasion as far as High Wycombe. This may have been an attempt to mislead the defenders as to the real target. The turning point was marked by red and white flares and the main force then headed back for London at full throttle in a shallow dive.

High above the capital, at 9,000m, a Ju 88S of *I/KG 66* released eighteen red marker bombs on Westminster. The main force bombers swept in at high speed, bombed, then headed towards the coast while continuing to descend. This high-speed escape made life very difficult for the RAF night fighters, but they still managed to inflict a high toll. In all, 72 bombers were lost during the month.

The pattern was broken during March when four raids on London were followed by attacks on Bristol, Hull and Portsmouth. Then, on 18/19 April,

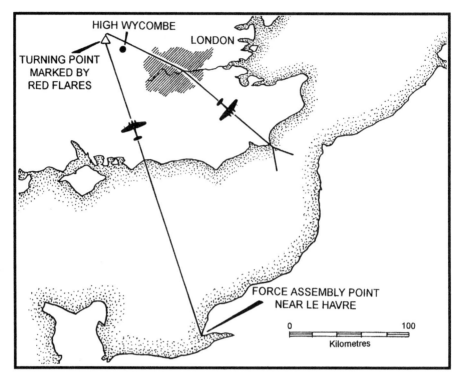

The attack on London, 24 February 1944.

came the last manned raid of the war on London. In a terribly unfortunate incident, North Middlesex Hospital in Edmonton was hit by five high-explosive bombs. The nurse's quarters were hit, the ward above the children's ward was set on fire and the x-ray rooms were destroyed. Nineteen people were killed, including several nurses, and 86 were injured. Many of the victims were trapped in the rubble for several hours.

What was it like on the receiving end? Eleven year-old Dorothy Bonfield, swathed in plaster from armpits to ankles and totally immobile, was in the women's orthopaedic ward at the time. She recalled:

> The drone of German bombers grew louder, and the defending guns started to bark. Soon we could hear the whistle and crump of bombs in the distance. They grew closer. Suddenly we heard more bombs. They were going to hit us; I knew beyond a shadow of a doubt. I lay there, waiting for the end! The noise grew to a deafening shriek. Then came a shattering roar which seemed to go on for ever. The ward rocked and danced, and my bed seemed to rise in the air. The lights went out, the windows blew in, and the curtains

streamed wildly. Outside, all was mayhem. The bells of the fire engines, the roar of the
flames, and the rumble of collapsing masonry.

Amazingly she was unharmed, and was one of 150 patients evacuated to York-
shire that same day.

The next attack came on 30 April, when 101 aircraft raided Plymouth. They
included a dozen Do 217s of *III/KG 100*, carrying the Fritz X guided bomb.
Their main target was the battleship *King George V*, but this was obscured by
the harbour smokescreen. Little damage was caused, for the loss of three bombers, two of them missile-carrying Dorniers.

'*Steinbock*' finally fizzled out in May. On 14 May 91 bombers raided Bristol but only succeeded in landing three tonnes of bombs on the city, losing six
bombers in the process. A few attacks were made on the invasion ports, but to
little effect. The campaign had, like the Baedeker Raids, been an almost total
failure, with more than 300 bombers lost for little result, apart from tying
down a considerable amount of defensive resources.

10. LAST STAND IN THE WEST

By the spring of 1944 the German High Command were well aware that the Allies would shortly launch the long-awaited Second Front, but a massive fighter umbrella over southern England prevented all air reconnaissance. Therefore they had no means of knowing where troop concentrations were, or which ports would be most heavily involved, or where the main attack would fall. The situation was not aided by some extremely clever dummy radio traffic from phantom divisions supposedly in Kent, nor by intensive Allied fighter-bomber and medium-bomber attacks against communications targets all over northern France. When, on 6 June, the blow finally fell on the Normandy coast, it was for a while thought to be a feint and that the real invasion would be directed at the Pas de Calais. When it was finally seen for what it was, it was too late: the Allies had secured their lodgement.

With hindsight, it seems amazing that such relatively large *Luftwaffe* resources were frittered away on *'Steinbock'* rather than being held back to meet the greater threat. But *Der Gröfaz*, acting as usual on intuition rather than reason, would have it so. On the final day of May, just one week before the invasion, the offensive units of *Luftflotte 3* were caught in a very weak posture and few reinforcements were available.

Virtually all the units which had taken part in *'Steinbock'* were seriously understrength. Low serviceability made matters much worse. *KG 2* had just 25 of its 55 Do 217s and Ju 88s serviceable. *KG 6* was slightly better, with 41 out of 84 Ju 88s and 188s, although *III Gruppe* was re-equipping with the Ju 188 at the time. *II* and *III/KG 26* could muster 41 out of 72 Ju 88s. *II/KG 51* was in better shape with seventeen out of 24 Me 410s available, but the *Stab*, *I* and *III/KG 54* could muster a mere fourteen out of 26 Ju 88s. *I/KG 66*, the Pathfinder *Gruppe*, was in the throes of re-equipping with the Ju 188, with twelve of 31 serviceable, while *6/KG 76* could manage just three out of twelve. *I* and *II/KG 77* were also at less than half strength, with 25 out of 53 Ju 88s, as was *III/KG 100* with thirteen of 31 Do 217s. Although re-forming, *II/KG 40* was in better shape, with 26 He 177s out of 30. Of the fighter-bombers, *III/SG 4* was near full strength with 36 FW 190s, but *I/SKG 10* had only nineteen out of 33.

It seems reasonable to speculate that had *'Steinbock'* been called off at an early stage—preferably before it had even begun, given the results of the Baedeker Raids—and the FW 190s and Me 410s used to keep pressure on the defenders, the bomber force could have been built up to full strength by the end of May. It would also have contained many experienced crews who had in fact been lost during *'Steinbock'*. Had the *Kampfflieger* then been flung in against the invasion fleet and the troops on the beach-heads, they might have done a great deal of damage. Of course, casualties would have been very high, given the huge amount of anti-aircraft fire that the Allied armada would have put up and the overwhelming night fighter presence in the surrounding area, but casualties had been high during *'Steinbock'* in any case. As it was, night bomber attacks over the invasion area amounted to little more than pinpricks, even though the congestion was such that it was hard not to hit something worthwhile either at sea or ashore.

Apart from operations in the East, *Luftwaffe* conventional bomber sorties were rapidly coming to an end, mainly because of a shortage of fuel, and in the autumn of 1944 most *Kampfgeschwader* were disbanded, their crews being transferred to fighters or, in many cases, to ground units. Fighter-bombers were still widely used, however, and continued to be so until the end of the war.

There were a few notable exceptions. Apart from a single He 177 which was modified to carry the German nuclear weapon, at such time when this could be developed, the carrying capacity of German bombers was very limited. There was no equivalent of the British Lancaster, which could be modified to carry the 12,000lb 'Tallboy' and the 10-ton 'Grand Slam'. Yet the Germans needed a more destructive weapon for use against hard targets such as battleships. Improvisation was the order of the day, and this duly emerged as the *Mistel* (Mistletoe) composite aircraft.

Then there was the Fi 103 flying bomb, variously known as the V1 or 'Doodlebug'. Normally launched from a ground ramp, this was range-limited, and to extend both range and versatility He 111s were modified to act as launch vehicles. Then there were the jets. The Messerschmitt Me 262 was used in the fighter-bomber role, while the Arado Ar 234 became the world's first jet bomber. Both were used in the dying days of the Third Reich and, thanks to their overwhelming speed and rate of climb, proved difficult to counter.

Mistel

After lengthy use, a warplane becomes what is known as 'war-weary'. No longer suitable for front-line operations, it can be scrapped and its materials recycled, or 'reduced to produce', in which case it becomes a source of spare parts. There is, however, a third alternative. It can be packed to the gills with high explosive, and crashed into a high-value target. This certainly produces a big bang, but not only is accuracy lacking, even with remote radio control from a mother ship, but the explosion tends to dissipate itself, taking the line of least resistance. In other words, much of the energy released expends itself on empty air. This was one of the problems encountered with the German remotely controlled bombs described in an earlier chapter. If they penetrated the outer shell of a warship, the effect was devastating, but, as we have seen, hits on heavily armoured warships did not guarantee their destruction.

Much the same problem had been encountered in tank warfare, where guns had proved largely inadequate to penetrate the heavy frontal armour of main battle tanks. The solution was the hollow-charge warhead. This was cone-shaped, with the high explosive contained behind a soft metal liner, copper for preference (though, as copper was in short supply, aluminium was often used). Detonated on impact, the explosive melts the liner and projects it forward at hypersonic velocity, cutting and burning through anything in its path, with all the energy directed linearly. Penetration is directly related to warhead diameter and not to impact velocity, which allows hand-held infantry anti-tank weapons to be effective regardless of range.

To destroy battleships, a large hollow-charge weapon looked a good bet, while the means of delivery selected was the Ju 88. The weapon tailored for it weighed 3,500kg, of which 1,725kg was high explosive—a mixture of Hexogen and TNT. Depending on size, hollow-charge weapons need a certain distance in which to develop their full lethal effect, and this was catered for by adding a detonator in a 3m long nose probe. When triggered, this would unleash a jet of molten metal 300mm in diameter, calculated to penetrate up to 7.5m of armour—far more than was carried by any battleship in the world. In fact, during trials it actually penetrated more than 18m of concrete!

Operationally, the *Mistel* was flown from a single-engined fighter, either a Bf 109 or an FW 190, mounted on pylons above the Ju 88. This could release itself once the weapon had been established on its attack path, after which the pilot would quickly make himself scarce. There were, however, other needs— training missions, and the need to ferry the *Mistel* combination to its attack base. In theory, this could have been done by the pilot of the upper aircraft, but, in practice, judging a safe landing would have taxed his abilities to the limit. Crashing a converted Ju 88 with a hollow-charge warhead on board was not a good idea, especially given the sting-like proboscis, which, if it had detonated the weapon, would have made a mess of the runway.

The solution was truly ingenious. The original crew compartment was re-moved and replaced by a new nose section which housed a two-man crew, with basic facilities for training missions. On training or ferry flights, both upper and lower aircraft were piloted, allowing the upper man to detach him-self and land separately. The new cabin was mounted with quick-release bolts which allowed a rapid changeover to the hollow-charge nose.

Final trials were completed in April 1944, and in that month the first *Mistel* unit, *2/KG 101*, was formed, under the command of Horst Rudat. Previously a He 111 pilot and *Staffelkapitän 2/KG 55* on the Eastern Front, Rudat had been awarded the *Ritterkreuz* on 24 March 1943. Now he applied himself to his new task.

Three primary targets were considered—Gibraltar, Leningrad and Scapa Flow. Gibraltar was eliminated on the grounds that the attack would have to overfly neutral Spain. Neither was Leningrad viable, first because of the diffi-culty of attaining surprise and secondly because, as the Soviet Fleet was bot-tled up in the Baltic, little military advantage would be gained. A raid on the British fleet anchorage at Scapa Flow was meticulously planned, with the

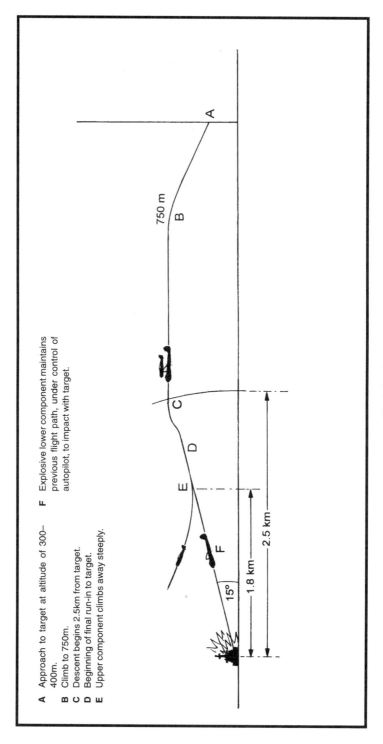

A Approach to target at altitude of 300–400m.

B Climb to 750m.

C Descent begins 2.5km from target.

D Beginning of final run-in to target.

E Upper component climbs away steeply.

F Explosive lower component maintains previous flight path, under control of autopilot, to impact with target.

The Mistel *attack.*

*Mistel*s scheduled to fly out at low level, navigating using radio beacons which had been previously laid.

This last was pre-empted by the Allied landings in Normandy in June, and *2/KG 101* was transferred to St Dizier in France to operate against the invasion fleet. The first attack, of four *Mistel*s led by Rudat, took place on the evening of 24 June. It went ill. 'Friendly' fire knocked out the port engine of Rudat's Ju 88, and, when he disengaged from it, it dived into the sea. Of the others, one scored a near miss against the headquarters ship HMS *Frith*, causing extensive splinter damage.

Only about six other *Mistel*s were launched against the invasion fleet, one of which is believed to have hit the elderly French battleship *Courbet*, which was used as a blockship for the Mulberry harbour off Arromanches. As this had already been scuttled and was resting on the sea bottom, it hardly counted. Then, on 9/10 August, a Ju 88 component impacted well inland near Andover, following an abortive shipping attack in the Channel.

This lack of success was hardly surprising. The approach was made at low level, below Allied radar cover. On reaching the target area, the *Mistel* pilot would pop-up to about 750m and select a ship to attack. Having lined up on it, at a distance of about 2½km he launched into a 15-degree dive. As the range closed to 1½km, he released the bottom half of the combo and pulled away. The explosive-packed Ju 88 then continued on its former course by autopilot to impact the target. But it usually did not!

Shortly afterwards *2/KG 101* was redeployed for the attack on Scapa Flow, and, with the addition of illumination and training *Staffeln*, was redesignated *III/KG 66*. The operation was mounted in October, but three of the five *Mistel*s crashed and the other two failed to find the target.

On 10 November *III/KG 66* became *II/KG 200*, with *6/KG 200* commanded by Walter Pilz, like Rudat previously an He 111 pilot with *KG 55* in the East, who had been awarded the *Ritterkreuz* on the same day. The Scapa Flow operation was finally abandoned when, on 12 November, the German battleship *Tirpitz* was sunk by RAF bombers. With the removal of this surface threat, the target, the British Home Fleet, decamped for the Pacific.

With no naval targets left, the *Mistel* force was next directed against the Soviet electrical generating industry in Operation *'Eisenhammer'*. In charge was bomber ace Werner Baumbach, who by now sported the *Ritterkreuz* with *Eichenlaub* and *Schwerten*. However, this plan was overtaken by events as the Soviet Army threatened and then overran the bases from which *'Eisenhammer'* was to have been launched.

By March 1945, slowing the Soviet advance by smashing the river bridges over first the Vistula, then the Oder, took priority. However destructive the giant shaped charge was, it was totally unsuitable for the task of destroying reinforced concrete bridges. Moreover, without radio command guidance, the system was too inaccurate. Like many other German schemes, it was simply not good enough.

Doodlebugs

No one who has heard a Doodlebug in flight is ever likely to forget it. A rattling noise like a two-stroke engine, coupled at dusk with a reddish glow against the clouds from its pulse-jet engine, made it unmistakable. The fact that it was a robot bomber, unthinking and unfeeling, somehow made it more horrific. One waited for the engine to stop, shortly to be followed by a very loud bang.

The first Doodlebug fell on London in the small hours of 13 June 1944. With a warhead containing about 850kg of high explosive, it was extremely destructive. Fortunately for the citizens of London (and other targets), the weapon was extremely unreliable and inaccurate, and less than one in four actually came down in the Greater London area, large though this was.

The Fieseler Fi 103 had more names and designations than any other machine in the Second World War. It was also known as the *Vergeltungswaffe Eins* (V1); the FZG 76, designed to mislead Allied intelligence into thinking that it was a target drone; *Maikaker* (Maybug); *Kirschkern* (Cherrystone); and *Höllenhund* (Hellhound). In Britain it was codenamed 'Diver', while the press knew it as the 'Buzz-Bomb' or 'Doodlebug'!

Most 'Doodlebugs' were launched from ground ramps in Occupied Europe, but this was a tactical limitation, both in range and direction. To give greater versatility, the He 111s of *III/KG 3*, based in Holland, and led by *Ritterkreuz* holder and anti-shipping *Experte* Martin Vetter, were modified as 'Doodlebug' carriers.

The air-launched 'Doodlebug' campaign started on 7 July 1944, with attacks on Southampton. Little damage was caused, mainly because the problems of accurate aiming were extreme. The 'Doodlebug' was carried inboard on the starboard wing. The asymmetric drag was easily compensated for, and the reduction in speed was not too significant, although at low speeds the Heinkel was a sitting duck for fighters. This meant that, realistically, attacks could only be made at night.

Outbound, the Heinkel cruised at about 270kph at low altitude, beneath British radar cover. On reaching its designated launch point—and, over the featureless wastes of the sea on a moonless night, finding it was the tricky part—it pulled laboriously up to about 500m. Once there, it had to accelerate to the minimum launch speed of 320kph and line up on an exact heading, making due allowance for wind direction and speed.

At that point, the pulse-jet of the 'Doodlebug' was started, lighting up the sky for miles around, until the missile could be released some ten seconds later. This was the most unpopular part of the mission: most Heinkel crews reckoned that the launch was a Mosquito magnet! Directly the 'Doodlebug' was on its way, the Heinkel pilot returned to sea level and headed homewards.

The Mosquito was rather too fast to intercept the low and slow intruders effectively, and at a later stage the Beaufighter was used against the V1-carrying Heinkels. Actually, on at least one occasion, a Heinkel crew was saved when the 'Doodlebug' pulse-jet was lit. A Mosquito crew had followed a Heinkel for miles at very low altitude, unable, as the radar operator said. 'to get a shot at him without swimming'. Then, when it pulled up to launch its weapon, the pilot got a visual sighting and lined up his gun sight. He recalled:

> I could even see the thing hanging under the wing. But before I could fire, somebody went and lit the blue touch paper. There was a dirty great flash as the bomb went whooshing off on its way, and for the next five minutes I could see sweet Fanny. I had to pull up in case I hit the deck, and that was that!

In October *III/KG 3* was redesignated *I/KG 53*. Shortly after this, two more *Gruppen* re-formed in the missile-launching role. On 24 December some 50 Heinkels tried to attack Manchester, but only 30 Doodlebugs crossed the English coast and, of these, only one hit the target. The air-launched 'Doodlebug' attacks ceased on 14 January 1945. Results were negligible, but 77 Heinkels were lost, sixteen to night fighters and the others to operational causes. So far as is known, only one *Ritterkreuz* was awarded to a member of the 'Doodle-bug' units—Walter Richter, an NCO flight mechanic with *5/KG 53*, who received his award on 28 February 1945.

Fighter-Bombers

Following the invasion of Normandy on 6 June 1944, the fighter-bombers, reinforced by units from Germany, were flung into the battle. They achieved little, mainly due to the overwhelming strength of Allied air power. In air superiority sorties alone, the *Luftwaffe* were outnumbered by six to one, while anti-aircraft fire from the beach-heads was intense. The German bases were continually bombed, communications broke down, supplies failed to get through and units were continually forced to retreat before the advancing Allied armies. The situation was aggravated by a severe fuel shortage from August. Not until autumn, when the Allies were beginning to outrun their supply routes, did the pressure ease.

The German Jets

The *Luftwaffe* managed to get jet aircraft, both bombers and fighters, into operational service before any other air arm. This promised to give them a significant qualitative advantage to offset, at least partially, their numerical inferiority. The two main types were the Me 262 fighter and the Ar 234 bomber, both of them twin-engined single-seaters.

Much has been made of Adolf Hitler's decision to produce the Me 262 as a fighter-bomber at a time when USAAF heavy bombers were pounding the Fatherland by day, accompanied by an effective shield of long-range escort fighters which could only be countered by the fast jets. However, this was not as potty as it is often made out to be. The *Führer*'s reasoning was that invasion was coming, and that it could only be stopped on the beaches. As he stated on 20 December 1943:

> The most important thing is that they get some bombs on top of them just as they try to invade . . . after half a day, our reserves will already be on their way. So if we can pin them down on the beaches for just six or eight hours, you can see what that will mean to us . . .

Hitler foresaw that the invasion would be accompanied by such a vast air armada that conventional aircraft would be hard-pressed even to scratch the surface. Given this, only the extraordinarily fast Me 262 would stand a chance of penetrating the defences.

In this he was correct. No less a military personage than *Generalfeldmarschall* Erwin Rommel, probably influenced by being hamstrung by Allied air power in the desert and now commanding the Western defences, agreed with him. He said: 'We must stop the enemy in the water and destroy his equipment while it is still afloat.'

In fact, the Me 262 entered service far too late to intervene in the invasion. As for the effectiveness of conventional *Luftwaffe* units, Hitler was again proved right. Two days before he was wounded and put out of the battle by RAF fighter-bombers, Rommel submitted a report to the *Führer* which contained the words: 'Our own air force has hardly entered the battle at all!' This was underlined by a German soldier who commented: 'Silver aircraft are American, camouflaged aircraft are British, and if we do not see them at all they are German!' Nor, as is often stated, did Hitler's decision to use the Me 262 as a fighter-bomber delay its entry into service by any great amount, as severe problems with engine life and reliability took a long time to overcome.

The first Me 262 unit, *EprKdo 262*, was formed in May 1944, mainly from pilots of *III/ZG 26* (Bf 110). The purpose of this was operational evaluation. It was followed on 6 June by *III/KG 51*, converting from the Ju 88. The first fighter-bomber unit to be declared operational was *3/KG(J) 51*, commanded by *Ritterkreuz* and *Eichenlaub* holder Wolfgang Schenk, the former *Kommodore* of *SG 2*. This was in fact far too early: the *Staffel* had had barely four weeks to learn about their new mount.

In the fighter-bomber role, the Me 262 carried two 250kg bombs. Forbidden at this time to descend below 4,000m over Allied territory, and with no effective bomb sight, the aircraft attacked targets in the Allied bridgehead from 27 July, aiming with the standard gun sight in a shallow dive. The results were pathetic: the Allies did not even notice and record their presence!

III/KG(J) 51 was declared operational in August, closely followed by *I/KG(J) 51*, with *II/KG(J) 51* in October. But with low serviceability due to unreliable engines, *KG(J) 51* was unable to mount more than pinprick attacks on Allied airfields and troop concentrations. The best results were achieved by using dispenser weapons to scatter bomblets over a wide area, and on 1 October five Spitfires of 127 Wing were destroyed on the ground at Grave in Holland by a lone raider. But, as the saying goes, one *Schwalbe* does not make a summer!

Meanwhile the Arado Ar 234 had entered service, initially in the reconnaissance role. Erich Sommer and Horst Goetz, whom we last met high over England in the Ju 86R, had flown many sorties, both over the invasion area and over England, largely undetected and completely unintercepted. The first jet bomber unit, *III/KG 76*, was formed on 6 December 1944 under the command of veteran bomber pilot Hans-Georg Bätcher, holder of the *Ritterkreuz* with *Eichenlaub*. At this point the critical fuel shortage had forced the disbandment of many conventional bomber units, and many highly experienced men were available.

The preferred method of attack with the Ar 234 was a shallow (about 30-degree) dive, during which the speed mounted to about 965kph. The bombs were aimed via a periscopic sight mounted in the cabin roof. Fast, low-level, lay-down attacks were also used, but, without even so much as a gun sight to assist, aiming was by eye—with plenty of 'Kentucky windage!' It was also possible to attack from high altitude in level flight. This was 'interesting' for the pilot, as he had to double as the observer, and it could only be carried out in exceptionally clear conditions. Having identified the target from some 30km back—less than three minutes' flying time away—he lined up and switched on the autopilot. He then disconnected the control column and swung it to one side, out of the way, before moving into the nose to use the *Lotfe* bomb sight. Fortunately this was coupled to the autopilot, which enabled him to make course adjustments. Having released the bombs, he then regained his seat and took over control. *Ritterkreuz* holder Robert Kowaleski, *Kommodore KG 76*, once attacked British tanks near Dortmund from about 9,000m using this method, in what can only be described as a triumph of optimism over expectation.

The first Arado operational mission was mounted on the morning of Christmas Eve. The *Staffelkapitän* of *9/KG 76*, Dieter Lukesch, a long-time *Geschwader* member who also held the *Ritterkreuz mit Eichenlaub*, led nine

Arados, each with a single 500kg bomb under the fuselage. After take-off, the aircraft initially stayed at low level in order to conceal their base. Then, climbing to 4,000m, they headed for targets at Liège and Namur in Belgium. Aiming in a shallow dive, they bombed from between 2,000 and 2,400m before heading homewards. Five hits were observed.

That afternoon they bombed the same target, but with only eight aircraft as one had been damaged while landing after the first mission. Results were not observed. On the following day two missions to Liège resulted in an Arado crash-landing after being attacked by an RAF Tempest, whilst two more were damaged on landing.

Over the next few days Ar 234s and Me 262s mounted harassing attacks on Allied ground forces in the Ardennes; poor weather precluded anything more ambitious. Then, on New Year's Day, Operation *'Bodenplatte'*, a massive attack on Allied airfields, was mounted at first light. This morning also saw the first ever night jet bomber mission, when Lukesch led four Arados over Belgium as a combined weather reconnaissance and decoy raid.

'Bodenplatte' was designed to catch the British and American air forces on the ground and inflict unacceptable casualties on them. The concept was badly flawed. While about 200 easily replaced Allied aircraft were destroyed, few not so easily replaced pilots were lost. This was in direct contrast to the *Luftwaffe*, which lost not only about 300 aircraft but 237 pilots, many of them very experienced. The casualties included Alfred Druschel, holder of the *Ritterkreuz*, *Eichenlaub* and *Schwerten*, who had been appointed *Kommodore SG 4* only three days earlier. He fell to light anti-aircraft fire. It was a catastrophe from which the *Luftwaffe* never recovered.

In January 1945 *KG(J) 54* started to re-equip with the Me 262; like *KG(J) 51*, this was also formerly a bomber unit. Day fighter units, notably *JG 7*, were in the process of converting to jets, but the problem here was that day fighter pilots had no blind flying training. This was a serious omission in the cloud-laden skies over Germany, and it was considered better to convert bomber pilots, who were well-versed in instrument flying, to fighters than to re-train fighter pilots in the art.

This was major error: *I/KG(J) 54* flew its first fighter mission on 9 February and lost six out of ten Me 262s to American escort fighters, including their

Kommodore, *Ritterkreuz* with *Eichenlaub* holder Volprecht *Freiherr* von und zu Eisenbach Riedesel. Another disaster followed on 25 February: twelve Me 262s were lost, half in air combat, four in a strafing attack and two in accidents. At this point Hans-Georg Bätcher was transferred from *III/KG 76* to take command.

By March only *KG(J) 51* and *III/KG 76* operated regularly as fighter-bombers, but never with the numbers needed to deliver a really damaging weight of ordnance. The swansong of the jet bombers effectively took place in March 1945, when American troops captured the Ludendorff Bridge over the Rhine at Remagen. Ar 234s and Me 262s made repeated attacks over several days, including a high-altitude raid using the *Egon* blind bombing system, but failed to drop it.

Once Allied fighters had taken the measure of the jets, casualties were high, but not all fell in the air. Rudolf von Hallensleben, *Ritterkreuz* holder and newly appointed *Kommandeur* of *I/KG(J) 51*, was killed when USAAF P-47s strafed his staff car near Leipheim on 21 March 1945.

Ludwig Albersmayer of *I/KG(J) 51* was awarded the final *Ritterkreuz* of the war, on 1 May 1945. Unlike most of his comrades, he survived.

11. THE BOMBER ACES

The German armed forces had an award system common to all three services. It started with the *Eisernes Kreuz* (Iron Cross) Second and First Class, awarded for certain well-defined achievements in the field. The most highly prized award of all was the *Ritterkreuz*, or Knight's Cross. For this award there was no discrimination between officers and other ranks: corporals and colonels, and for that matter U-boat commanders, could wear the *Ritterkreuz* with equal pride as members of the same fraternity. In the *Luftwaffe* this marked the *Experte*, or ace. The *Ritterkreuz* tended to be awarded for achievements over a period of time, including leadership. In the *Jadgflieger* it became formalised into a points system based on aerial victories (see the author's companion volume *Luftwaffe Fighter Aces*). For bomber and attack pilots matters were not so clear-cut, and a minority of awards appear to have been fairly arbitrary. It is nevertheless the basis on which a bomber, Stuka or attack pilot could be deemed an *Experte*, or ace, and has been so adopted in the current work.

Unlike Allied decorations, the *Ritterkreuz* could not be awarded twice. This led to a series of grades—the *Eichenlaub* (Oak Leaves) and *Schwerten* (Swords). Beyond this lay the *Brillianten* (Diamonds), which were awarded but rarely. The *Führer* personally invested awards of the *Eichenlaub* and upwards; the *Ritterkreuz* was normally bestowed by the local *Luftwaffe* commander.

By 1941 so many *Ritterkreuze* had been handed out to all services that the award appeared in danger of being devalued. As a result, an interim award was instituted—the *Deutsches Kreuz*, or German Cross in Gold. This notwithstanding, the bomber aces in this section all have the *Ritterkreuz* as a minimum.

Only a handful of Allied bomber pilots flew 100 operational sorties. This contrasts with the *Kampfflieger*. Heinkel pilot Rudolf Müller flew an incredible 682 sorties, against France, Britain, Malta and North Africa and in the

East. He was closely followed by Hans-Georg Bätcher, with 658 sorties, many of them in the West. Bätcher progressed from the He 111 to the Ar 234 jet bomber, then to the Me 262 *Jabo*. Four other *Luftwaffe* bomber aviators are recorded as having topped 500 sorties, and a further eighteen between 400 and 500, although, as the records are incomplete, the total may well be higher. Although most *Ritterkreuz* holders were pilots, many were observers: as we have noted, in the early years of the war the observer was the aircraft captain, and many *Geschwader Kommodoren* flew in this capacity. A small but significant minority flew as flight mechanics, radio operators or gunners.

Comparison of the records of German and Allied fighter aces has led some commentators to believe that Germans were intrinsically better in air combat, whereas the truth is that they had many more opportunities to score. The same trap is evident in the huge number of sorties that many German bomber aces managed to achieve. It must, however, be recognised that, for the most part, they operated in more benign conditions than did their Allied counterparts. This is not to denigrate their achievements: the fact is that, over England from mid-1943 and over the Western Front from 1944, *Luftwaffe* bomber sorties became ever less successful in the face of a strong air defence system. It must also be stressed that *Luftwaffe* aviators were not unfeeling robots, as they have sometimes been portrayed, but human, with human feelings and emotions. Many, 'flown out', had to be removed from front-line units and sent to less demanding positions. Others continued until they exhausted their physical and mental resources, and died in action. Just a few, a tiny minority, kept going and notched up incredible sortie totals.

Enemy assets destroyed credited to individuals are those credited in *Luftwaffe* records. As with the *Jagdflieger*, they are frequently overstated, but, despite this, they were generally made in good faith. Unless otherwise indicated, the aces listed were pilots, and were commissioned. Their ultimate fate is given where known. Where it is not, in most cases it can be presumed that they did not survive the war.

Antrup, Willi

A communications pilot with the Condor Legion in Spain, Antrup began the war as technical officer with *Stab/KG 55* (He 111), flying in the Battle of

Britain and later in the Blitz. He was appointed *Staffelkapitän 5/KG 55* and went to the Eastern Front in 1941. He was awarded the *Ritterkreuz* on 22 November 1942 for close support of the Army and was appointed *Kommandeur III/KG 55* on 8 August 1943 and *Kommodore KG 55* on 11 May 1944. On 21 June 1944 a large USAAF shuttle raid landed at Poltava in Russia and other nearby airfields. That night Antrup led elements of *KG 4, KG 27, KG 53* and *KG 55* in a very destructive raid on the Soviet airfields. Some 44 out of 72 B-17s were destroyed and 26 more damaged, plus several P-51s. In addition, munitions dumps and fuel stores were hit. It was the last really devastating *Luftwaffe* raid of the war. Antrup was awarded the *Eichenlaub* on 18 November 1944. He survived more than 500 sorties.

Bätcher, Hans-Georg

A qualified pilot, Bätcher flew as an observer over Poland with *KG 4* (He 111), making low-level attacks east of Warsaw. In the French campaign he reverted to pilot, but his aircraft was attacked by five French Morane MS 406 fighters near Rouen and both engines were shot up. Desperately, he hung on to his formation and bombed the target—troop concentrations—before making a forced landing. Taken prisoner, he was released at the Armistice and rejoined his *Gruppe* on 3 July 1940, in time for the Battle of Britain and the Blitz. He was transferred to *1/KGr 100* pathfinders on 1 July 1941; his Heinkel was badly damaged by a night fighter just nine days later, and only an exemplary piece of flying enabled him to regain the French coast (see Chapter 5).

He was appointed *Staffelkapitän 1/KGr 100* on 15 July, but shortly after this *KGr 100* was transferred to the Eastern Front. On the night of 4/5 November he led a devastating night raid on the Gorki engine factory in Moscow with SC 1800 bombs, starting huge fires. This was just one of sixteen raids that he flew against the Russian capital. Soon afterwards *1/KGr 100* was withdrawn to Germany for refresher training. On New Year's Day the unit returned to the East, to join the assault on Sevastopol.

By 5 July 1942 Bätcher had demonstrated incredible physical and mental toughness and established himself as an outstanding bomber pilot by flying 206 sorties in just five months. He was awarded the *Deutsche Kreuz* on 17 July 1942. From August *1/KGr 100* supported the advance to Stalingrad and ranged as far afield as the Caspian. He was awarded the *Ritterkreuz* on 21 December 1942. He was appointed *Kommandeur I/KG 100* on 6 October 1943 and in the following month became the first bomber pilot to complete 600 sorties. Award of the *Eichenlaub* followed on 24 March 1944. After a spell at the War Academy, he was appointed *Kommandeur III/KG 76* (Ar 234) on 6 December 1944 and flew his 682nd and final sortie on 21 February 1945. He survived the war.

Baumbach, Werner

Baumbach began the war as an He 111 pilot over Poland, then transferred to *I/ KG 30*, the first operational Ju 88 unit. He flew against the British Fleet from October 1939 and in April 1940 established a reputation as an anti-shipping specialist. He supported the invasion of Norway, attacking British naval units at Aandalsnes and Narvik, often in appalling weather. His handling of the tricky Ju 88 was however rather suspect, as on two occasions he crashed while attempting to land.

He was awarded the *Ritterkreuz* on 9 May 1940. On the following day he attacked targets in south-west Holland. He was appointed *Staffelkapitän* on 1 June but shortly afterwards was sent to Japan on a special mission. He returned at the end of September, in time to take part in the Blitz. When in 1941 this gave way to the Battle of the Atlantic, he was credited with sinking many Allied ships. He was awarded the *Eichenlaub* on 14 July and five days later was appointed *Kommandeur I/KG 30*. In spring 1942 *I/KG 30* was deployed to the Crimea but in August returned to Norway to interdict the Murmansk convoys.

Baumbach was awarded the *Schwerten* on 18 August, his *Gruppe* by now credited with sinking 300,000 tonnes of shipping, then he was posted to Sicily to take part in the campaign in the Mediterranean. This was not a happy time. Upset by what he considered haphazard targeting, he complained to Hans Jeschonnek, the *Luftwaffe* Chief of Staff. Relieved of his command on 12 December 1942, he was posted to Berlin for special duties, later being appointed *Kommodore KG 200* and *General der Kampfflieger*. He commanded the *Mistel* programme. He survived the war but died on 10 February 1954 in Argentina while testing, of all things, a Lancaster bomber.

Beust, *Freiherr* Hans-Henning von

A veteran of the Condor Legion, von Beust was *Staffelkapitän 2/KG 88* (Ju 52/3m) in 1936 and was awarded the Spanish Cross in Gold with Swords. At the outbreak of war he was a *Staffelkapitän* with *KG 27* (He 111) and flew eleven sorties over Poland. He flew 29 sorties in the West, then, as *Kommandeur II/KG 27*, made more than 70 night attacks in the Blitz on England in 1940–41. Deployed to the Eastern Front, he led his *Gruppe* in the advance to Stalingrad. He was awarded the *Ritterkreuz* on 7 September 1941. He was appointed *Kommodore KG 27* from 1 March 1942, from the attempted resupply of the Stalingrad pocket to its disbandment in autumn 1944, and was awarded the *Eichenlaub* on 25 November 1943. He survived 420 sorties.

Bradel, Walter

Observer and *Staffelkapitän 9/KG 2* (Do 17) at the outbreak of war, Bradel took part in raids on France and England. He was awarded the *Ritterkreuz* on 17 September 1941 after leading his unit to stop a huge Soviet armoured attack near Grodno and was appointed *Kommandeur III/KG 2* (Do 217) from 1 July 1942. Re-deployed to the West and appointed *Kommodore KG 2*, he led several Baedeker attacks but was killed in a crash-landing due to engine failure at Amsterdam on 5 May 1943 following a raid on Norwich.

Forgatsch, Heinz

Forgatsch joined *EprGr 210* as a pilot in June 1940 and flew more than 50 *Jabo* sorties against England, being credited with sinking a 14,600-tonne transport in the English Channel. He was awarded the *Ritterkreuz* on 14 June 1941. He was appointed *Staffelkapitän 3/SKG 210* (Bf 210) but was killed while testing this aircraft at Rechlin on 23 September.

Harlinghausen, Martin

'Iron Gustav', as he was widely known, commanded *AS/88* (He 59) in Spain, where he specialised in anti-shipping attacks. In particular his name is forever linked with the low-level 'Swedish Turnip' method of attack, although it is doubtful whether he originated it. A staff officer at the outbreak of war, he set a personal example by flying reconnaissance sorties as an observer in the He

115 floatplane and later in the He 111. His usual pilot was Robert Kowaleski (q.v.). Harlinghausen became the foremost anti-shipping and torpedo bomber specialist. He was awarded the *Ritterkreuz* on 4 May 1940.

As Chief of Staff of *Fliegerkorps X* in the Mediterranean, Harlinghausen led the first (and fairly disastrous) raid on the Suez Canal (Chapter 6). He was awarded the *Eichenlaub* on 30 January 1941, the first bomber crewman to be so honoured. In March 1941 he was appointed *Fliegerführer Atlantik*. In November Harlinghausen's Heinkel was very badly damaged while, still leading from the front, he attacked a transport in the Irish Sea and only just managed to limp back to the coast of France before ditching. Seriously injured, 'Iron Gustav' spent the next three months in hospital. He was then appointed *Kommodore KG 26*, a He 111 torpedo bombing outfit which later deployed to Norway to counter the Murmansk convoys. In November 1942 he was sent to Tunis to co-ordinate tactical air support in North Africa and on 6 February 1943 replaced *General* Loerzer. He was relieved of his command on 16 June and sat out the war in a succession of staff appointments. Promoted to *General*, he survived the war.

Helbig, Joachim

Helbig flew as an observer with *II/LG 1* (He 111) over Poland and later against the British Home Fleet and Norway. In a low-level attack on the latter, his port engine was shot out by anti-aircraft fire and his flight mechanic seriously wounded. He converted to the Ju 88 in April 1940 and became a pilot. Appointed *Staffelkapitän 4/LG 1*, he flew against Holland, Belgium and France and was wounded over Dunkirk by Spitfires on 25 May 1940. On 13 August *II/LG 1* attacked the airfield at Worthy Down. Flying at the rear of the column, Helbig's *Staffel* was intercepted by fighters and its defensive formation broken. Only the alertness of his NCO radio operator/gunner, Franz Schlund, who continually called breaks, saved Helbig, although the port motor was shot up, the braking system was damaged and both Schlund and the gunner were wounded. Schlund was awarded the *Ritterkreuz* on 30 August 1940, the first radio operator to be so honoured.

Helbig had to wait until 24 October for his own *Ritterkreuz*, by which time he was flying night raids against England. Transferred to Sicily at the end of the year, he took part in the attack on the aircraft carrier *Illustrious* in January. Raids on Malta and Benghazi followed, then on Greece, during which Schlund fought off a night fighter attack, and Crete. In November 1941 Helbig succeeded Kuno Hoffmann as *Kommandeur I/LG 1* and was awarded the *Eichenlaub* on 16 January 1942, after 210 sorties. Then on 10 May he led the attack which sank three out of four British destroyers off Crete. For this success he was awarded the *Schwerten*, which he received on 28 September.

He continued to operate in the Mediterranean and Italy and was appointed *Kommodore LG 1* in August 1943. He was recalled to Germany late in 1944 to command a battle group and ended the war commanding the *Mistel* attacks against bridges on the Eastern Front. He survived the war with 480 sorties.

Herrmann, Hans-Joachim (Hajo)

Herrmann was a veteran of the Spanish Civil War, where he flew bombing sorties with *1/K 88* (Ju 52/3m); he re-joined *III/KG 4* (He 111) on his return. He flew eighteen sorties over Poland in 1939, returning on one engine on 2 September after a fighter attack. His usual observer was Heinrich Schmetz, who was awarded the *Ritterkreuz* as a pilot in 1944. Hermann flew against Norway in 1940 and in May that year converted to the Ju 88, which he flew against France and the Low Countries. Shot down by Hurricanes over Dunkirk on 31 May, he crash-landed unhurt in shallow water.

At about this time *III/KG 4* was redesignated *III/KG 30* and in June 1940 Herrmann was appointed *Staffelkapitän 7/KG 30*. Many raids on England followed, by day and by night, in which he developed a remarkable skill in using cloud cover. It was on 22 July that he had his memorable encounter with a balloon over Plymouth (see Chapter 5). He was injured in a take-off accident on 18 October and hospitalised for six weeks. He was awarded the *Ritterkreuz* on 30 October. His unit deployed to Sicily in February 1941 and he raided Malta, Greece—including the devastating attack on Piraeus on 6 April—Crete and North Africa. A brief spell in a staff job followed, then in August Herrmann was appointed *Kommandeur* of his old *Gruppe*, based in France and flying once more against Britain. At Christmas he went to Norway, to interdict the Murmansk convoys, then, in July 1942, he once more joined headquarters. After 320 bomber sorties, his career moved into the world of night fighting.

He was awarded the *Eichenlaub* on 2 August 1943 and the *Schwerten* on 23 January 1944. He survived the war as *Kommandeur* of *Fliegerdivision 9*.

Hogeback, Hermann

Hogeback flew more than 100 sorties with *K 88* (He 111) in the Spanish Civil War, for which he was awarded the Spanish Cross with Swords. Already in an attack on 13 September 1938, his Heinkel was set ablaze by Republican anti-aircraft fire and one motor stopped. Streaming smoke, he was forced to land between the lines. He was rescued by Nationalist troops, seriously injured, and spent two months in hospital.

A pilot with *III/LG 1* (He 111, then Ju 88), Hogeback flew against Poland in 1939, then in the West and against Britain, including 28 sorties over London. In 1941 he was in the Balkans, where he was appointed *Staffelkapitän 9/LG 1*. He flew over Greece and North Africa. Once his Ju 88 was so badly riddled that he was forced to make a belly-landing in the desert; this was during the retreat, but he and his crew managed to escape. He was awarded the *Ritterkreuz* on 8 September 1941; uniquely, all his regular crew later received the same award.

Transferred to the Eastern Front, Hogeback flew against Leningrad, Kersch, the Crimea and Sevastopol. He was appointed *Kommandeur III/LG 1* in July 1942. In September the *Gruppe* was redesignated *III/KG 6* and transferred to France, where he flew in the Baedeker and *'Steinbock'* raids. He was awarded the *Eichenlaub* on 20 February 1943, having completed 416 sorties. Then, on 12 August, he was appointed *Kommodore KG 6*, succeeding Walter Storp. He converted to the Ju 188 in the summer of 1944 and was awarded the *Schwerten* on 30 April 1945, by which time his unit was converting to the Me 262. He survived the war.

Höflinger, Karl

A pilot with *9/KG 77* (Ju 88), Höflinger specialised in the so-called *Piratenangriffe*, or pirate raids, against British targets in 1940–41. On one occasion he attacked an engine factory at Birmingham in spite of a cloud base of barely 100m, in the teeth of driving snow and balloon and gun defences; then, on 19 January 1941, he scored three direct hits on another in Coventry. He was awarded the *Ritterkreuz* on 7 March 1941 but failed to return from a sortie on 18 April.

Kindler, Alfred

Kindler was a pilot with *II/KG 2* (Do 17) at the outbreak of war, and flew against Poland, France and Britain. His unit converted to Do 217s early in 1941. Appointed *Staffelkapitän 6/KG 2*, he was shot down over Birmingham by anti-aircraft fire and taken prisoner on 31 July 1942, on his 230th sortie. He was awarded the *Ritterkreuz* on 24 September.

Kowalewski, Robert

Beginning the war on the staff of *Fliegerkorps X*, Kowalewski flew extensively with the staff flight as pilot to Martin Harlinghausen, with whom he refined the 'Swedish Turnip' attack. By November 1940 the pair were credited with the destruction of more than 83,000 tonnes of Allied shipping, a British cruiser damaged and a fighter and a flying boat shot down. Kowalewski was awarded the *Ritterkreuz* on 24 November. He also piloted Harlinghausen on the disastrous raid on Suez in 1941 (see Chapter 6).

He was appointed *Kommandeur II/KG 26* (He 111), an anti-shipping outfit in the Mediterranean, in July 1941, *Kommandeur III/KG 40* (FW 200) from August 1941 to September 1943, and *Kommodore ZG 76* (Me 410) in February 1944, but this last unit was disbanded in July. He was *Kommodore NJG 2* (Ju 88 night fighters) until November, then *Kommodore KG 76* (Ar 234 jet bombers). He survived the war.

Kühl, *Dr* Ernst

While combat flying is no place for elderly gentlemen, *Dr* Kühl was the exception which proved the rule. He survived the war with a tally of 315 sorties at the age of 57. An artillery officer in the Great War, and a private pilot between the wars, in 1939 he was a *Luftwaffe* reservist. He flew with *Stab/KG 55* (He 111) against Poland and France, then later against Britain. On 30 September 1940 he was shot down into the Channel by fighters and spent an exhausting 36 hours in a dinghy with his crew before being rescued. Appointed *Kommandeur II/KG 55* in March 1941, he transferred east for the invasion of Russia in June. He was appointed *Kommodore KG 55* in September 1942 and awarded the *Ritterkreuz* on 25 November that year. He commanded the transport force in the abortive attempt to keep the troops encircled at Stalingrad supplied by air. 'Uncle Ernst', as he was affectionately known, relinquished command in August 1943 to become *Fliegerführer Nord*. He was awarded the *Eichenlaub* on 18 December 1943.

Lindmayr, Alois

A Slovenian-born observer, Lindmayr began the war as *Staffelkapitän 7/KG 76* (Do 17), leading his unit in the French campaign, attacking airfields at low level, during which he was credited with the destruction of 28 aircraft on the ground. He also hit an ammunition train in Rennes station, causing great devastation. He was awarded the *Ritterkreuz* on 21 July 1940. Appointed *Kommandeur III/KG 76*, he flew in the Battle of Britain and led *KG 76* on the noon raid of 15 September, surviving against fearful odds (see Chapter 5).

Mevissen, Kurt

Mevissen was an NCO pilot with *9/KG 1* (Ju 88) who by 4 March 1942 had flown 221 sorties, mainly on the northern sector of the Eastern Front. Among other things he was credited with the destruction of eleven tanks, nine gun batteries destroyed or damaged and eight trains knocked out and with leaving an armoured train in flames. He was awarded the *Ritterkreuz* on 21 September 1942.

Müller, Philipp

A pilot with *KG 55* (He 111), Philipp Müller flew against Poland, France and Britain and then on the southern sector of the Eastern Front, where he often undertook reconnaissance missions with the *Stab*. He was appointed *Staffelkapitän 1/KG 55* on 7 September 1942. On 14 November he crashed and died near Morosovskaya. It was his fourth sortie of the day, and the physical and psychological strain is thought to have been the main factor. A posthumous *Ritterkreuz* was awarded on 2 April 1943.

Müller, Rudolf

Beginning the war as pilot and *Staffelkapitän 1/KG 27* (He 111), Rudolf Müller flew many sorties against airfields in France and England in 1940. He was appointed *Kommandeur I/KG 27*. In the course of intensive anti-shipping operations his *Gruppe* was credited with sinking some 60,000 tonnes and seriously damaging another 45,000 tonnes. He was transferred to the southern sector of the Eastern Front in June 1941, where aircraft factories and other industrial facilities were the main targets. He also flew continuous day and night operations against Sevastopol. He received the *Ritterkreuz* on 6 July 1942. He went to Sicily in 1943 with *Fliegerkorps II*, where he continued to fly against Malta and North Africa. He survived the war with the incredible total (for a *Kampfflieger*) of 682 sorties.

Paepke, Heinrich

Staffelkapitän 7/KG 30 (Ju 88) on the first day of the Norwegian campaign, Paepke later flew against the Low Countries and France and took part in raiding Dunkirk, where he was credited with sinking a large freighter and an AA ship. His *Staffel* was also successful, claiming a heavy cruiser, three light cruisers, three destroyers, a minelayer and five transports, plus five enemy fighters. In the Battle of Britain he once returned with 180 bullet holes in his aircraft and his rudder badly damaged. He was awarded the *Ritterkreuz* on 5 September 1940. He transferred to Sicily in early 1941. Appointed *Kommandeur II/KG 77* and returning to the north, he flew against Britain and later Murmansk. In spring 1942 he returned to the Mediterranean and flew against Malta, Cairo, Suez, Tobruk and Alexandria. He was shot down and killed near Malta by a Spitfire on 17 October 1942, being posthumously awarded the *Eichenlaub* on 10 December that year.

Rösch, Rudolf

Rösch was a pilot and *Staffelkapitän 9/KG 51* (Ju 88) on the Eastern Front, where he flew several hundred sorties. He was awarded the *Ritterkreuz* on 26 March 1944 for landing 80km behind the front line to rescue his shot-down *Kommandeur*. He converted to the Me 262 late in 1944 and flew with *1/KG(J) 51*. He was shot down and killed by anti-aircraft fire while making a low-level attack on an airfield near Helmond.

Roewer, Herbert

An NCO pilot with *KG 3* (Do 17/Ju 88) from 10 July 1941, Roewer was shot down while on a weather reconnaissance flight on 18 July that year but escaped by parachute. Then, on 26 January 1942, he returned safely with one engine shot out. When the railway specialist *Staffeln* were formed he joined *9(Eis)/KG 3* and was credited with the destruction of 59 locomotives, fourteen transport and ammunition trains, eighteen tanks, 90 trucks and many aircraft on the ground. He was awarded the *Ritterkreuz* on 3 July 1943 after 305 sorties.

Sattler, Georg

A silversmith and gifted watercolour painter prewar, Sattler joined *LG 1* as a Ju 88 NCO pilot in time to fly against Britain. Then in 1941 he went to the Balkans, where he attacked the Metaxas Line defences. In April he was shot down behind the lines by Greek anti-aircraft fire, but he returned on foot after five days evading capture. He then took part in the destruction of Yugoslav headquarters in Skopje, and later the capture of Crete. Based in the Eastern Mediterranean, he ranged over North Africa as far as Suez. In June 1941 a night fighter set an engine on fire and, forced to ditch off Tobruk, he swam ashore. Shortly after this he was coned by searchlights over Alexandria. Diving steeply to evade, he was hit by anti-aircraft fire which damaged his instruments, but he managed to pull out low over the rooftops and escape. One of the 'Helbig Flyers', Sattler was awarded the *Deutsches Kreuz* in January 1943 and commissioned. This was followed by the *Ritterkreuz* on 5 February 1944. Appointed *Staffelkapitän 1/LG 1*, he failed to return on 30 August. He was posthumously awarded the *Eichenlaub* on 6 December.

Schäfer, Karl

Schäfer was an NCO gunner with *KG 55* (He 111) on the Eastern Front from May 1942, then with the railway specialist *Staffel 14(Eis)/KG 55* from February 1943, with whom he completed 193 sorties. He re-trained as an observer in April 1944. He was awarded the *Ritterkreuz* on 3 April 1945 after 420 sorties in total.

Thurner, Hans

An Austrian, Thurner was by reputation one of the coolest pilots in *KG 55* (He 111). In 1940 he flew in the West and against Britain, both by day and by night. On the night of 14/15 February 1941 RAF radio countermeasures confused the navigation of his crew, leading them to believe that they were over France. He is believed to have touched down at three RAF airfields in quick succession, but each time discovered his mistake while still rolling. Opening the throttles wide, he quickly escaped into the darkness before finally returning safely to base. He was awarded the *Ritterkreuz* on 6 August 1941. Later appointed *Kommandeur I/KG 6*, the Pathfinder outfit, he took part in the *'Steinbock'* raids. He failed to return from a sortie over England on 11 June 1944 and was awarded the *Eichenlaub* posthumously on 20 September following.

Vetter, Martin

Born in New Guinea, Vetter commenced the war as *Staffelkapitän 1/KG 26* (He 111) and in September 1939 claimed a direct hit on the British battlecruiser *Hood* in the Firth of Forth. He was appointed *Kommandeur II/KG 26*, and on 9 April led it against the British Fleet north of Bergen, then near Narvik. On one occasion, near the Shetlands, British fighters put 150 holes in his aircraft and he was lucky to return home. Awarded the *Ritterkreuz* on 16 May 1940, he was appointed *Kommodore KG 40* (He 177/FW 200) in 1943 and flew in the Battle of the Atlantic. From late 1944 he led *III/KG 3*, one of the 'Doodlebug'-carrying units.

Wittmann, Herbert

Wittmann flew with *K/88* (He 111) in the Spanish Civil War and was *Kapitän Stab/KG 53* (He 111) in 1939. In May 1940 took part in attacks on the Maginot Line, and later against Britain. He went to the East in 1941, where he stayed for the next three years, credited with the destruction of 30 supply trains, ten tanks and two gunboats, in addition to damaging rail links and marshalling yards. He also bombed Moscow on seven occasions. He was awarded the *Ritterkreuz* on 23 November 1941 and appointed *Kommandeur II/KG 55*. He flew at least 467 sorties, during which he was forced to bale out many times. He was awarded the *Eichenlaub* on 1 February 1945.

12. STUKA AND SCHLACHT ACES

The definition of *Kampfflieger* in the previous section has been largely determined by the titles of the *Geschwader* involved. For this reason, the Ju 88, which was both a level bomber and a dive bomber, was defined as being under this heading. Ideally we should have split *Stukaflieger* and *Schlachtflieger* into separate headings, but this was not practicable, because from 1943 onward *Stukageschwader* became *Schlachtgeschwader*. In consequence, a majority of dive bomber pilots became attack pilots at this time, and the inevitable duplication would have only led to confusion.

There were of course *Schlachtgeschwader* from the very outbreak of war, but these were few and far between. The waters were muddied at an early stage by the introduction of *Jabos*, or fighter-bombers, which often, but not always, flew close air support missions. As bomb-droppers, these were primarily attack pilots. Therefore the author has had no alternative but to combine the two under a single heading.

Close air support missions were of very short duration—typically minutes rather than hours—because the bases were very close to the front. Consequently, it was not unusual for crews to fly up to eight sorties in a single day, while the maximum appears to have been about seventeen. This was of course in 'surge' operations, unsustainable in the long term not only because of the wear and tear on aircraft and crews but also because of the logistics difficulties involved. Keeping a *Gruppe* supplied with fuel, ordnance and spares was a major operation.

Several Stuka crews flew more than 1,000 sorties. The psychological strain of this was enormous. Taking off to fly against the enemy eight times a day, risking being shot down in flames, or being captured by the unforgiving soldiers of the Red Army was bad enough, but day after day . . . !

With the *Kampfflieger*, other members of the crew—the observer, radio operator and flight mechanic—doubled as gunners. The main function of radio operators in the Ju 87, apart from acting as living protection for the pilot, was to man the guns in rear defence. For this reason, in this section they are referred to as gunners rather than radio operators. Their task was unenviable: facing rearwards, they were unable to see what the crazy driver was doing, and if he was hit and incapacitated they had no option other than to join him in making a hole in the ground.

The *Kampfflieger* section was listed in alphabetical order, but with the *Sturzkampfflieger* one man was so outstanding that he has been given pride of place—the most decorated soldier of the Third Reich, Hans-Ulrich Rudel.

Rudel, Hans-Ulrich

Rudel flew a total of 2,530 operational sorties, nearly all on the Eastern Front. When one considers that only a handful of other Stuka pilots topped the 1,000 mark, this is absolutely astounding. The obvious question is, how? The answer is twofold—opportunity and survival. From the moment that he was appointed a *Gruppenkommandeur*, he made his own opportunities. On his return from a mission with his *Gruppe*, he would frequently have his own and one other aircraft refuelled and rearmed quickly and take off for another attack while the rest of the unit was readied for the next strike. Invariably he led his unit into action, and if his aircraft was damaged, which it often was, he would take whatever was available. This was especially the case during the great retreat of 1943–44, when at the end of an exhausting day hardly any aircraft were serviceable, and often he would end up leading a mere *Kette*, or even a pair—all that remained of his whole *Gruppe*. In December 1942 he flew seventeen sorties in a single day. He flew when he should have been incapacitated by illness or wounds. Finally, he refused to accept orders grounding him, even from the *Führer* himself.

The truly amazing thing is that he survived so many sorties. Three factors entered the equation. The first was determination: he was the son of a priest, and his motto was 'He only is lost who gives himself up for lost!' The second was physical fitness. Rudel was teetotal, a non-smoker and addicted to exercise. Fitness and stamina played a large part in his survival. The third, and

213

arguably the most decisive, was sheer luck. Time and again he ran the gauntlet of intense anti-aircraft fire. He was shot down more than 30 times and his aircraft was badly damaged on many other occasions. Fortunately he usually regained the German lines before coming down, although once he was rescued from behind enemy lines by Helmut Fickel, another *Ritterkreuz* winner. On six occasions he landed behind Russian lines and rescued downed comrades. In all he was wounded six times, twice seriously, and he lost a leg on 9 February 1945. Despite this, he returned to operations at the end of March, even though his stump had not properly healed.

'Uli' Rudel trained as a Ju 87 pilot prewar but was a slow learner. Nor did his habit of milk-drinking endear him to his comrades, who took the opportunity of 'volunteering' him for a reconnaissance course. At the outbreak of war he was an observer with *Fernaufklärungsgruppe 2(F) 121* and flew long-range reconnaissance sorties over Poland. He reverted to Ju 87s in spring 1940, but his inability to learn quickly told against him and he did not reach *I/StG 2* in France until September, by which time Stuka attacks over England had all but ceased. When, in 1941, *StG 2* was deployed to the Balkans and the Mediterranean, he was posted to the training and reserve *Gruppe* in Austria. It was here that the penny finally dropped and he mastered his craft. Soon after Easter he joined *I/StG 2* in Greece, only to find that his old reputation had preceded him. Grounded by a biased *Kommandeur*, he sat out the assault on Crete. Transferred to the Eastern Front, he flew his first operational sorties with *3/StG 2* and was shot down by ground fire, just managing to regain the German lines before force-landing. Under the tutelage of *Staffelkapitän* Ernst-Siegfried Steen, who later earned a posthumous *Ritterkreuz*, he gained experience which was later to stand him in good stead. In August Rudel was transferred to *III/StG 2*, to find that Steen had just been appointed *Kommandeur*. He had a narrow escape shortly after this when he lost control of his Stuka during a thunderstorm, pulling out blind with just inches to spare and returning to base with a birch sapling embedded in either wing.

On 21 September he sank the battleship *Marat* in Kronstadt harbour with a direct hit from a 1,000kg bomb. By Christmas 1941 Rudel had flown 500 sorties, an average of nearly three a day, and was awarded the *Deutsches Kreuz*. The *Ritterkreuz* followed on 6 January 1942, and he was posted to a training unit as an instructor. He arrived in the Crimea in summer 1942 and was soon in action, although a spell in hospital in November with jaundice slowed him up. He flew against Stalingrad, and was appointed *Staffelkapitän 1/StG 2* on 22 November. On 10 February 1943 he flew his 1,000th sortie. He was awarded *Eichenlaub* on 14 April 1943, then went to Rechlin to evaluate experimental anti-tank aircraft. He returned to the Crimea with the Ju 87G but on 10 May sustained a direct hit from anti-aircraft fire on his first sortie. He took part in the Battles of Kursk and Orel and on 5 July knocked out twelve tanks with the cannon-armed Stuka. He was appointed *Kommandeur III/SG 2* on 17 July, succeeding Walther Krauss, who had been killed by bombs from night nuisance raiders, and was awarded the *Schwerten* 25 November.

On 20 March 1944 Rudel landed behind the Soviet lines to pick up a downed Stuka crew, but his aircraft bogged down in mud. The four men headed for German lines on foot but, pursued by Soviet troops, had no option but to swim the wide and icy Dniester river. Tragedy ensued. *Ritterkreuz* holder Erwin Hentschel, who had flown as Rudel's gunner from October 1941 and had amassed more than 1,400 sorties, drowned. The three survivors continued, but encountered more Soviet troops. In the gathering dusk, Rudel made a run for it. Hit in the shoulder by a bullet, he managed to evade capture and, after walking barefoot all night, returned to safety and was back in the air the very next day. He was awarded *Brilliante* on 29 March—the tenth soldier so honoured.

That summer he completed 2,000 sorties, and converted on to the FW 190, although he also continued to fly the Ju 87G. He was appointed *Kommodore SG 2* on 1 August. He was awarded the *Golden Eichenlaub*, a unique decoration, on 1 January 1945. As previously stated, he was shot down and lost a leg on 9 February 1945, but he returned to the front at the end of March and flew his 2,530th sortie on the last day of the war. In addition to *Marat*, he was credited with sinking a cruiser, a destroyer and more than 70 landing craft; with the destruction of four armoured trains, more than 150 artillery and anti-aircraft guns and more than 800 road vehicles; and with destroying many bridges and rail links. His main claim to fame is, however, as a tank-buster, with 519 claimed destroyed. Postwar he settled in Argentina and is reputed to have acted as a consultant for Fairchild Republic in the 1960s in the design of the A-10A Warthog close air support and anti-tank aircraft, although enquiries have failed to turn up any record of his involvement or input.

Bellof, Ludwig

An NCO pilot with *1/NSGr 3* (Go 145 and Ar 66), Bellof flew these tiny biplanes on constant night harassment raids on the Eastern Front between 1943 and 1945, apparently with great success. He was awarded the *Ritterkreuz* on 28 January 1945.

Boerst, Alwin

A pilot with *I/StG 2* (Ju 87) at the outbreak of war, Boerst flew 39 sorties against Poland. In 1940 he took part in the assault on Eben Emael and flew 113 sorties in the campaign in the West, then flew in the Battle of Britain. He was transferred to the Balkans in 1941, where he flew 22 sorties over Greece, including Larissa and Piraeus harbour, then against Crete, where he sank a destroyer and badly damaged another.

He was appointed *Staffelkapitän 3/StG 2* in time for the move to the Eastern Front and was awarded the *Ritterkreuz* on 5 October 1941. He attacked Volkhov, Demyansk and Cholm, and supported the advance to Stalingrad through Voronezh and Rostov. He was awarded the *Eichenlaub* on 28 November 1942 after 624 sorties. In 1943 he took part in the Kursk and Orel battles and was shot down in October by anti-aircraft fire and hospitalised in Bucharest. He then succeeded Bruno Dilley as *Kommandeur I/SG 2*. Having flown his 1,000th sortie on 29 January 1944, he was shot down and killed by ground fire over Romania on 30 March 1944 while flying the Ju 87G. He was awarded *Schwerten* posthumously on 6 April. With him died his regular gunner, NCO Ernst Filius, who was awarded a posthumous *Ritterkreuz* on 19 May after more than 900 sorties.

Dilley, Bruno

Pilot and *Staffelkapitän 3/StG 1* (Ju 87), Dilley flew the first sortie of the war at 0445 hours on 1 September 1939 to launch the invasion of Poland. His next sortie was against the radio station in Warsaw. In all, he flew 24 sorties against Poland before leading his *Staffel* against Norway in April 1940, raiding Oslo,

Namsos and Narvik. On 1 May his aircraft was badly damaged by ground fire and barely managed to make base. On 14 June he was deployed to France for the assault on Britain. On 13 August 1940, *Adler Tag*, his Ju 87 sustained 55 hits from British fighters but returned safely. In the autumn, the *Gruppe* deployed to the Mediterranean.

On 16 January 1941 Dilley led the first raid on Malta, then from 16 March attacked targets in Yugoslavia, Greece and Crete. On 7 April he force-landed in the Yugoslavian mountains but regained friendly lines. In May he was transferred to North Africa, where he supported Rommel's advance into Libya. From January 1942 he flew as an instructor, then in February went to the Eastern Front, where in the course of his first sortie, a low-level attack, he suffered a direct hit from anti-aircraft fire; force-landing behind enemy lines, his Ju 87 turned over, knocking Dilley unconscious. His gunner dragged him clear, and after three days and nights the pair regained German lines at Demyansk.

Dilley was awarded the *Ritterkreuz* on 10 June 1942 and was appointed *Kommandeur I/StG 2*. He was shot down for the third time in the winter of 1942/43. He was awarded the *Eichenlaub* on 8 January 1943 after more than 600 sorties. He was shot down in flames by anti-aircraft fire near Kersch on 23 April 1943, but he and his gunner baled out into no man's land. He flew his final sortie on 16 October 1943, then commanded the flight school at Metz. He survived the war.

Enneccerus, Walter

Pilot and *Staffelkapitän* with the Condor Legion in Spain (He 51), Walter Enneccerus flew against Poland in 1939 as *Staffelkapitän* with *II/StG 2*. He was appointed *Kommandeur II/StG 2* for the campaign in the West and attacked road convoys, troop concentrations, artillery batteries, fortified areas (including the Maginot Line) and rail targets, and shipping at Dunkirk, Le Havre and La Rochelle. He flew in the Battle of Britain and was awarded the *Ritterkreuz* on 21 July 1940. In December 1940 he went to Sicily, leading the attack on the aircraft carrier *Illustrious* in January as well as sinking the cruiser *Southampton*. He later supported Rommel's advance in the desert. He flew in the Balkans and against Crete, then on 26 May 1941 led the attack on the aircraft carrier *Formidable*. On 13 October 1942 he was appointed *Kommodore StG 77* on the Eastern Front but was deprived of his command on 1 March 1943 for refusing to order his pilots to carry out what he regarded as a suicidal mission. He survived the war as a *Generalmajor*.

Fischer, Siegfried

Fischer was an NCO pilot with *6/StG 1* (Ju 87) who made his operational début against Malta in 1941. Then he went to the Eastern Front, first in the 5th then the 6th *Staffel*, and finally in *9/SG 1*. His narrow escapes were legendary. On 8 July 1941 he jumped from his blazing Ju 87 into marshland 40km behind the front, and although his face and hands were badly burned he returned to friendly territory. In all, he force-landed 25 times, twice behind Soviet lines, and was wounded three times. He was awarded the *Deutsches Kreuz* on 17 October 1943, converted to the FW 190 in 1944 and was awarded the *Ritter-kreuz* on 28 February 1945. On his 713rd sortie a direct hit from anti-aircraft fire damaged his controls near Frankfurt-an-der-Oder and he was injured in the ensuing crash landing. He was taken prisoner by the Russians in his hospital bed but he survived the war.

Haker, Theodor 'Bubi'

Haker was a pilot who joined *7/StG 77* (Ju 87) in France in autumn 1940. He made his combat début in Yugoslavia on 6 April 1941, then went to the Eastern Front. He was appointed *Staffelführer 3/StG 77* in summer 1942, then *Staffelkapitän 6/StG 77* in 1943. He was awarded the *Ritterkreuz* on 29 February 1944. After more than 900 sorties he was shot down in flames by American Mustangs on 25 July; he survived but was blinded. Captured by partisans, he was shot.

Henze, Karl

A pilot with *2/StG 77* (Ju 87), Henze flew against Poland, France and Britain. On 18 August 1940 he was very lucky to return: attacked by fighters, his hydraulics were damaged, his dive brakes would not retract and a spent bullet had lodged against his skull. At one point his wheels touched the sea, but fortunately his Stuka bounced back into the air. He crawled back to France at low speed and wave-top height, to crash-land. He then went to the Balkans and Crete, and finally to the Eastern Front in June 1941. He was awarded the *Deutsches Kreuz* in January 1942, was appointed *Staffelkapitän 1/StG 77* and was awarded the *Ritterkreuz* on 15 July 1942. *Kommandeur I/SG 2* from 2 March 1943 to 15 November 1944, he was awarded the *Eichenlaub* on 20 May 1944. He survived 1,098 sorties.

Hozzel, Paul-Werner

Commencing the war as *Kommandeur I/StG 1* (Ju 87) against Poland, Hozzel took an active part in the Norwegian campaign, where his *Gruppe* was credited with sinking 60,000 tonnes of shipping. He was awarded the *Ritterkreuz* on 8 May 1940, the first *Stukaflieger* so honoured. He flew in the Battle of Britain, then went to the Mediterranean, where his unit took part in the devastating attack on the aircraft carrier *Illustrious*. He flew against Greece and Crete, then was transferred to the Eastern Front. He was appointed *Kommodore StG 2* on 16 October 1941. He supported the advance to Stalingrad in 1942, then in February 1943 was given command of elements of two other Stuka units to form a battle group against a massive Soviet breakthrough. Exhausted, he relinquished command on 1 March 1943 and was succeeded by Ernst Kupfer. He was awarded the *Eichenlaub* on 14 April. Hozzel survived the war.

Jaekel, Egbert

A pilot with *2/StG 2* (Ju 87) from the outbreak of war, Jaekel flew in the Mediterranean and against Crete, where he contributed to sinking a heavy cruiser and a destroyer and damaged another cruiser and an AA ship. Then he went to the Eastern Front, where he was appointed *Staffelkapitän 2/StG 2*. He was awarded the *Ritterkreuz* on 14 May 1942. A comedian by inclination, he maintained that his Stuka was particularly fast, and he developed a habit of attacking Russian fighters on sight. On his 983rd sortie, on 17 July 1943, he did this once too often and was shot down and killed by an La-5.

Kupfer, *Dr* Ernst

An elderly but dynamic personality, Kupfer joined *7/StG 2* in France on 7 September 1940 and was appointed *Staffelkapitän* on 1 October. His operational début came in the Balkans in 1941, and he sank a British cruiser off Crete with a direct hit, for which he was awarded the *Deutsches Kreuz*. Then he moved to the Eastern Front, where he sank a Soviet cruiser with a direct hit in the teeth of almost impenetrable anti-aircraft fire, a near miss by which caused heavy damage. The propeller blades were half shot away, and the Ju 87 was barely controllable. Having made a smooth landing, he led five aircraft back to Kronstadt, where he damaged the Soviet battleship *Oktober Revolution* with a direct hit. Then, at the end of September, again over Kronstadt, he took a hit in his engine from anti-aircraft fire. He managed to stretch his glide to safety but was injured in the crash-landing and hospitalised. He was awarded the *Ritterkreuz* on 23 November 1941.

Appointed *Kommandeur II/StG 2* on 1 April 1942, he took part in the battle for Stalingrad and was awarded the *Eichenlaub* on 8 January 1943. He was appointed *Kommodore StG 2* on 1 March 1943 and participated in the actions at Kursk and Orel that summer. After 636 sorties he was appointed *General der Schlachtflieger*. He was killed in a crash in an He 111 north of Salonika in appalling weather on 6 November. *Schwerten* were awarded posthumously on 11 April 1944.

Lang, Friedrich (Fritz)

Lang was a pilot with *I/StG 2* (Ju 87) at the outbreak of war and flew against Poland. In the West, he supported the attack on Eben Emael on 10 May 1940, then the breakthrough at Sedan. He operated against Arras and a French armoured force near St Quentin and later bombed Calais and Dunkirk, where he encountered British fighters. Then, on 8 June, in a wild mêlée with French fighters south-west of Soissons, he was hit in the back. Although he returned safely to base, the wound was severe enough for him to be hospitalised until the end of August and so he missed the assault on Britain. He went to the Balkans in early 1941 and raided Piraeus harbour and airfield near Athens. Then he flew against Crete, where he scored hits on two British destroyers.

Lang was transferred to the Eastern Front in June 1941, at first to the northern sector against Leningrad and Kronstadt then to the central sector against Smolensk. He was appointed *Staffelkapitän 1/StG 2* on 7 October and awarded the *Ritterkreuz* on 23 November. After a brief rest, his *Gruppe* returned to the front, supporting the advance through Voronezh and the Don basin. By the end of October 1942 they were outside Stalingrad, and Lang operated over the Kuban bridgehead. He was awarded the *Eichenlaub* on 30 November. He was appointed *Kommandeur III/StG 1* on 1 April 1943, and led this unit in the battles of Kursk and Orel and for the next year over the central sector of the Eastern Front while converting to the FW 190. Then came the great retreat.

Lang commanded a training school from the end of April 1944, after 1,007 sorties. He was awarded the *Schwerten* on 4 July. He was recalled to command *SG 2* when Rudel was wounded on 9 February 1945 but he flew only one more sortie, on the 13th, when he overshot while landing his FW 190. He survived the war, and in 1,008 sorties he never once was shot down, baled out or force-landed—a truly remarkable record.

Mahlke, Helmut

Helmut Mahlke was a pilot and *Staffelkapitän 2/Trägergruppe 186(T)* (Ju 87T), the carrier unit for the *Graf Zeppelin*, at the outbreak of war, and flew against France. He was appointed *Kommandeur* when this unit was expanded to a full *Gruppe* on 9 July 1940 and redesignated *III/StG 1*. He flew in the Battle of Britain, but when the Stukas were withdrawn after the débâcle on 18 August this unit remained in northern France and in early November Mahlke carried out shipping attacks in the Thames estuary, usually with a huge fighter escort. Losses were, however, heavy, and *III/StG 1* was soon withdrawn. He was transferred to Sicily on 23 February 1941 for attacks on Malta. Three days later a direct hit by anti-aircraft fire tore a huge hole in one wing. As he limped unsteadily away he was attacked by a Hurricane, but this was beaten off by Mahlke's gunner. Then, on 21 May, the *Gruppe* was transferred to Greece and made heavy attacks on Crete.

Mahlke was transferred to the central sector of the Eastern Front in June but in less than three weeks he was shot down in flames behind enemy lines three times. In each case he was quickly recovered by the advancing German Army, but while on the first two occasions he was unhurt, on the third he was gravely injured. It was his 145th and last sortie. He was awarded the *Ritterkreuz* on 16 July 1941 and the Italian Silver Medal for Bravery on 20 November. He survived the war in a succession of staff postings.

Malapert, *Freiherr* Robert-Georg von

Pilot and *Staffelkapitän* with *II/StG 1* (Ju 87) at the outbreak of war, Malapert flew against Poland and France. In the attack on Britain he was credited with the destruction of 20,000 tonnes of shipping. In June 1941 he went to the central sector of the Eastern Front; he was awarded the *Deutsches Kreuz* in December and the *Ritterkreuz* on 6 January 1942. Soon after this he was appointed *Kommandeur II/StG 1*. He supported the advance on Moscow, then, in a low-level attack on 21 May (his 510th sortie), he sustained a direct hit by anti-aircraft fire and, his coolant system damaged, he was forced down in no man's land. While trying to regain the German lines he and his gunner were shot by Soviet snipers. Malapert was awarded the *Eichenlaub* posthumously on 8 June 1942.

Nordmann, Theodor

A pilot with *2/Trägergruppe 186(T)* (Ju 87T) at the outbreak of war, Nordmann flew 60 sorties over France. His unit was redesignated *7/StG 1* on 9 July 1940 but he flew only six sorties in the Battle of Britain. He went to Sicily early in 1941, where he twice had 'soldier's luck'. Over Malta on 26 February he was hit in the oxygen supply by anti-aircraft fire, which ripped his fuselage open. Then, on a transfer flight to North Africa, engine failure forced him to ditch in the sea; after two days in his dinghy he was rescued by an Italian flying boat. In May he flew in the assault on Crete, then in June went to the Eastern Front. He was awarded the *Ritterkreuz* on 17 September.

Nordmann was appointed *Staffelkapitän 8/StG 1* at the end of the 1941. He was awarded the *Eichenlaub* on 16 March 1943 and was appointed *Kommandeur III/SG 1* in 1944, which converted to the FW 190 in May; his regular gunner had been Gerhard Rothe, who was awarded the *Ritterkreuz* on 12 November 1943. Nordmann then transferred to the northern sector of the Eastern Front and in August reached the grand total of 1,111 sorties. Awarded the *Schwerten* on 17 September 1944, he was killed in a mid-air collision near Insterburg on 19 January 1945.

Panse, Werner

A pilot with *9/StG 1* (Ju 87), Panse joined this unit on the Channel coast in February 1941 and flew 21 night sorties against shipping in the Thames Estuary. He then went to Sicily for the assault on Malta. Transferred to the Eastern Front in February 1942, he attacked bridges over the Neva, armoured trains and rolling stock. Seriously wounded by anti-aircraft fire, he managed to bring his stricken aircraft back to the German lines, where he crashed. He went to the central sector in 1943, where he took part in the battles of Kursk and Orel and was involved in mopping-up operations after a Soviet armoured break-through had been halted. He was appointed *Staffelkapitän 9/SG 1* in March 1944 and converted to the FW 190. He was awarded the *Ritterkreuz* on 4 May. On 4 August he set off on his 836th sortie, a low-level attack against the Baranov bridgehead. A direct anti-aircraft hit set the fuel tank beneath his seat on fire. Barely conscious, he crash-landed his FW 190 in the German lines more or less by instinct but never flew operationally again. He survived the war.

Plewig, Waldemar

Plewig was a pilot and *Staffelkapitän 8/StG 2* against Poland. He was ap-pointed *Kommandeur II/StG 77* on 15 May 1940 to replace *Graf* Clemens von Schönborn-Wiesentheid, who had been elevated to *Kommodore* follow-ing the death in action of Günter Schwartzkopff the previous day. He sup-ported the assault on Eben Emael and the Maas river crossing near Antwerp and raided the Maginot Line, Calais and Dunkirk. He then took part in convoy raids in the Channel. On 8 August he was shot down off the Isle of Wight by Hurricanes while attacking convoy 'Peewit'. Seriously wounded, he was taken prisoner. He was awarded the *Ritterkreuz* on 14 December.

Pölz, Hubert

An Austrian pilot who joined *6/StG 2* (Ju 87) at the front in January 1941, Pölz flew his first sortie in February against Malta, then moved to North Af-rica to support Rommel. On 24 June he sank the destroyer *Auckland* north of Tobruk with a direct hit but his Stuka was set on fire. He force-landed near Gambut but his gunner was killed. Returned to Sicily, he flew intensively against Malta between December 1941 and May 1942 and was appointed *Staffelkapitän* on 1 March. Then he went to *II/StG 3* in Tunisia. Awarded the *Deutsches Kreuz* on 2 October 1942, he was shot down and wounded by fighters on 3 April 1943 over El Guttar, his gunner being killed. Months in hospital followed, but Pölz was then posted to his original unit, *II/SG 2*, in the East, on 18 July. He took part in many major actions—Kursk, Orel, Kharkov, Bryansk, Poltava, Dniepetrovsk and the Kuban. He was appointed *Staffelkapitän 7/SG 2* on 28 September and awarded the *Ritterkreuz* on 5 February 1944. He was then transferred to the northern sector, converting to the FW 190 in July. He was awarded the *Eichenlaub* on 25 November and was subsequently appointed *Kommandeur I/SG 151* (FW 190). He survived a total of 1,055 sorties, during which he was shot down four times and wounded thrice.

Schenck, Wolfgang

Schenck was a South African-born pilot who commenced the war with *I/ZG 1* (Bf 110), with which he flew against Poland and France. He transferred to *I/ EprGr 210* (Bf 110) on its formation and flew *Jabo* sorties against England. He was appointed *Staffelkapitän* in September 1940. His *Gruppe* was re-designated *I/SKG 210* in April 1941 and Schenck flew trials of the Bf 210, then went to the Eastern Front for low-level attacks. He was awarded the *Ritterkreuz* on 14 August.

He was appointed *Kommandeur* on 1 January 1942 but shortly after this the unit was redesignated *I/ZG 1*. He was awarded the *Eichenlaub* on 30 October. He was with *II/SG 2* (FW 190 and Hs 129) in the Mediterranean and North Africa between 3 January and 10 October 1943, then moved to a staff job. He supervised bombing trials with the Me 262 from June 1944, and was then posted to reorganise *KG(J) 51* on 1 November, although he is believed not to have flown the Me 262 operationally. Schenck survived the war.

Sigel, Walter

As pilot and *Kommandeur I/StG 76* (Ju 87) on 15 August 1939, Sigel had an incredible escape in the training disaster at Neuhammer when thirteen Stukas crashed (see Chapter 2). He flew against Poland on the first day of the war and fought in the West in 1940, attacking troop concentrations in southern Belgium, attacking the Maginot Line south of Sedan and supporting the advancing army. He attacked shipping at Calais and Dunkirk. His unit was then redesignated *I/StG 3*. Awarded the *Ritterkreuz* 21 July 1940, Sigel led his

Gruppe in the last great Stuka attack on England on 18 August 1940. He was transferred to the Mediterranean and North Africa in 1941 and was appointed *Kommodore StG 3*. He took part in the assault on the Free French stronghold of Bir Hacheim in July 1942 and was awarded the *Eichenlaub* on 2 September. He relinquished his command on 1 April 1943 and was appointed to the staff in Norway. He was killed on 8 May 1944 when his Storch crashed in Trondheim Fjord.

Tonne, Günther

Tonne was initially a Bf 110 pilot with *II/ZG 1* who flew against France and England; he was credited with 20 victories. His unit was redesignated *III/ZG 76*, then, in early 1941, *II/SKG 210*. He went to the central sector of the Eastern Front for the invasion of the Soviet Union in June, making low-level attacks. He was appointed *Staffelkapitän*, and his *Staffel* was credited with the destruction of 138 Soviet aircraft on the ground. He was awarded the *Ritterkreuz* on 5 October. The *Gruppe* was then redesignated *II/ZG 1*, with Tonne as *Kommandeur*.

In December 1942 Tonne was appointed *Kommodore SKG 10* (FW 190), at first in the West, where casualties were heavy, then later in the Mediterranean theatre for night attacks on the Allied invasion fleet off Sicily. After more than 300 sorties Tonne died in a crash at Reggio on 15 August 1943 when he suffered an engine failure on take-off. He was awarded the *Eichenlaub* posthumously on 29 October.

Weiss, Otto

Pilot and *Staffelkapitän 4(Schlacht)/LG 2* (Hs 123) at the outbreak of war, Weiss flew against Poland and was appointed *Kommandeur II(Schlacht)/LG 2* on 9 September 1939 when the previous incumbent failed to return. In the West from May 1940, he supported the assault on Eben Emael and the Maas river crossing and helped to halt a French armoured attack near Cambrai and a British one near Arras. Then he turned south to support the Army. He was awarded the *Ritterkreuz* on 18 May, and his unit re-equipped with Bf 109 *Jabo*s in September to raid England. Reverting to the old biplanes, his unit moved to the Balkans in 1941, then to the East, supporting the advance in the central and northern sectors. He was awarded the *Eichenlaub* on 31 December. Weiss was appointed *Kommodore LG 2* in January 1942 but relinquished command on 18 June. He then moved to various staff and evaluation jobs. He survived the war.

APPENDIX: MAIN LUFTWAFFE BOMBER AND ATTACK AIRCRAFT

Arado Ar 234 Blitz

The world's first jet bomber, the Ar 234 was a twin-engined single-seater. Originating in a specification for a high-speed reconnaissance aircraft, it was first flown on 15 June 1943. Given the limitations of the early jet engines, every effort was made to save weight, with the result that it took off from a jettisonable trolley and landed on an extending skid. The operational limitations of this were soon apparent, notably the immobility after landing, and later models were fitted with wheels. The pressurised cabin was fitted with an ejection seat. Use of the *Lotfe* tachometric bomb sight is described in Chapter 10.

Initial operational use commenced on 20 July 1944, in the reconnaissance role. The first bomber unit to become operational was *Stab/KG 76*, commanded by Robert Kowaleski, closely followed by *6/KG 76*. *I* and *III/KG 76* were next, in February 1945. However, although its overwhelming speed made it almost immune from interception at high altitude, it achieved little, mainly due to the difficulties of accurate bomb aiming, which were compounded by sheer speed.

Maximum speed 742kph; service ceiling 10,000m; maximum range 1,215km; typical bomb load 2,000kg carried externally, which significantly reduced performance.

Dornier Do 17Z

Originating in a specification for a high-speed mail plane, the twin-engined Do 17 first flew in 1934. The potential for a fast bomber was evident, and Dornier 17Es and Fs received their baptism of fire in the Spanish Civil War. The most important variant was the Do 17Z. This carried a four-man crew and differed from previous variants in having a 'beetle eye' glazed nose. With its radial engines less vulnerable to battle damage than water-cooled types, its excellent view from the cockpit and its low wing loading, which made it extremely manoeuvrable, it was well suited both to low-level operations and to formation flying. Its greatest failing was its small bomb load—a mere 1,000kg. For this reason it was already being phased out in the summer of 1940 and by November 1942 had vanished from the scene.

Maximum speed 345kph; maximum cruising speed 300kph; service ceiling 8,200m; tactical range 330km.

Dornier Do 217

Rather larger than the Do 17, from which it was derived, the Do 217 first flew in August 1938. The first bomber variant was the Do 217E, which entered service with *II/KG 40* in March 1941 in the anti-shipping role. These aircraft were later modified to carry two Hs 293 missiles. Next was *KG 2*, which played a large part in the Baedeker raids. The Do 217K had a completely redesigned cabin, while the K-2 was equipped to carry two Fritz X missiles.

The type took a leading role in Operation *'Steinbock'* but shortly afterwards began to be phased out, although a handful soldiered on until the end of the war.

Maximum speed 516kph; maximum cruising speed 416kph; service ceiling 9,000m; range 2,300km; typical war load 2,500kg, or one LT 950 torpedo and two mines, or two Hs 293 or Fritz X guided missiles carried externally.

Focke-Wulf FW 190

A single-engined, single-seat fighter, the robust FW 190 was quickly adopted for the *Schlacht* mission, replacing the Ju 87 which was proving far too vulnerable to ground fire to be viable. In the West in 1942 *10(Jabo)/JG 2* and *10(Jabo)/JG 26* received the FW 190A-3 fighter bomber, which could carry a single 500kg bomb under the fuselage. These later became *14* and *15/SKG 10*. Many other *Jabo* units followed, and gradually the bomb load crept up to 1,750kg. Next came specialised *Jabo* variants with added armour protection, the FW 190F and G. The latter could carry a single 1,800kg bomb beneath the fuselage, whilst the F variant could take eight 50kg bombs on underwing racks.

Maximum speed 654kph; cruising speed 480kph; service ceiling 11,400m; range 805km.

Focke-Wulf FW 200 Condor

Designed as an airliner, this four-engined aircraft first flew on 27 July 1937. Structurally strengthened for military use, and with defensive armament added, it had but two advantages, range and endurance, to fit it for the anti-shipping mission. Flying with *KG 40*, it became the scourge of the Atlantic from 1940. Offensively it carried four 250kg bombs on underwing racks, although the carriage of two 1,000kg mines made it too unwieldy to be viable. A few aircraft were modified to carry a pair of Hs 293 missiles, but this marriage was not a success. On occasion, Condors encountered RAF four-engined aircraft, Liberators and Sunderlands, and a battle of the heavyweights ensued, usually to the detriment of the Condor. It was produced only in small numbers, and structural weakness was a major failing.

Maximum speed 360kph; cruising speed 335kph; service ceiling 6,000m; range 3,560km; endurance up to 17 hours.

Heinkel He 111

The He 111 was a close contemporary of the Do 17, its first flight taking place on 24 February 1935. Twin-engined, and with a crew of five or six, it made its combat début in the Spanish Civil War. Its original stepped cabin was re-designed with a fully-glazed nose which, oddly enough, was asymmetric in shape, and this featured on all later models, the 111P and 111H, the latter the most common variant in the war. This had the disadvantage of causing annoying reflections at night, or when the sun was astern. To overcome this, particularly for landing, the pilot's seat could be raised to the point where his head, shielded by a small retractable screen, projected through a hatch in the roof. To enable him to see his instruments in this position, the panel was mounted high against the cabin roof. This gave the strange effect that, when in normal flight with his seat lowered, he looked up rather than down at his instruments. This apart, the He 111 handled well, and in fact had a rather lower wing loading than the Bristol Beaufighter, its regular opponent in the latter part of the Blitz.

The internal weapons bay carried the bombs nose-up, a feature which not only restricted the size of the bombs that could be carried but meant that, when released, they toppled into a nose-down position. This was hazardous, as the bombs could collide, and did nothing to aid accuracy. The standard load was eight 250kg bombs. In some later H models, the internal bay was replaced by fuel tanks and external provision was made for the carriage of weapons up to 2,500kg. Other variants could carry the Hs 293 missile, two torpedoes or the 'Doodlebug'. From 1944 most Heinkel bomber units were disbanded and those aircraft remaining were used as transports.

Maximum speed 420kph; cruising speed 381kph; service ceiling 7,500m; range 1,500km.

Heinkel He 177 Greif

In the Second World War, the greatest deficiency in the *Luftwaffe* was the lack of a true strategic bomber. The He 177 was the nearest the service ever got to it, although compared to contemporary British and American heavy bombers it was far short of ideal. The 1938 specification stated a warload of 2,000kg over a radius of 1,600km at a speed of 500kph. This aircraft duly emerged as the He 177, which made its first flight on 19 November 1939, piloted by Carl Francke, the man who 'sank' the *Ark Royal*.

In an attempt to improve performance by minimising drag, it was powered by two pairs of coupled engines, which gave only half the frontal area of a conventional four-engined bomber, for the same power. In concept this was not too far removed from the ill-fated British Avro Manchester, which used two monster 24-cylinder Rolls Royce Vultures which were effectively two 12-cylinder engines mounted above and below a common crankshaft—and with much the same results: unreliability, overheating, and in-flight fires. But whereas the Manchester was quickly abandoned in favour of the more conventional Lancaster, the *Luftwaffe* persevered. This was a major error. Losses due to engine fires were unsustainable, and while a handful of He 177s entered service, notably with *I/KG 40* from July 1942, delays mounted while solutions to the problems were sought. Eventually they were found, but by then it was far too late.

The He 177 was used to carry up to three Hs 293 missiles in the antishipping role; it was also used during *'Steinbock'* and on the Eastern Front, but never on true strategic missions. One aircraft was modified to carry a nuclear weapon, ready for when and if this should be developed. A German engineer is said to have remarked: 'If we succeed in this, we shall rule the world!'

Maximum speed 488kph; cruising speed 415kph; service ceiling 8,000m; range 5,000km plus.

Henschel Hs 123

The *Luftwaffe's* last operational biplane, the *'Ein-Zwei-Drei'* first flew in the spring of 1935. It was originally designed as a dive bomber, but its operational importance far exceeded its numbers. In the Spanish Civil War it was used for close air support rather than for its original function. With its radial engine overspeeding it made a shattering noise which demoralised troops under attack, making it far more effective than the physical damage it caused. It served until mid-1944.

Maximum speed 341kph; cruising speed 317kph; service ceiling irrelevant; range 860km; typical bomb load 92 SD 2 anti-personnel bombs.

Henschel Hs 129B

The Hs 129, first flown in spring 1939, was designed as an assault aircraft, with the accent on survivability. It was a twin-engined single-seater with the fuselage cross section minimised, with the result that the cockpit was tiny and cramped while the view 'out of the window' was poor to the front and sides—a characteristic not helped by a 75mm thick bullet-proof windshield—and non-existent to the rear. The engines and cockpit were armoured, at the cost of a heavy weight penalty. Armament was typically a single 30mm MK 101 cannon, and a variety of small bombs.

Not popular with its pilots, the Hs 129 was underpowered, unhandy and unreliable, the last the fault of the engines. First used in North Africa, it was not a success. Meanwhile hordes of Soviet tanks were causing problems on the Eastern Front, and an effective anti-tank aircraft was desperately needed to counter them. The Hs 129B was up-gunned with the 37mm BK 3.7 in time to take part in the Battle of Kursk. Still later, the 75mm Pak 40L gun was fitted, carried in a fairing beneath the fuselage. While this could penetrate the armour of many Soviet tank types, it carried a mere twelve rounds, the rate of fire was one shell every 1½ seconds and the formidable recoil gave the pilot a nasty jolt every time it was fired. Only a handful entered service, from late 1944. But, however big the gun, performance was still inadequate, manoeuvrability was lacking, reliability was poor, and losses of up to 20 per cent were frequent.

Maximum speed 355kph; service ceiling irrelevant; range 560km.

Junkers Ju 87D Stuka

By far the most effective dive bomber of the early years of the war, the Ju 87 first flew in spring 1935. A single-engined two-seater, its distinguishing features were the cranked wing and fixed, 'trousered' main gear. These, allied to its generally sinister, angular appearance, marked it as a bird of ill omen to those on the receiving end. It made its combat début in the Spanish Civil War from December 1937, flown by the *'Jolanthe'* (a cartoon pig) *Kette*.

Successful against Poland, and later in the West, Stukas suffered heavy losses to British fighters in the summer of 1940 and for all practical purposes were withdrawn after 18 August. They achieved further successes in the Balkans and the Mediterranean in 1941, and to a lesser degree in the Western Desert until 1942. They spearheaded the invasion of the Soviet Union in 1941–42.

The most widely used variant was the Ju 87D, which began to replace the B model from the end of 1941. A more powerful engine enabled it to carry an 1,800kg bomb beneath the fuselage and two 500kg bombs beneath the wings—a great advance on the 1,000kg bomb load of the Ju 87B. The final important variant was the Ju 87G, a dedicated tank-buster which carried two 37mm Flak 18 cannon underwing. These reduced both performance and manoeuvrability and called for an expert and experienced pilot. Only one *Gruppe* and four *Staffeln* were so equipped. As Soviet anti-aircraft fire improved, so Stuka losses rose to the point where the type was no longer viable, and production ceased in September 1944.

Maximum speed 400kph; cruising speed 300kph; range typically 600km.

Junkers Ju 88A

Designed as a high-speed bomber capable of making steep diving attacks, the Ju 88 was arguably the most versatile aircraft on the *Luftwaffe*'s inventory. First flown on 21 December 1936, it was twin-engined, with a crew of four or five. The normal warload of the A variant consisted of ten 50kg bombs internally and either four 250kg or two 500kg bombs externally on underwing racks. Its combat début came in September 1939, against the British Fleet in the Firth of Forth.

The Ju 88 was a 'hot ship' and was considered tricky to handle, especially with one engine out. In fact bomber ace Werner Baumbach twice crashed in poor weather though on both occasions escaped unhurt. Nor was it very easy to fly a tight formation, the projecting engine nacelles seriously interfering with visibility. Later models carried heavier loads, typically two 1,000kg bombs or mines and two 500kg bombs.

The Ju 88 flew extensively against Britain in 1940–41, against Malta and in the Mediterranean, against the Arctic convoys and off Norway as a torpedo bomber, and on the Eastern Front. In 1944 it was used in Operation *'Steinbock'*, but by the end of that year it was being phased out, mainly because of a shortage of fuel. Its final role was as a *Mistel* pilotless bomber.

Maximum speed 470kph; cruising speed 370kph; service ceiling 8,200m, range 1,790km.

Junkers Ju 188A

Intended to replace both the Ju 88 and the He 111, the Ju 188 was a development of the former aircraft, with a greater wingspan, a completely redesigned cabin and a larger, remodelled empennage to correct instability problems. The typical warload consisted of two torpedoes or up to 3,000kg of bombs. The type's operational début came over England on 18 August 1943, and in the following year it took part in Operation *'Steinbock'*. Production ended early in 1944, and the Ju 188 disappeared from service later that year.

Maximum speed 500kph; cruising speed 375kph; service ceiling 9,300m; range 1,950km.

Messerschmitt Bf 110D

In the 1930s a fashion arose for long-range strategic fighters and bomber escorts, which had of necessity to be twin-engined. There was the American P-38 Lightning, the Dutch Fokker G-1 and the German Bf 110—Goering's 'Ironsides'. No one had apparently considered what would happen when these large and unmanoeuvrable fighters encountered agile single-engined defenders, as they inevitably did. That is neither here nor there. What is important is that the Bf 110D was pressed into service as a *Jabo*, carrying two 500kg bombs on racks beneath the fuselage.

The first unit was *EprGr 210*, established on 6 July 1940, its number refer-
ring to the Bf 210, the type which it was intended to clear for service. Against
England casualties were heavy, and the final attack came on 27 September. In
fact the Bf 210 was a disaster, and saw little service, forcing the Bf 110 to
soldier on as a *Jabo*. It was widely used on the Eastern Front, and the Bf 110G
could carry four 50kg bombs as well as the two 500kg weapons, but by 1944
it was obsolescent.

Maximum speed 550kph; service ceiling 8,000m; range 775km.

Messerschmitt Me 262A *Sturmvogel*

The Me 262 was the world's first operational jet aircraft, and much has been
made of Hitler's decision to use this as a *Jabo* rather than a fighter. However,
the reasons for this are stated in Chapter 10. Typical air-to-ground weapons
were either a single 1,000kg or two 500kg bombs. These were carried externally, which severely limited the otherwise sparkling performance of this aircraft. The main problem was of course accurate aiming at very high speeds,
and the best results were often obtained by scattering cluster bombs at diffuse
targets such as airfields.

Maximum speed 868kph; service ceiling 11,000m; range 845km.

Messerschmitt Me 410A Hornisse

When the Bf 210 was abandoned it was replaced by the Me 410A, a twin-
engined, two-seat light bomber. Very similar to the Bf 210, it was first flown
at the end of 1942. Bomb loads varied: two 1,000kg bombs could be carried
internally, but more usually eight 50kg bombs were carried internally with
another four under the wings. The 410 entered service in May 1943 and operated at night against England, where its sheer speed made it very difficult to
intercept, especially during Operation 'Steinbock'. But, like all *Luftwaffe* bombers of this period, accuracy was lacking and its effect was more of nuisance
value than actually damaging.

Maximum speed 625kph; service ceiling 10,000m; range 2,330km.

Note: As a rule of thumb, operational radius is generally about one quarter of
the stated range, or in some cases even less when carrying external loads.

BIBLIOGRAPHY

Becker, Cajus D, *The Luftwaffe War Diaries*, Macdonald (London, 1967).

Brütting, Georg, *Das waren die deutschen Kampflieger-Asse 1939–1945*, Motorbuch Verlag (Stuttgart, 1975).

———, *Das waren die deutschen Stuka-Asse 1939–1945*, Motorbuch Verlag (Stuttgart, 1976).

Camelio, Paul, and Shores, Christopher, *Armée de l'Air*, Squadron/Signal Publications (Warren, Michigan, 1976).

Collier, Richard, *Eagle Day*, Hodder & Stoughton (London, 1966).

Foreman, John, and Harvey, S. E., *The Messerschitt Combat Diary: Me 262*, Air Research Publications (Walton-on-Thames, 1995).

Green, William, *Famous Bombers of the Second World War*, Macdonald & Jane's (London, 1975).

Herrmann, Hajo, *Eagle's Wings*, Airlife (Shrewsbury, 1991).

Hooton, E. R., *Eagle in Flames*, Arms & Armour (London, 1999).

———, *Phoenix Triumphant*, Arms & Armour (London, 1994).

Lamb, Charles, *War in a Stringbag*, Cassell (London, 1977).

Liddell Hart, B. H., *History of the Second World War*, Cassell (London, 1970).

Mason, Francis K., *Battle over Britain*, McWhirter Twins (London, 1969).

Poolman, Kenneth, *Scourge of the Atlantic*, Macdonald & Jane's (London, 1978).

Price, Dr Alfred, *Battle of Britain Day*, Sidgwick & Jackson (London, 1990).

———, *Blitz on Britain 1939–1945*, Ian Allan (London, 1976).

———, *The Bomber in World War II*, Macdonald & Jane's (London, 1976).

———, *German Air Force Bombers of World War 2*, 2 vols, Hylton Lacey, Windsor, 1968/1969.

———, *The Hardest Day*, Macdonald & Jane's (London, 1979).

———, *The Last Year of the Luftwaffe*, Arms & Armour (London, 1991).

———, *The Luftwaffe Data Book*, Greenhill Books (London, 1997).

Ramsey, Winston G., (ed), *The Battle of Britain Then and Now*, After the Battle (London, 1982).

Rawnsley, C. F., and Wright, Robert, *Night Fighter*, Collins (London, 1957).

Rudel, Hans-Ulrich, *Stuka Pilot*, Euphorion (Dublin, 1952).

Smith, John R., and Kay, Antony, *German Aircraft of the Second World War*, Putnam (London, 1972).

Smith, Peter C., *Impact!* William Kimber (London, 1981).

————, *Stuka Squadron*, Patrick Stephens (Wellingborough, 1990).

Stahl, Peter, *The Diving Eagle*, William Kimber (London, 1984).

Townsend, Peter, *Duel of Eagles*, Weidenfeld & Nicholson (London, 1970).

Wakefield, Kenneth, *The First Pathfinders*, William Kimber (London, 1981).

Winton, John, *Air Power at Sea 1939–45*, Sidgwick & Jackson (London, 1976).

Young, Desmond, *Rommel*, William Collins (London, 1950).

INDEX